Adorno and the Ends of Philosophy

Adorno and the Ends of Philosophy

Andrew Bowie

polity

Copyright © Andrew Bowie 2013

The right of Andrew Bowie to be identified as Author of this Work has been asserted in accordance with the UK Copyright, Designs and Patents Act 1988.

First published in 2013 by Polity Press

Polity Press
65 Bridge Street
Cambridge CB2 1UR, UK

Polity Press
350 Main Street
Malden, MA 02148, USA

All rights reserved. Except for the quotation of short passages for the purpose of criticism and review, no part of this publication may be reproduced, stored in a retrieval system, or transmitted, in any form or by any means, electronic, mechanical, photocopying, recording or otherwise, without the prior permission of the publisher.

ISBN-13: 978-0-7456-7158-1
ISBN-13: 978-0-7456-7159-8 (pb)

A catalogue record for this book is available from the British Library.

Typeset in 10 on 11.5 pt Palatino by
Servis Filmsetting Ltd, Stockport, Cheshire
Printed and bound in Great Britain by Clays Ltd, St Ives plc

The publisher has used its best endeavours to ensure that the URLs for external websites referred to in this book are correct and active at the time of going to press. However, the publisher has no responsibility for the websites and can make no guarantee that a site will remain live or that the content is or will remain appropriate.

Every effort has been made to trace all copyright holders, but if any have been inadvertently overlooked the publisher will be pleased to include any necessary credits in any subsequent reprint or edition.

For further information on Polity, visit our website: www.politybooks.com

Contents

Preface	vii
Acknowledgements	ix
Introduction: Contemporary Alternatives	1
1 Negative Philosophy?	22
2 Contradiction as Truth-Content: Adorno and Kant	38
3 Immediacy and Mediation: Hegelian and Adornian Dialectics	54
4 Nature	75
5 Freedom	96
6 Aesthetics and Philosophy	135
Conclusion	175
Notes	189
References	198
Index	205

Preface

Adorno has been intriguing and irritating me since the mid-1970s, and at times in the intervening period I have given up on him as a major source for my philosophical reflections. The present book is not intended as any kind of definitive account of Adorno, which would anyway be at odds with basic assumptions of its subject. Rather, the reason for my writing it is that changes in the focus of attention of contemporary philosophy, as well as recent political and economic developments, made me appreciate that there was more to Adorno, above all as a philosopher, than I had sometimes thought. Increasing numbers of contemporary philosophers on both sides of the institutional divide between European and analytical philosophy have started to realize that this divide makes little sense. Where change has begun to happen, the reasons often have to do with a new willingness to look at the ways in which philosophy can inform pressing concerns of social, political, and cultural life. It is here that Adorno has come to seem very relevant, in ways which were previously not always apparent.

The further factor leading to the book has been the intellectual, but sadly not the political and real, demise of the neo-liberal model of capitalism that has wrought such destruction since the 1970s, and the need to rethink the contemporary historical, political, and economic situation of the world. This might sound wildly generalized, but Adorno's connection of philosophy to the idea that modern capitalism makes the world into a totality, in which systemic factors deeply affect aspects of everyday life all over the globe, has become hard to ignore. Whatever problems there are with this Marx-derived conception, it helps to suggest that the metaphysical aim of seeing how sense can be made of things, as A.W. Moore puts it, 'at the highest level of generality' (Moore 2012, p. 7) is connected to the concrete functioning of the socio-historical world. Adorno's work is predicated on the idea that the traditional metaphysical aim of grasping things at the highest level of generality is likely to obscure or repress what does not fit into the metaphysical picture. For Adorno the concrete realization of the highest level of generality in modernity is actually the wholesale commodification of the natural and human worlds. This situation creates the difficulty for philosophy of seeking to do justice to the inherent particularity of things and people, at the same time as realizing that the world is more and more dominated by universalizing forms. Adorno's perception that the task of philosophy is to negotiate such contradictory perspectives contrasts with many approaches to philosophy, because resolving such contradictions is for him not a conceptual issue, but a political and social one. This is why Adorno should be looked at in terms of the ambiguous notion of the 'end of philosophy'. What Adorno offers here is flawed in some respects, but he confronts head-on things that never appear on the agenda of too much philosophy as practised today. At the same time, the contemporary changes in philosophy, epitomized in particular by the revival of Hegelianism and developments in pragmatism, have made it possible to think of new ways of addressing Adorno's concerns, so shifting the agenda of contemporary philosophy in directions which address issues that interest more than a small number of professional philosophers.

Acknowledgements

Because of the book's long gestation period, the number of people who have contributed is enormous, from Klaus Laermann in seminars on Adorno at the Free University of Berlin in the 1970s, to those who have invited me to give talks based on the book in Bosnia, Denmark, Germany, and elsewhere in recent times. The book would not have been possible without an extension of my Alexander von Humboldt Fellowship at the invitation of Christoph Menke to work at the University of Potsdam while mining the Adorno Archive in Berlin. Michael Schwarz at the Archive was the perfect host, offering immediate, friendly assistance and scholarly insight, and the Archive was an ideal place to work. While I was at the Archive, Eberhard Ortland offered some valuable insights, and conversations, coffee, and beer with Josh Robinson made days at the Archive enjoyable, as did the wonderful Wednesday jam session run by Robin Draganic at the B-Flat jazz club up the road in the Rosenthaler Strasse. A term's research leave from Royal Holloway in 2012 enabled the final push.

The list of those who contributed (in some cases a considerable time ago) to what I have to say would, if complete, be enormous, so I apologize as usual to those who don't appear. Karl Ameriks, Jay Bernstein, Scott Biagi, Arnfinn Bø-Rygg, Liz Bradbury, Tony Cascardi, Peter Dews, Robert Eaglestone, Richard Eldridge, Michael Forster, Manfred Frank, Victor Garcia Priego, Neil Gascoigne, Steve Giles, Kristin Gjesdal, Lydia Goehr, Jørgen Hass, Stephen Hinton, Stephen Houlgate, Jonathan Lewis, Nanette Nielsen, Peter Osborne, Ian Pace, Robert Pippin, John Rundell, Kiernan Ryan, Martin Seel, Asger Sørenson, Jakub Stejskal, Ferdia Stone-Davis, Corinna Stupka, Mark Tomlinson, Nick Walker, Jeff Warren, Albrecht Wellmer, and many others, were invaluable interlocutors. Thanks go to my colleagues in the German Department and other colleagues in the School of Modern Languages,

Literatures, and Cultures at Royal Holloway, and a special thanks to Richard Pym, the Head of the School, for his friendly, calming influence and geniality. I hope the book will contribute to a flourishing new culture of Philosophy at Royal Holloway, where the students remind one by their enthusiasm and engagement why one keeps pursuing philosophical questions. I would also like to thank the regular members of my Sunday night jazz group in Cambridge: Ric Byer, Laurence Evans, Jon Halton, Joel Humann, Ben Pringle, Derek Scurll, and Pete Shepherd (and other members of the Cambridge jazz scene), who help me combine theory and practice in ways which increasingly inform my philosophical thinking. Sarah Lambert, Emma Hutchinson, and Justin Dyer at Polity provided prompt, friendly, and helpful editorial assistance and advice. A final thanks to Jamie for showing me how much we can learn from children about what matters in philosophy, as well as for making me laugh so much.

Introduction: Contemporary Alternatives

In an essay on 'The Wider Significance of Naturalism', Akeel Bilgrami (2010) suggests why the ends of contemporary philosophy are shifting in significant ways. What makes the essay startling is that a philosopher known for his work on specialized aspects of analytical philosophy addresses head-on central concerns of European philosophy which have been neglected in the analytical tradition. Bilgrami's criticisms of contemporary scientism echo *Dialectic of Enlightenment*, one of the most well-known (and problematic) books, written together with Max Horkheimer, by the philosopher, social theorist, and music theorist Theodor Wiesengrund Adorno (1903–1969).[1] In order to understand the contemporary debate about the scope of naturalistic explanations, Bilgrami insists on a genealogy of the tendency to regard nature, including the human world, in mechanistic terms that exclude considerations of human value. He focuses on events in the development of modern science in the seventeenth century in Britain which paved the way for Nietzsche's announcement of the 'death of God', and the 'disenchantment' of nature, one of whose manifestations is contemporary reductive naturalism.

Like Adorno, Bilgrami is not interested in hopes for a return of theology, or in questioning the validity of advances made by the modern sciences. He is concerned rather with how a particular questionable version of the idea of disenchantment comes to dominate thinking about nature. His genealogy focuses on a paradigmatic split between the 'Newtonians', such as Robert Boyle and Samuel Clarke, who 'began to dominate the Royal Society' (ibid., p. 38), and the 'dissenters'. The split originated in differences over theology, but had wider ramifications. The theological difference lay in the fact that the Newtonians removed God from nature, in the form of 'an exile into inaccessibility from the visions of ordinary people to a place outside the universe' (ibid., p. 36), while the dissenters were essentially Pantheists, believing in God's 'availability to the visionary temperaments of all those who inhabit his world' (ibid.). The latter were not 'anti-science', because they too played an active role in the genesis of modern science, but they objected to the '*metaphysical* outlook' (ibid., p. 38) of the Newtonians.

Clearly the theological debate here no longer has any great call on our philosophical attention. However, the implications of what lay behind the debate have considerable contemporary resonance, as well as directly echoing aspects of *Dialectic of Enlightenment*: '[S]ome of the dissenters argued that it is only because one takes matter to be "brute" and "stupid", to use Newton's own term, that one would find it appropriate to conquer it with nothing but profit and material wealth as ends, and thereby destroy it both as a natural and a human environment for one's habitation' (ibid., p. 39). This latter view, Bilgrami argues, is too often conflated with a general 'Enlightenment' view of the exclusive superiority of scientific explanation, in order to reject any form of criticism of the potential consequences of the metaphysical assumptions behind the Newtonians' idea of nature as something to be conquered.

Neither the Newtonians' nor the dissenters' conceptions of nature are necessary for a 'thin' notion of modern scientific rationality, which both shared in any case: 'What was in dispute had nothing to do with science or rationality in that sense at all. What the early dissenting tradition was opposed to is the metaphysical orthodoxy that grew around Newtonian science and its implications for broader issues of culture and politics' (ibid., p. 47). The outcome of this genealogy is manifest in 'the fact that Weber and Marx were able to mobilize terms such as "disenchantment' and "commodification" and "alienation"' (ibid., p. 49) against the descendants of the Newtonians' conception. Bilgrami suggests that '[t]hese are all terms that describe how our relations to the world were impoverished in ways that desolate us, when we severed these deep connections in our conceptual and material lives' (ibid.), and he asks how much the 'wider significance of the dispute about naturalism in the early modern period [. . .] survives *in our own time*' (ibid.). He concludes by suggesting that analytical philosophers should address this question and 'come out of their more cramped focus and idiom' (ibid., p. 50) to do so.

The fact that Bilgrami makes such a demand can be seen as part of a contemporary sense that some of the concerns and methods of Anglo-American analytical philosophy are themselves a product of a 'Newtonian' attitude, and that they are therefore part of the problem he identifies. As Bilgrami's essay implies, even within analytical philosophy there are signs of dissatisfaction of the kind just suggested. Anyone wishing to reflect on issues associated with questions of alienation and disenchantment, such as the meanings of modern art, questions of ethics after the Holocaust, or why epistemology became so dominant in modern philosophy, is these days unlikely to make their first port of call theories by analytical philosophers of art, ethics, or epistemology. The ever-growing volume of radically incompatible theories in such areas suggests that something is awry with seeing philosophy predominantly in terms of theory construction based on the 'analysis' of concepts.

This situation is one source of the interest in the work of European/Continental philosophers elsewhere in the humanities, arts, and social sciences. One cannot simply give up the attempt to arrive at adequate responses via conceptual clarification to issues which we cannot ignore. Philosophy has never been noted for its production of consensus, and as such it is doubtful whether a methodological line can really be drawn between 'analytical' and 'European/Continental' philosophy. However, the fact is that that attempts to arrive in the analytical manner at solutions in the form of theories defining the real nature of the object of the theory produce more and more contradictions. This should give pause for thought, not least, as Bilgrami contends, because there are areas of the natural sciences which do produce substantial degrees of durable consensus.

Evidently science progresses via the destruction of untenable consensuses, and theories may never be definitive, but problem-solving technological advances show that science can produce predictable effects based on warranted agreements, even if the level of agreement tends to differ, especially with regard to issues concerning living beings. In philosophy, in contrast, the debate, say, over 'realism' and 'anti-realism' generates ever more books and articles, but it is by no means clear that the substance of the debate has many effects outside philosophy.[2] Given that most thinkers on both sides of that debate do not doubt the validity of well-confirmed scientific theories, it is sometimes hard to see exactly what is at stake, and the participants rarely spell it out in a way which would make it clear to non-philosophers. The debate here is in some respects an echo of the differences between the Newtonians and the dissenters, insofar as neither side tends to be 'anti-science' in any significant sense. As we shall see, such a difference would in Adorno's terms therefore be more interesting for what it reveals about contemporary culture than for whether it settles the issue of 'realism'.

A stance which no longer sees such debates as decisive is sometimes, though, seen as leading into what is often referred to in terms of 'postmodernism'. The pursuit of truth as something universal and timeless is here renounced in favour of a concentration on difference, particularity, and a renunciation of many of the traditional goals of philosophy. The appeal of such an approach lies in the sense that its aim is to keep open the response to the 'Other'. Does such an aim, though, require the rejection of 'Western rationality', as *necessarily* involving repression of the Other, with which it is often associated? There might seem to be an unbridgeable distance between, on the one hand, analytical positions which seek answers to supposedly perennial questions about truth, meaning, and rationality and, on the other, positions deriving from Nietzsche and others in the European tradition which seek to show that rationality is a manifestation of the attempt to exercise power over the Other. However, more and more analytical philosophers, like Bernard Williams and John McDowell, have extended the scope of their work to take in the European tradition, including Hegel, Nietzsche, and Heidegger. The question suggested by Bilgrami's demand to his fellow analytical philosophers is how to respond to the apparent gulf between some 'analytical' and some 'European' approaches, and it is here that I am interested in looking at the work of Adorno in new ways.

Adorno has played at best a minor role in the recent interest in the European tradition on the part of analytical philosophers. He is notorious for contending that we live in a 'universal context of delusion' brought about by the effects of capitalism on modern society. For him only dissonant avant-garde music and other radical modernist art is appropriate to the modern cultural situation, because it expresses what is obscured by an unjust and destructive cultural status quo. The books in which he advances such views are characterized by an at times unnecessary complexity, and his philosophical arguments are sometimes either implausible or insufficiently elaborated. The reasons he advances for his extreme positions also often seem less than convincing: if, for example, the 'context of delusion' is total, how can he reveal its delusory nature? Given such problems, it might, then, seem odd that I want to suggest that Adorno can be a major resource for contemporary philosophy.

Isn't it rash, moreover, even to think that one can generalize sufficiently to talk of the state of contemporary philosophy in this way? Hasn't philosophy become a discipline requiring specialized training? That academic philosophy in the Western world has turned out this way is clear. However, complexity, difficulty, and specialization in philosophy have different significances in differing historical contexts. Kant, Fichte, Schelling, Hegel, and others were hardly immediately accessible to the uninitiated, but they still played a significant role in shaping aspects of modern culture. Many forms of contemporary analytical philosophy, by contrast, cannot be regarded as playing a major cultural role (though their progenitors in the Vienna Circle and elsewhere sometimes did play such a role). This diminished cultural role may come about either because these forms require considerable specialized knowledge and technical expertise, or because the claims made in such philosophy often have so few consequences for other human practices. Among those approaches to philosophy that see themselves as closely connected to the methods of the natural sciences, there seems, then, to be a mismatch between their aims and methods and their results.

The contemporary situation of philosophy in relation to the sciences can, though, be interpreted in a variety of ways. The reason for the phrase 'the ends of philosophy' in my title, with its play on the idea of 'aims' and the idea of 'conclusions', is that one can interpret the development of contemporary philosophy both in terms of competing goals and in terms of the notion that certain kinds of philosophy, most notably those based on large-scale, positive metaphysical claims, and those based on the empiricist assumptions characteristic of many kinds of analytical philosophy, are ceasing to be living options. Adorno can be used as part of a challenge to contemporary philosophical attitudes because of how he responds to the ways in which philosophy generates more and more contradictions, rather than producing new consensuses. A still very widespread perception of philosophy is that it consists in proposing arguments about metaphysics, ontology, epistemology, ethics, aesthetics, and so on, based on such fundamental oppositions as those between idealism and materialism, which will lead to a resolution of an opposition in favour of one of its sides. This approach has the advantage that there is always something to do, because there is no philosophical agreement on virtually any of the competing positions. A book or essay which has some coherent argumentative moves in favour of one side of a conflict will generally find a philosophical audience.[3]

Adorno does advance philosophical arguments, and engages in close examination of concepts, but this does not constitute the core of his approach to philosophy. It is impossible to do philosophy without making assertions which can command or fail to command assent, but if one thinks of the later Wittgenstein's manner of philosophizing, which is not based on arriving at argumentative conclusions, a different perspective emerges. Both Adorno and Wittgenstein pose the question as to what sorts of alternatives there are to what for many people is the only real way to do philosophy. Some philosophers despair of how Adorno produces texts which do not proceed in an argumentative straight line. Indeed, many of his published texts may not justify the complexity of their construction and their style. However, there is a decisive point here, which relates to the issue of contradictions. The core of many established approaches to philosophy is precisely the resolution of contradictions, hence the basic approach of offering theories defending idealism, materialism, and so on, which seek to overcome what seems lacking in one position in favour of another. In terms of a logical approach to contradiction, this is a necessary stance: contradictions do not involve determinate thoughts and, as such, are in a strictly logical sense meaningless.

What, though, of the fact that the contradictions that recur in the history of philosophy never seem to be definitively resolved by philosophical arguments? The dominant professional response here is to continue making moves in the particular argumentative game that constitutes a philosophical 'problem'. From this perspective the main alternative response is not really philosophy at all, being rather the 'history of ideas', in which one traces the moves in past versions of the game. 'Real' philosophy therefore consists in making new moves.[4] In order to indicate the alternative direction in which Adorno's approach leads, let us briefly consider his notion of 'experience' (see Foster 2007 for Adorno on experience).

Adorno does not think of experience in the empiricist sense, where it consists of probably mythical 'sense-data', but in the sense of what is required if one is really to comprehend something. Understanding therefore cannot be established in terms of clear, final definitions, as the basis of any such definition has to be constituted in experience itself, which is a complex weave of sometimes contradictory factors. The weave is not resolvable into a series of propositions, because the sense of the terms in such propositions will shift in relation to the other terms. This might sound unlikely to be philosophically convincing, though since Quine the basic idea should be familiar. Think, however, of something as familiar as how one experiences another person: this can be distorted by the attempt to establish a fixed idea of the person, even though some degree of stability is also required in order to be able to engage with someone successfully.[5] The experience of contradiction in the sense intended here, where opposed judgements coexist without being able to be resolved, is, then, very much part of everyday life, and is constitutive, for example, of the way characters become manifest in great novels. Most, if not all, of us live with contradictory stances on a whole swathe of issues and people, without ever being able to bring the contradictions to a definitive end. This kind of living with contradiction is, nevertheless, as the remarks above suggest, strikingly at odds with many prevalent attitudes to philosophy.

It might be objected here that if philosophy does not propose stances on issues, it is likely to end up with either 'relativism' or 'syncretism'. However, when one looks at the ways in which philosophical problems are manifest in real contexts, things are not so simple. The contemporary debate on, for example, whether the 'mind is the brain' seems to generate contradictory stances in such a way that adjudicating between claims does not lead anywhere which does not itself involve further contradictions. Take a crude version of a standard objection in the debate. If the mind is just the brain and the brain is a 'machine', as it would appear to be from the point of view of some versions of neuroscience, this gives us no purchase on the dimensions of mental life involving self-determination, deliberation, creative imagination, and so on. The question that generates the contradictions is how to see the world in terms of these two incompatible accounts. One of the most interesting and original aspects of Adorno's thought will be his rethinking of the notion of nature, and this will throw a different light on questions of free-will and determinism that arise in relation to neuroscience and the philosophy of mind (see Cook 2011; Stone 2006).

It is precisely the sense that these differing factors involved in understanding human action are both ineliminable and potentially incompatible that is philosophically significant, as is the sense that one needs ways of negotiating the consequences of these incompatibilities. These ways cannot consist just in arguments that resolve the dispute in favour of one side against another. In Adorno's terms, such contradictions become the very content of our self-understanding. The implication here is that there are meta-philosophical questions inherent in any such issue, and the task is therefore to understand how the issue relates to the world of which it is a part. The meta-philosophical reflections involved need not lead to a new kind of answer, but neither do they have to lead to a regress of meta-philosophies; that would only be the case if one gave the meta-philosophical position the same foundational status one is denying to the original position.

The difficulty here can be suggested by the fondness in Anglophone philosophy for asking questions of the form 'Can lying/violence ever be justified?' This sort of question will generally give rise to a lively seminar, but is largely vacuous if the assumption is that one is striving for a definitive answer. It is in Adorno's terms more interesting to ask why philosophy of this kind could get so stuck in a mode of questioning which has too little connection to the dilemmas faced by real-world actors. Just asking what follows from the positive or negative response to the abstract question can make clear what I mean: without locating the response in relation to practices in law and elsewhere, one is left with a bit of mere moralizing.

The failure to see that the history of a philosophical problem is itself part of what that problem *is* vitiates significant amounts of contemporary philosophy. The assumption that what Plato meant by art is the same as what we, in the light of modernism, Dada, and so on, mean is, for example, simply untenable, though some analytical aestheticians seem unaware of this. There is, however, a further important twist here, on which Adorno repeatedly insists: if there were no continuity at all between Plato's concerns and ours, even the claim that what he meant by art differed from what we mean would be incomprehensible. Concepts are seen by Adorno as inherently involving movement, but that also entails them having some kind of identity, if what moves is not to dissolve into its successive moments. It might seem as if all we are now left with is a to and fro between competing viewpoints, each of which reveals some inadequacy in the others, but none of which can be definitively established. The fact is that this seems to me, if it is understood in the right way, precisely where one should be with regard to such issues. Establishing why such a stance might be defensible, and what consequences this has for the idea of the ends of philosophy, will be a major task in what follows. Why, though, should Adorno be so significant in this context?

Who is Adorno?/Which Adorno?

The following sketch of Adorno's life can be complemented by the wealth of biographical material in Claussen (2003), Jäger (2005), and Müller-Doohm (2005). Adorno was born in Frankfurt am Main in 1903. After showing early talent as a musician he began lessons in composition at the age of 16, and by the age of 18 was studying philosophy, music, and psychology at university, and publishing music criticism. Having completed a largely derivative Ph.D. on the phenomenology of Edmund Husserl in 1924 under the supervision of Hans Cornelius, he moved to Vienna in 1925 to study composition with Alban Berg. After returning to Frankfurt he withdrew, on the advice of Cornelius, a *Habilitation* dissertation on 'The Concept of the Unconscious in the Transcendental Doctrine of the Soul', the last part of which manifests a new Marx-influenced concern with the relationship between the emergence and adoption of philosophical theories and socio-economic developments. At the end of the 1920s, while editing the musical journal *Anbruch* ('Dawn'), Adorno encountered Georg Lukács's *History and Class-Consciousness* and developed a more intensive contact with Walter Benjamin, whom he had got to know in 1923. In 1931 he completed his *Habilitation* (later published) on *Kierkegaard: Construction of the Aesthetic*, which bears many of the traits of his mature work and is influenced by Benjamin. Adorno at first regarded the seizure of power by the Nazis as a merely passing phenomenon, and continued to visit Germany until 1937, while working as an 'advanced student' at Merton College, Oxford (an environment he found pretty intolerable). In 1938 he moved to America to work with Max Horkheimer as a member of the Institute for Social Research, living in New York until he moved to Los Angeles for the years 1941–9. During this time he wrote *Dialectic of Enlightenment* with Horkheimer, completed *Minima Moralia*, a collection of short pieces which bears the subtitle 'Reflections from Damaged Life', and *Philosophy of New Music*, which deals mainly with the work of Schoenberg and Stravinsky and which influenced Thomas Mann's novel *Doktor Faustus*, and he was a member of the group that wrote *The Authoritarian Personality* as part of the Berkeley 'Project on the Nature and Extent of Antisemitism'. Adorno returned to Frankfurt in 1949, where he finally gained his first (and only) tenured professorship, at the re-established Institute for Social Research, in 1956. In the early 1960s he was involved, along with, among others, his academic assistant Jürgen

Habermas, in the 'Positivism Dispute in German Sociology', in which his main opponents were Karl Popper and Hans Albert.[6] Throughout the 1960s he was engaged in writing major works, such as *Negative Dialectics*, *Aesthetic Theory*, and a host of other projects, some of which remained incomplete. He died on holiday in Switzerland in 1969, at the time of disturbances associated with the Student Movement.

The intention here is not to provide another survey of Adorno's thought, of which there are plenty already (see Brunkhorst 1999; Buck-Morss 1977; Jarvis 1998; Jay 1984; Wilson 2007; see also Gibson and Rubin 2002 and Huhn 2004 for representative selections of essays), let alone of his character or his life. For the time being the most we need to infer from the biographical details is that Adorno lived through a time of the utmost disruption and crisis, though he managed to do so whilst himself remaining, given what happened to so many people, comparatively unscathed. What is beyond doubt is that Adorno had a significant effect on post-war German society and culture, and assessing how his philosophy relates to some of its performative effects will be important for the present account. There is no simple way of matching philosophical contentions with the effects of those contentions in real historical contexts. There must, though, be an ethical dimension to philosophy, which sustains an awareness that making theoretical contentions is a form of practice which can involve ethical consequences. Adorno is concerned with precisely the kind of gap between the desire for complete knowledge of what such consequences could be and the sceptical sense that there is no way of knowing how philosophy has its effects. His best work confronts the contradictions generated by the idea that positive metaphysics which makes sense of things as a whole is no longer possible, but that the needs on which it was based have not and cannot go away, and so demand new responses.

Adorno's own life provides an obvious example of the relationship between philosophical theory and social practice. Even though he regarded the Student Movement of the later 1960s as generally misguided and naïve, his ideas played a major role in its rejection of the post-war West German consensus which repressed the fact that Germany had done little to come to terms with the Nazi period. The political aims of the Movement itself may have been for the most part illusory, but its enduring liberating effect on the nature of German society is unquestionable. The fact is that the Movement's inflated political stances often had more to do with the younger generation's reactions to Nazism than with an adequate appraisal of the contemporary issues which formed its immediate focus. Justified outrage at events in Vietnam and elsewhere was intensified by unarticulated outrage at the failure in Germany to confront the deeds of the preceding generations. Adorno's refusal to take the economic success of post-war Germany as a reason to pass over the horrors that preceded it was, along with some of the effects of the Student Movement, part of what led to a liberal German culture for which coming to terms with the Holocaust remains a central goal.

Adorno had a more problematic effect on German and other European musical culture, where his often dogmatic preference for a certain kind of musical modernism created something of a strait-jacket for many composers from the 1950s onwards. At the same time, his concern to connect music to social issues made possible debates which kept alive theoretical discussion of music in Germany and elsewhere, and helped sustain an innovative musical culture. Adorno's influence on discussion of music outside Germany has generally been a much more recent phenomenon. It seems clear that this influence often has to do with the questioning of a predominantly empirical approach to the history and practice of music that relates to philosophical changes of perspective which will concern us in what follows (see de Nora 2003).

When it comes to Adorno's impact on philosophy the questions become more complex. A prominent contemporary German philosopher once wrote to me that Adorno was not really a philosopher, though he might be more than a philosopher. What he meant was that Adorno tended not to address philosophical issues in a consistent manner; this did not mean that his work might not still offer a great deal, just that it did not do so in a way which was 'strictly philosophical' in that it provides theoretically elaborated arguments. What appears here as a deficit from one perspective is, however, seen by defenders of Adorno as germane to his thinking: they often cite the writing style of his published work as a reason not to see him in the same terms as one sees mainstream philosophers. The complex web of the writing is meant to be part of the content of what he is saying. Adorno himself makes this point concerning philosophical style, when he insists, following Walter Benjamin, that '*Darstellung*', the manner of its 'presentation', is part of what a work of philosophy means. That the manner of his writing affects how we understand Adorno's philosophy (or anybody else's, for that matter) is unquestionable, but there are two important points here.

The first is that it is arguable that Adorno's failure to become part of mainstream debate may be a result of his manner of writing sometimes getting in the way of adequate engagement with the durable substance of his work. The second, related, point is that Adorno's thinking exists not just in the form of written texts, but also as transcripts of lectures and other kinds of text. The transcripts of lectures from the later 1950s until the later 1960s are very often of improvisations from quite minimal notes on the topics which then became the books, or on topics dealt with in his essays and books. Topics which in the books are often cryptic, unexplained, unnecessarily exaggerated, very often appear in a lucid, developed form in the lectures. Adorno himself has lots to say about why he does not trust lecture presentation, and about why only the written text can appropriately convey his message. However, it seems evident that his pedagogical talent thrived on the dialogical situation, and being compelled to formulate difficult ideas in a manner accessible to students brought out this talent. When he reverts to reading out a text there is often a sense of moving from the dialogical communication of ideas that matter to an esoteric stance in which ideas have to be formulated in a way that makes any kind of coherent summary difficult.

It is important to remember here that Adorno's considerable influence on and reputation in post-war German society could not in fact have rested on his major theoretical works, because they only appeared at the end of his career – indeed, in the case of *Aesthetic Theory* after his death. Even *Dialectic of Enlightenment* (first published 1947) was out of print for most of the time until 1969 (illegal copies admittedly circulated before then), and much of his other work was not easily accessible. Adorno's influence in fact largely rested on his talks on the radio and elsewhere, and on his lectures and his participation in public debate. As such, it seems invidious to insist that we only get the true Adorno in the 'canonical' texts, such as *Aesthetic Theory* (1970) and *Negative Dialectics* (1966). The opening of critical perspectives on German society achieved by Adorno in the 1950s and 1960s may, then, be more significant than any supposedly durable philosophical conclusions, of a kind which he himself regarded as unattainable anyway. Responses to his work are, therefore, more likely to develop in productive directions if we keep in mind that his work can have performative effects which depend on the ways the differing forms in which it appears influence how an issue is understood.

Although Adorno defended theoretical stances with no immediate practical import, he also, as we just saw, did have considerable effects on German post-war culture. My aim here is to bring Adorno into the mainstream of debate about the 'ends of philosophy', and, as such, it is the texts which can most easily be made to communicate with that debate on which I shall focus. This approach does not involve any dogmatic divisions between kinds of text, but does offer some new perspectives, not least because, along with reference to already published texts of all kinds by Adorno, I shall refer to unpublished lectures, some of which will only appear in print some years hence.[7] The criterion for my use of the texts is simply the degree to which they illuminate the issues at hand.

History and Truth

Adorno often fails to make it into wider philosophical discussion because some of his most well-known claims seem so dogmatic and all-encompassing that there appears to be no room for debating them, unless one already accepts a whole series of contentious assumptions. From a contemporary perspective, much that Adorno says is, I think, indeed indefensible, but just making such a judgement in this form already involves taking one side in a crucial conflict which is far from resolved. The issues here are often seen in terms of the fear of 'relativism'. By seeing the importance of philosophical stances as lying in their articulation of key aspects of the history in which they emerge, one is regarded as being likely to surrender the specific content of philosophical claims. Because there is an obvious objection to claiming that truth is relative to historical context – the claim itself is similarly relative, and so supposedly self-refuting – people are often wary of seeing philosophy in terms of its relations to history.

Many approaches to philosophy work on the apparently self-evident assumption that the answers which they seek to philosophical questions must be true, and so must always be true. What makes this seem a compelling stance is the fact that the idea that 'true' means 'true in these particular historical or other circumstances' is contradicted by the everyday understanding of truth. When we say 'The sky is blue' we don't mean 'I think the sky is blue today, but I may be wrong about this at some point in the future.' We may be wrong, but if truth is as inseparable from meaning, as is often contended, our being contingently wrong has no effect on our basic sense of truth. By isolating a particular semantic approach to truth, one therefore seems to arrive at a philosophical position which is immune to history. Philosophical debates about truth then revolve around exactly how to cash out the relationship between truth and meaning. The common alternative to such approaches seems to result in a 'performative contradiction': by asserting that truth is relative to context, I undermine the truth of my own claim. This might all seem fairly obvious, but it is not clear that one settles questions of truth in this context as simply as this. Adorno is himself implacably opposed to 'relativism', but not necessarily for the same reason as the one just cited. Although he is convinced of the historical relativity of all philosophical investigation, he wishes at the same time to sustain a non-relativistic sense of truth.

It is clear that the history of philosophy does not resolve the contradictions of which it can be said to consist. The core attitude of the analytical tradition has, despite this, been that philosophy has to resolve contradictions by producing true arguments. It is consequently hardly surprising that so much of that tradition is obsessed with finding an answer to a narrowly conceived epistemological scepticism (see Gascoigne 2002). The demand for definitive resolutions of philosophical questions generates a fear that the whole enterprise may be in vain, which the historical perspective's revelation of philosophy as the continual failure finally to overcome contradictions can seem to justify. The strange thing here is just how little meta-reflection there has been within the analytical tradition on the fact that in carrying out one's philosophical pursuit of the truth one is in all likelihood doomed to failure.

One response to this situation is to see oneself as part of an ongoing larger story, in which a specific problem is the underlying ground which sustains the contradictions. It is perhaps no coincidence, then, that, after being ignored for most of the twentieth century, Hegel has recently become vital to some new directions in analytical philosophy (see Redding 2007). Hegel precisely combines the sceptical moment, which sees positive theories as inherently prey to being contradicted by subsequent theories, with the sense that this process of negation can itself become positive. This is possible if the moments of the process are in fact connected as part of a larger story, in which the sceptical attitude can be shown to result in a position that generates more justifiable truths than those which are refuted in the process.

In the empirical sciences the revision of theories generally results in theories with better predictive capacity or which explain more of the phenomena. Maintaining that philosophy can progress in this manner seems, however, rather questionable. Was logical atomism the advance on Hegelian Idealism that it claimed to be? Conversely, didn't logical atomism, which helped lead to the ideas of the Vienna Circle, achieve something which its failure as a philosophical theory does not invalidate? The importance of the Circle's role in articulating a stance suspicious of grand philosophical claims, in the name of reliance on scientific methods, should not be underestimated, and Adorno himself praises the Vienna Circle in the 1930s for clarifying what should come within the remit of philosophy. He does so in order to distance himself from tendencies in philosophy at the time which are linked to an irrationalist, anti-science position. His evaluation is an endorsement not of the Vienna Circle's verificationism, but rather of its excluding 'all questions which, as specifically scientific questions, are appropriate for individual sciences and which cloud philosophical questioning' (Adorno 1973, p. 333).[8] Adorno's later animus against 'positivism' seems hard to square with this evaluation, and is often indefensible, being based on an often imprecise caricature of what is being attacked. However, his change of position is consistent with his core assumption that no philosophical position is immune from being misused for repressive purposes.

This assumption suggests why Adorno offers a challenge to some often unquestioned presuppositions about the aims of philosophy, because he does not accept the idea that there is an essential philosophical task which takes precedence over all others. Why this is the case can be made clear by thinking about one of the more well-known aspects of his thought. One of the reasons Adorno may seem so extreme in his claims is that he makes the Holocaust central to his consideration of many philosophical questions. He therefore apparently makes something empirical into a foundation for his philosophical investigations. Leaving aside the argument as to whether such an approach is legitimate, the key point here is that the Holocaust plays almost no role in large parts of Anglo-American philosophy. This striking difference is germane to my seeking to make Adorno part of mainstream philosophy.[9]

There is a danger here of thinking that if one deals with the Holocaust one is going to say something of deep philosophical significance, when what is first required is a demonstration that one is justified in involving the Holocaust in philosophical discussion at all. There is, conversely, also a danger that, by failing to consider philosophical issues in relation to the extremes of history, one is dealing in mere abstractions when using philosophy to understand human action. This danger forces one to consider how history is inseparable from an understanding of what philosophy can contribute to moral life. It puts in question the sort of moral theorizing which spends its time dissecting a few key concepts or seeking to decide between deontological, utilitarian, and other stances mainly on the basis of conceptual considerations or thought experiments.[10] A further manifestation of this danger is the kind of discussion in moral philosophy which seeks to reduce moral issues to choices between very clear alternatives, and so obscures the kind of complex and diverse pressures that play a role in nearly all moral behaviour.

The essential tension here arises, then, from the dual demands of seeking to respond to philosophical dilemmas which have immediate practical consequences for how we relate to the world and other people, and of acknowledging how those dilemmas cannot be adequately understood without seeing that they arise in historical contexts that affect their very nature. Adorno challenges us no longer to assume that there are discrete 'philosophical problems', to which one can expect theoretical solutions. In deconstruction, conceptual oppositions are similarly seen as impossible to specify in a definitive manner, because the opposed terms depend on each other and change their significance via this dependence. However, this tends to lead to an exaggerated attention to the undecidability of metaphysical and philosophical problems which takes too little account of the pragmatic functioning of communication that succeeds despite the aporias of metaphysics. While showing how conceptual transparency of the kind demanded in many kinds of philosophy is a myth, Adorno still regards himself as a defender of rationality. He also interprets the contradictions generated by the history of metaphysics as expressions of historical tensions, rather than just seeking to show how metaphysics can be deconstructed.

In a world where the need for openness to other ways of thinking generated by the rapid increase in the speed and volume of global communication has become inescapable, negotiating incompatibilities between ways of thinking requires resources which are lacking in many ways of doing philosophy. This lack relates to an essential tension in the ways in which language is conceived, between the 'formal mathematically inspired tradition' and 'an anthropological, natural-historical, social-practical' approach (Brandom 2008, p. 8), which has, at last, begun to become a focus of more sustained philosophical attention.[11] Gadamer argues that, although the natural sciences are indispensable to human survival, 'this does not mean that people would be able to solve the problems that face us, peaceful coexistence of peoples and the preservation of the balance of nature, with science as such. It is obvious that not mathematics but the linguistic nature of people is the basis of human civilization' (Gadamer 1993, p. 342). The question is, then, how this linguistic nature is conceived. In Anglo-American philosophy, language has too often been reduced to what can be investigated in terms of constative utterances, ignoring the fact that communication depends on how we share expressive resources *beyond* the inevitable and sometimes irresolvable conflicts over what we would assert as true or regard as legitimate.

The tensions between approaches to language can be regarded in roughly analogous terms to the relationship between 'freedom', in the broad sense of human self-determination and self-expression,[12] and 'nature', in the sense of what can be explained in causal, law- or rule-governed terms. In both cases the contrasting conceptions cannot be resolved into a higher synthesis. If language becomes the object of an explanatory science, the aim is to account for its workings in a theory which explains language as rule-bound phenomenon. Such an approach has, though, to confront the fact that language is always already the condition of possibility of any such theory, and so inherently exceeds such objectification. A key argument here, which is first made clear by Kant's reflections on judgement, is that rules for language cannot be self-applying, because that would involve the rule for the application of a rule, and so on, so generating a regress that would render communication impossible. At the same time, without linguistic rules there could be no elaborated forms of communication; the question, therefore, is the status of such rules. Either one seeks to resolve this dilemma by pursuing a theory which would overcome the contradiction by finally incorporating the practical dimension of language-use into what can be formulated in terms of linguistic rules, or one makes the contradiction itself constitutive for one's conception of language. The former stance leads in the direction of analytical semantics, the latter to a conception which can use insights from analytical approaches, but which seeks to show how they may have significant real-world effects by their exclusion of vital aspects of language (see Wellmer 2004, 2007).

Once one ceases to regard some linguistic practice, such as the making of assertions, as foundational for language as a whole, one is in a position to see how the interplay and tension between the practices in real contexts may be as significant as the analysis of assertions. Brandom says of analytic philosophy that its 'characteristic form of question is whether, and in what way, one can make sense of the meanings expressed by *one* kind of locution in terms of the meanings expressed by *another* kind of locution' (Brandom 2008, p. 1). This may work as a theoretical explication for some kinds of language-use, but it does not work for the expressive, musical, and gestural dimensions of communication which inform and influence most interpersonal exchange, or for the wider contexts which are necessary to comprehend many concrete instances of language-use. The expressive dimensions of language often have to be *enacted* in ways which only partially translate into discursive idioms. What is at issue here can be indicated by the fact that a piece of music cannot be replaced by its description in verbal language. This does not mean that sense cannot be made of the music in terms of another form of locution: what someone says about a piece can change my understanding of it. In terms of a non-analytical view, though, what cannot be thus made sense of in music can be precisely what makes most sense, rather than being a contingent addition to its articulable semantic content.

It is at this point that the expressive resources of poetic language come into play, which can provide a better means of understanding in some contexts than conventional language-use. Wittgenstein talks of the importance of 'these words in these positions' in such cases, precisely in order to suggest that poetic meanings cannot be fully made sense of by being expressed by another locution. Now it might be countered here that there is no certainty that 'music' should count as a language at all. The counter to this claim is that we have no certain concept of a language either, precisely because of what is at issue here (see Bowie 2007): which language does one use to draw the boundaries of language? The musical, in the sense of the tonal, the rhythmic, the gestural, and so on, is inherently part of actual vocal exchanges (and, in a different way, of written communication), and has performative and semantic effects. If one insists that language be understood primarily in terms of conceptual content, this insistence will have to be grounded in the stipulated aims of a particular philosophical project, rather than in a definitive drawing of the language/non-language boundary.

Mark Johnson sums up his frustration with the focus of the analytical tradition in this respect:

> It radically distinguishes linguistic meaning from all other types of symbolic interaction, and it assumes that if any of those forms of expression (e.g. painting, music, sculpture, architecture, dance, sign-languages)

have meaning, then it must be in some second-rate sense, as being parasitic on linguistic meaning (where 'linguistic' is always a severely limited selection from the full scope of actual linguistic meaning). (Johnson 2008, p. 271)

If one keeps the concept of language more open, in order to encompass kinds of meaningful articulation that are not restricted to the verbal, one does not need to define in advance what counts as linguistic. This emerges instead via the engagement with the piece of articulation: for some purposes this will be assertion, but to take this as fundamental from the beginning already prejudges too many issues. Underlying what I am suggesting here is the notion of 'dialectical' thinking. This still contentious notion can be clarified via an exploration of Adorno's relation to certain responses to the issue of contradiction in philosophy.

Adorno has an apparently contradictory relationship to Hegel's philosophy. On the one hand he is committed to a Hegel-derived refusal to draw a philosophical line between the subjective and the objective: what the subject is is inseparable from the world through which it seeks to determine itself and by which it is determined. Language illustrates what is meant here: it is part of the world which helps determine who we are, but is also that via which subjective individuality can realize itself. On the other hand Adorno is opposed to Hegel's and others' 'Idealism'.[13] The danger Adorno sees in 'Idealism' is that, while it rightly questions the notion that there is an uncrossable epistemological gap between our thinking and the world, it seeks to resolve the mind–world relationship in terms of one side of that relationship, dissolving the objective resistance of the world into subjectivity. Hegel saw what he was doing as offering a definitive response to the sceptic, whereby what gives rise to sceptical doubts becomes, via the notion of 'determinate negation',[14] the basis of an anti-sceptical position, in which the philosophical truth is manifest in a logic of how positive theories come to be negated. It might seem, then, that Adorno is seeking to reinstate scepticism, but it is this kind of alternative that his work can suggest ways of circumventing.

This aspect of Adorno can shed some light on recent developments in analytical philosophy. In certain quarters the assumption is now widespread that the big metaphysical questions are back on the agenda, after the apparent demise of metaphysics in the face of logical positivism and the 'linguistic turn' (see, e.g., Williamson 2007). The idea that, because certain arguments in philosophy may point towards a revival of a certain kind of metaphysics, there will be a reorientation in thought, in which the tensions between thinking and reality characteristic of modernity are overcome, would appear simply mistaken to Adorno. For him philosophy, even though it must strive to transcend its historical situation if it is to be philosophy at all, and so retain a certain kind of metaphysical impulse, cannot *claim* to be more than a response to that situation, and so cannot hope to achieve the traditional aims of metaphysics. These aims are what he sees as being finally destroyed by the traumatic experiences of modernity: the fact that the Holocaust occurred means we have to interrogate our thinking for all the ways in which it could be complicit in what made the Holocaust possible and what would enable something like it to happen again. Adorno therefore would not think the issues now addressed in the return of metaphysical debate are all that significant: the pragmatic success of the sciences means that concerns about realism and the like are to be read primarily as a symptom of other social and historical developments, rather than as the search for a definitive answer to how we gain access to 'Reality'.[15] Adorno is quite happy to accept the truth of well-confirmed scientific theories; his philosophical concern is rather with how those truths affect human culture in the face of the failure of societies in modernity to achieve just social arrangements.

Adorno does not subscribe to the anti-metaphysical approach characteristic of certain scientistically oriented members of the Vienna Circle. Metaphysics has for him to do with what makes human lives worth living by their being located in a whole that makes sense, which has little to do with the epistemologically oriented critiques of Neurath and others. Metaphysics has this sense for Adorno because history has put in question all the traditional answers to questions about the point of life. The Holocaust destroys any residual sense of the meaning of human existence as being something about which philosophy could say anything substantial: concerns about realism seem in the light of this situation to be, at best, a subordinate matter. Adorno cites the dictum that 'life no longer lives', and what he seeks is what enables meaningful life to continue: Adorno's 'negative metaphysics' is generated out of the 'fall' of positive metaphysics. This might all seem like changing the subject in relation to the concerns of many contemporary Anglophone philosophers, but what emerges in relation to Adorno's ideas is not irrelevant to those concerns. The Adornian response would be to ask why those concerns have become the central ones. In a world where the increase in the number of warrantable scientific theories seems, for the foreseeable future, unstoppable, why should so much philosophical energy be expended on epistemological and metaphysical questions? It is not that such questions should be proscribed: they are one complement to reflection on the nature of scientific truth. The question is why they should be the predominant ones that are asked to the often wholesale exclusion of many others.

What concerns Adorno can be reductively characterized as follows. The success of the natural sciences depends on the exclusion of qualitative particularity, in the name of establishing general laws. The application of the same kind of approach to many areas of society and culture can also be vital to their efficient functioning. This approach relates to the concerns of analytical metaphysics and epistemology, insofar as they seek general ways in which we can classify and manipulate the world. To what extent, though, can the exclusion of qualitative particularity also be an element in the planning and carrying out of industrialized genocide? What lies behind Bilgrami's worries about the effects of disenchantment becomes apparent here. The Holocaust employed the rationalized means of technologically developed societies to enable what would otherwise have been impossible. One aspect of this was precisely the fact that these rationalized means allowed many of those contributing to the horror to exclude the kind of thoughts and feelings which would have prevented them from contributing.[16] They did so by reducing the victims to ways of thinking which wholly objectify them, by abstracting from their nature as individual sufferers. Planning train timetables to the gas chambers, or carrying out barbarous medical experiments, was, in the view of the perpetrators, often rendered justifiable by adherence to technical norms of established practices. Writing in Germany in the 1950s and 1960s, Adorno is, of course, aware that many doctors and natural scientists who were involved in the barbarism held respected academic and scientific posts in the Federal Republic.

The obvious – and in many respects justified – rejoinder here from traditional metaphysicians is that they can't see any possible connection between what interests them and Adorno's ideas. There are so many steps in between, which indeed there are. However, it is still worth asking whether the concern with analytical precision which is indispensable in many philosophical and scientific approaches might, in the kind of complex circumstances characteristic of modernity, where the systematic social and political consequences of ideas and practices are so hard to grasp, make it harder to see the kind of connections suggested by Adorno. An Adornian approach need not involve a moralizing judgement on those who think concentration on technical development in philosophy is akin to scientific development, and so see it as akin to 'blue skies' research. Adorno is clear that so much of what happens in the social world is the product of competing forces, where individual actors will find it very hard to judge what the implications and consequences of their ideas and actions are. Precisely because it is so hard to judge such matters, a narrow analytical focus can, though, become a problem. An example of the dangers of certain kinds of analytical focus became apparent in the contemporary world economic crisis: virtually the whole of academic economics failed to see the crisis coming, when non-economists had been worried for a long time about the effects of the growth of certain kinds of credit on the wider economy.

Adorno's aim is to gain access to whatever conceptual and other resources reveal what matters most about a pressing issue, and this demands more than a purely 'analytical' approach, though it will involve analytical elements. To this extent there has to be a different kind of temporality involved in philosophizing about questions of the kind at issue here from that assumed in traditional metaphysical inquiry. Something like this idea informs Heidegger's ideas about temporality and philosophy, which suggest that philosophy is also about what happens through the attempt to philosophize, rather than just about the truths it seeks. Otherwise the result tends to be the history of philosophy as the history of error, which makes it hard to grasp how people successfully inhabited a world which their philosophies interpreted in ways that are false from a contemporary perspective. Given the unlikelihood of metaphysical inquiry coming to any sort of definitive conclusion, meta-questions about how such forms of thought might actually be complicit in making possible inhuman practices cannot simply be dismissed. Evidently questionable is the rigid alternative between, on the one hand, a historical relativism that is widely assumed to be inherent in conceptions which take seriously how people lived with ideas that are now found to be false and, on the other hand, the assumption that one is working towards the one true account by engaging in the major questions which dominate contemporary debate in some area of philosophy. This is the case even though the alternative to this alternative involves a contradiction between sustaining both a demand for a non-relative conception of truth and the sense that in concrete terms truths *are* relative to the practices of the communities in which they are believed.

My basic idea is that there are good reasons to try to develop ideas which Adorno himself did not always articulate in their most plausible form. In order to do so I shall not attempt to fit Adorno's conceptions into the standard framework of epistemology, ethics, aesthetics, ontology, metaphysics, or whatever, not least because the dividing lines between these areas are often disputed. Aesthetics, for example, is regarded in the analytical canon as a minor subsidiary area, but philosophers as diverse as Kant, Cavell, and Adorno give it a major role which has consequences for most areas of philosophy. Rather than just extract a series of arguments from Adorno's work which can then be assessed in the area of contemporary philosophy to which they might be seen to pertain, I want to examine certain areas in which his ideas are played out, and show how we might use these ideas to change some of the perspectives in these areas. The areas are philosophy, nature, freedom, and culture. The point behind this approach is that, as suggested above, received contemporary ways of doing philosophy can lead to a reduction of notional topics which may be better understood in terms of their connection to other topics than by an analysis of the specific terms of the topic.

The Adorno to be encountered in what follows will not necessarily be a familiar one to some readers, though I hope some familiar but apparently implausible ideas might be made more plausible by my approach. What I say is anchored in texts produced by Adorno, but I am not concerned to follow every version in Adorno's work of the issues I examine, let alone every major concern of Adorno's thought.[17] What interests me, as it did Adorno much of the time, is what a critical reading of philosophical texts can do to our understanding of ourselves and the world we inhabit. The truth of the texts is what emerges as they are read in relation to subsequent philosophy and history, not something that somehow inheres in the texts themselves: Adorno will talk about this in terms of their 'truth-content'. Adorno has come into and gone out of fashion since the 1960s, and this is, as he would also argue, to be expected in relation to any philosopher. The present state of the political and social world, where a deep sense of insecurity has become widespread, has led to renewed attention to him, and I hope to bring out some of the resources he offers for responding to that sense of insecurity. My choice of approach should make it clear that I don't think such responses will be appropriate if they attribute any kind of canonical status to Adorno and so keep on repeating even his worst ideas. A fair amount that is good in Adorno seems to me not always to have formed the focus of discussion of his work so far, and my use of often neglected or so far somewhat inaccessible texts seeks to remedy that situation.[18]

1
Negative Philosophy?

Philosophical contradiction

Adorno is well known for such claims as the one in *Negative Dialectics*, that philosophy 'remained alive' because 'the moment of its realization' was missed (Adorno 1997, 6, p. 15; see also Honneth 2008, pp. 93–111; O'Connor 2004). The difficulties involved in understanding the remark often lead to criticism of Adorno for his failure to offer substantial perspectives either for positive social and political change or for the concrete practice of philosophy. It seems as if there must be a clear notion of what 'philosophy' is, and that it had the potential to be 'realized', but if we ask what precisely this refers to we are pretty much left in the dark. Moreover, such an appraisal of philosophy seems unlikely to constitute more than the kind of over-generalized thinking that analytical philosophers despair of in European philosophy.

However, if one looks at some possible contexts of the remark, a more plausible story can emerge. The remark might be understood, for example, in relation to Marx's thesis on Feuerbach, that philosophy should be realized by changing the world, rather than interpreting it, a realization that has been associated with the perversion of the idea of philosophy as praxis in the Soviet bloc. In the *Lectures on Negative Dialectics*, Adorno says: '[B]y the fact that the turning of philosophical theory into practice did not happen, philosophical theory also cannot any longer be seen as obsolete, antiquated, superfluous, as it was supposed to be in that Marxian conception' (Adorno 2003, p. 69). Alternatively, the remark might also be seen in terms of the perceived failure of the Enlightenment goal of self-determination to render the world a more humane place, which Adorno particularly associates with the ways in which 'instrumental' means/ends reason helped make the Holocaust possible. The idea of the 'realization of philosophy' can also be made more specific by considering another of its connotations, namely the idea of the 'end of philosophy', an idea which, in one of its versions, actually plays a key role in aspects of the history of analytical philosophy.

If philosophy is seen as 'metaphysics', in the sense of an account of the timeless true world underlying the changing world of appearances, the idea of its end has in varying forms been a theme of philosophy since the Young Hegelians attacked Hegel for the way his rationalist philosophical system was able to serve as an ideological cover for an unjust social and political status quo. This theme, as we saw, emerged in a different form in the Vienna Circle's politically admirable, but philosophically flawed, attempt to exclude all metaphysical claims from philosophy in order to counter irrationalist attacks on well-warranted science. The idea of the end of philosophy is now part of recent pragmatist attempts, such as those of Richard Rorty, to reorient analytical philosophy away from its obsession with epistemology, on the grounds that epistemological reflection increasingly blocks more important social, cultural, political, and existential concerns. Adorno makes much the same point, employing a core dialectical assumption of his thinking, namely that any way of thinking can turn into its opposite in changed circumstances:

> Epistemology is indeed not only a means of enlightenment, but in certain circumstances virtually another means of withdrawing from enlightening reflection. There is nothing in the world, even something as apparently as objective as epistemology, which, should the occasion arise, could not take on a social significance, a function in society, which transforms it into the opposite of what it once originally knew itself as. (Adorno 2008, p. 104)

This brief sample of ways in which the issue of the 'end of philosophy' is manifested brings us closer to the way Adorno sees the concrete practice and nature of philosophy.

The question is how the philosophical issue relates to the social and political issues which are part of what brings a particular philosophical stance to the fore. What Adorno seeks in philosophy are ways of transcending the world as it presents itself to us in specific historical circumstances, where the pressure of those circumstances can blind people to more humane alternatives. Adorno's combination of argument about the specifics of issues with a meta-perspective on how those issues became the focus of philosophical concern is central to what can be learned from him for the contemporary practice of philosophy. The contradictions this combination involves are not something which Adorno sees as susceptible to a definitive resolution. They are rather themselves an expression of what is inherent in attempts to resolve real contradictions generated by the modern world, which must be seen both in terms of their historical genesis and in terms of the legitimacy of the arguments and practices advanced to resolve them. The gap *between* these two aspects and the way they affect each other is as significant as either considered on its own terms: a division of the problem into genesis and validation is not the solution to what is at issue here.

A good way to get an initial sense of the alternative offered by Adorno is to look at a few aspects of his lectures 'Introduction to Philosophy' ('Einleitung in die Philosophie', unpublished, given in 1959–60), and some other introductory lectures, notably on Kant's *Critique of Pure Reason* (1995, given in 1959). These are intended to show to students of philosophy how doing philosophy is possible in the face of the idea of the end of metaphysics. Adorno insists to his listeners that 'what I would like to convey to you is not supposed to be a so-called negative philosophy, which is just as trivial as a positive one, but rather that you completely refuse to adopt this unfortunate manner of thinking' (Adorno 1959–60, p. 4972). On the issue of whether what he proposes is 'idealist', 'realist', 'materialist', 'spiritualist', and so on, he suggests that 'one should not get involved in these labels [*Fichets*], as I'd like to call it [*sic*], which in a sense compete with each other' (ibid., p. 4790), such that one ends up talking in the manner: 'I as *x* [i.e. idealist, materialist, etc.] must think in the following manner' (ibid., p. 4791). This stance might seem to lead to an untenable refusal to fulfil the commitments entailed by whatever Adorno claims about philosophy, and so to relativism. However, this assessment would not do justice to his approach.

All but the most dogmatic thinkers can and do find some positions plausible which are incompatible with their current conceptions. The most apt response to this situation need not be either simply to work hard enough on one's existing arguments in order to overcome other, incompatible conceptions, to adopt the other conception if one's own arguments come to seem untenable, or to find a mediating position between the two. All these approaches presuppose both that the issue that generates the contradictory conceptions is identifiable as the same issue, and that some kind of end-point to the contradiction is the required goal. The problem is that, as the history of philosophy shows, issues often turn out not to be as unified as they first appeared, and such end-points never seem to be definitive. On formal logical grounds one cannot make a positive claim based on the idea that contradiction, rather than resolution, seems constitutive in the history of philosophy. However, the awareness of the inherence of contradiction in philosophy has played a vital, if too often neglected, role in modern philosophy. Hegel can be seen as attempting both to incorporate and to overcome this awareness, by only eliminating contradiction at the end of his system, but this is precisely what Adorno opposes in Hegel. So what exactly does Adorno propose?

Adorno's idea is simply that what counts is the reality of the issue which generates the contradiction. 'Reality' here is meant in a sense that involves no substantial philosophical commitment, thus not in terms of a philosophical realism of the kind that arises from the desire to escape scepticism about the 'external world'. Adorno is pointing to the need to take account of all the decisive factors involved in whatever is being investigated, a need which may very well never be fulfilled, because of the obstacles to inquiry encountered in relation to any important issue. In a more philosophically reflexive sense, what he means is an echo of the Heidegger of *Being and Time*. Heidegger maintains that the standard claim that mathematics is a stricter discipline than history only applies because the existential foundations of mathematics are so much narrower.[1] Neither Heidegger nor Adorno seeks to question the truth of mathematical propositions, but the analytical narrowing involved in mathematics brings with it exclusions, which can be an obstacle, or worse, to understanding a key issue. Stephen Toulmin says in *The Uses of Argument* that '[p]hilosophers have often held that arguments in some fields of inquiry are intrinsically more open to rational assessment than those in others: questions of mathematics and questions about everyday matters of fact, for instance, have been considered to have a certain priority in logic over (say) matters of law, morals or aesthetics', but, he asserts, 'there is [. . .] a complete parallelism between arguments in all these different fields, and no grounds are yet evident for according priority to mathematical and similar matters' (Toulmin 2003a, p. 37). Claims to validity require grounds, and there is no essential difference in the way grounds of legitimacy are presented in the differing disciplines; if there were, it would be hard to see how those outside a discipline could ever enter it and contest or confirm its claims. However, since Hamann's critique of Kant's view of the synthetic a priori in the 1780s, the tension between, on the one hand, a view of the world in which the mathematically constituted natural sciences are the basis of reliable truth and, on the other, one in which natural languages are seen as the indication that one cannot reduce the world to what can be grasped on the basis of mathematically grounded explanation has been part of what would become the European/analytical divide.

Adorno deals with this tension as part of what he intends with the notion of 'non-identity', which relates to two different ideas. On the one hand, there is the Leibnizian idea that no entities are ever absolutely identical with each other, which is part of what led Kant to make identity a function of the categories of thought. The sense that identity is in some way a function of subjectivity will be vital in Adorno's complex critical relationship to Kant. On the other hand, there is the Hegelian idea that, because the determinacy of things depends on their relations to other things, they can never be definitively subsumed into a timeless classificatory concept which expresses their essential identity. This idea gives rise to Hegel's particular version of the 'concept/notion' (*Begriff*), as a dynamic structure of inferences that encompasses the changing status of things which results from their shifting relations to other things. Now such reflections can lead to a metaphysical concern with extrinsic and intrinsic properties, external and internal relations, and the like, which would land one in the midst of precisely the kind of thinking that Adorno seeks to get beyond. It is not that all such philosophical debates must be merely fruitless; they can concretely influence how an issue is responded to. The point is rather that one can be more interested in the debates for the reasons suggested by John Dewey in the following remark, than as topics which generate more and more conflicting arguments: '[T]he distinctive office, problems and subject-matter of philosophy grow out of stresses and strains in the community life in which a given form of philosophy arises, and [. . .] accordingly, its specific problems vary with the changes in human life that are always going on and that at times constitute a crisis and a turning point in human history' (quoted in Bernstein 2010, pp. 220–1). Given the dissonance between the aim of settling philosophical contradictions and the historical fact that they are not settled in the manner of the contradictions between Ptolemaic and Galilean cosmology, this should be at least an arguable approach.

The clashes between versions of atomism and holism, for example, which helped generate divisions between analytical and European philosophy, seem at present to be leading towards the widespread acceptance of versions of holism. Although many, like Jerry Fodor, will no doubt object, it is a measure of how holism has largely won out in many areas that other disciplines in the humanities and beyond see little future in atomist philosophical approaches. Seeing semantics in terms of how words represent things and regarding this as the decisive aspect of language, rather than seeing representation as only one part of what happens in language, offers too few productive avenues of inquiry for the understanding of human culture. What is interesting for an Adornian approach is why such a divide became constitutive for philosophical activity in so many places at the time it did. Toulmin (2003b) has suggested that the logicist, atomist approaches that developed in philosophy with Frege and Russell can be linked to trends in modernism which sought to arrive at a kind of intellectual purity that countered the ambiguity and complexity of the real social and historical world.[2]

Now there is no doubt that the results of such purity can be valuable: some of the focus on logic deriving from Frege has played a decisive role in the development of computing and other areas of application which have transformed and are transforming the modern world. The successes of applications of modern logic are, however, not a legitimation of an analytical focus as *philosophy*, especially not in its own terms of arriving at a theory of meaning which would provide answers to key epistemological and other questions. The same aspects of analytical approaches have also led to an image of language which excludes much of what is involved in human communication, from all the expressive and symbolic forms such as music, to ethical issues in interpretation, and so on (see Bowie 1997, 2007; Forster 2010; Johnson 2008). This image clearly impoverishes many crucial debates about human self-understanding, and leads to the kind of semantic approaches that attempted to suggest that cognitive science will answer the decisive questions about language which are now coming to be seen by many to have been a failure. Such approaches are precisely an example of what Adorno means when he says in the *Introduction to Dialectics*: 'There is no construct [*Gebilde*] in the world, not the highest constructs of philosophy, not the highest of art, which could not, by holding onto them in an isolated manner, be misused to keep people away from other things, to deceive people about other matters' (Adorno 2010, pp. 80–1). As Forster (2010) suggests, the contemporary moves in certain areas of analytical philosophy against the 'linguistic turn' (e.g. of Timothy Williamson and others) are not least a result of the image of language in much analytical philosophy being so impoverished.

In this perspective philosophy is necessarily involved in a continuous process of course-correction generated by the way in which focusing on certain issues turns out to lead to the neglect of what may be more important issues. Adorno says at one point: 'The history of philosophy is not just a history of problems and solutions, but in part also a rhythm of remembering and forgetting' (Adorno 1959–60, p. 4988). The idea of course-correction might sound rather banal and obvious, but the potential dangers of an atomist approach do not seem to have been the least bit obvious in key areas of modern thought, where the method of reducing what is at issue to objects of specific, often mathematical, analysis has regularly led to serious problems.

The basic danger of an atomist analytical focus is apparent in the way that brilliant mathematical economists came up with formulae which nearly destroyed the world economic system in 2008. One example, given by John Lanchester in his hugely entertaining and informed account of the crisis, has precisely the characteristics which Adorno sees as central to 'dialectical thinking', where a phenomenon turns out to be the opposite of what it is supposed to be once it is involved in complex links to real-world factors. 'Credit Default Swaps' were invented to spread risk by locating it in many parts of the financial system, so preventing one part of a system concentrating all the risks and taking everything down with it if it went wrong. The trouble was that the risk was spread in a way nobody could keep track of, so 'this tool, the CDS, which had been invented as a way of making lending safer, turned out to magnify and spread risks throughout the global system' (Lanchester 2010, p. 65), with catastrophic effects. The point is not just that any intellectual tool can, in the wrong circumstances, produce disaster, but that the reason for the disaster is that the tool is employed to the exclusion of what lies outside its frame of reference. The whole trend of much modern economic theory, in which mathematical models are built which eliminate consideration of what people are actually known to do in real contexts, has now, in the light of such effects, led to a crisis in the subject. Richard Bronk (2009) has convincingly argued that economists could do worse than read Romantic literature and philosophy in order to begin to understand how people really act.

Another manifestation of this tendency is the fondness in analytical philosophy for so-called 'thought experiments', such as the 'Trolley Problem' (do you switch the track for a runaway railway trolley about to kill five people to a track that would kill one person? What if stopping the trolley killing the five could be achieved by pushing a fat man off a bridge onto the line?). In real circumstances does anyone think they will base their behaviour on the principle they decide should be inferred from this piece of pure abstraction which masquerades as a concrete example to test utilitarian theories? The objection to such theorizing, which is based on people's actual counterfactual reflections, in which they necessarily engage all the time in order to make narrative sense of what they do and should do, is the idea that what is being conducted is an 'experiment' that has isolated the core of the problem and so can proffer a theory to solve it in the manner of a chemical theory. Models of the kind used in 'thought experiments' may play a useful role in the physical sciences, but the kind of debate engendered in the human sciences by such models is more often an obstacle to insight than an illumination, because it fakes a conceptual clarity which the complexity of real circumstances precludes. History tells us we often don't know what ultimately motivates people to do morally praiseworthy things, but it also tells us a lot about what makes them do appalling things, and that will be the point of departure for Adorno, rather than the search for a mythical philosophical criterion to defuse moral dilemmas.

It is, of course, important to remember that it is not just an atomistic analytical focus which can be the source of problems caused by that focus's occlusion of decisive phenomena. A totalizing explanatory system can also result in systemic blindness. If philosophy seeks to eliminate contingency either by isolating problems to be analysed in highly specialized terms, or by offering totalizing systematic conceptual answers, it may in this sense echo the effects of innovations in modern capitalism which are initially seen as the new big answer to perennial problems. Adorno's linking of philosophical systems, like Hegel's, to the way modern capitalism integrates everything into itself as an exchangeable commodity was sometimes regarded until very recently as a regrettable neo-Marxist residue of his thought. Recent events have, though, made at least some aspects of such links seem all too prescient. However, in the light of these initial remarks, it should also be clear that philosophical thinking seems to be suspended between, on the one hand, the need to avoid a narrow focus which fails to see how connections of an issue to other issues change the very nature of that issue and, on the other, the need to avoid a totalizing focus which subsumes too much into a prior system that blinds one to what lies outside the system. The example of the latter approach for Adorno will be Hegel, although his relationship to Hegel is a mixture of assimilation of much of Hegel's method and rejection of his conclusions. So how, then, does Adorno characterize the tasks of philosophy, if the result is not to be merely 'negative philosophy'?

Philosophical practice

The apocalyptic aspects of Adorno's philosophy, most apparent in *Dialectic of Enlightenment* and *Negative Dialectics*, tend to make his thinking seem cut off from engagement with less dramatic modes of thinking. This is why attention to texts of his that are generated in part by the demands of teaching can offer a different perspective. A course of lectures, like 'Introduction to Philosophy', given to students in a Federal Republic of Germany rapidly recovering, at the economic level at least, from the Nazi disaster, will clearly still bear traces of the trauma. At the same time, the course has to offer perspectives that can profitably engage students of philosophy, rather than plunging them into the sense of despair associated with Adorno's post-Holocaust reflections. Even *Negative Dialectics*, especially when seen in the light of the lectures, is actually, as we shall see in the Conclusion, an attempt to counter despair whilst renouncing metaphysical and theologically based forms of hope.

In the lectures Adorno does not define 'philosophy', but rather offers a series of reflections which let what he means emerge, beginning with the idea that philosophy is 'the comprehensive obligation not to be naïve' (Adorno 1959–60, p. 4793).[3] The lectures do not consist of a systematic introduction to 'key questions in philosophy', of the kind familiar on most Anglo-American introductory philosophy courses. Instead, Adorno reflects on what he thinks the tasks of philosophy should be, if many traditional assumptions about its nature can no longer be justified. A good example of what this means occurs when he talks about the distinction between 'appearance' (*Schein* – the meaning of the German word is generally ambiguous between 'appearance', and 'illusion') and 'reality/essence'. Adorno often turns metaphysical questions into empirical ones, because responding to them involves investigation of historical and social factors, rather than thinking that what is at issue can be resolved by philosophical argument about fundamental concepts. Instead of beginning with a defence of realism or anti-realism, or any of the contemporary variants of answers to the epistemological question of how mind and world relate, Adorno looks at how the appearance/essence distinction is manifest in modern culture: '[T]he whole way our life is set up is so much oriented to deception about what [...] lies behind it that the aim of knowing the essence and not being satisfied with the appearance corresponds to nothing less than the requirement for the intellect today' (Adorno 1959–60, p. 4798). Philosophical texts can, he maintains, 'only be understood by seeing them in the force-field in which they are located' (ibid., p. 4799), which is constituted by what they are opposed to.

Applied to Adorno's own preceding remark, the force-field of his comment would be the concentration of so much philosophy on abstract versions of the appearance/reality relationship, be they empiricist construals, such as phenomenalism, phenomenology's noesis and noema, or dialectical materialist models of base and superstructure, and so on. Such approaches seek a philosophical answer to the question of the relationship between the real and how it appears. Adorno's point is, though, that they do so in a period of history when there is a widespread failure to see through the deceptions inherent in modern societies, such as the projection by Nazis and others onto the Jews of the results of destructive effects of the crises of modern capital. But isn't the insistence on empirical versions of a break between appearance and reality just creating a false alternative, because the aims of philosophical inquiries into the issue since Plato are wholly different?

Adorno's argument would be wholly trivial if it just meant that people get things wrong a lot of the time, which has nothing to do with the substance of the metaphysical question about the relationship of appearance and reality. The real point is that he is suggesting links between the idea of a metaphysical solution to the question and the way that in modernity systematic distortion of how people see the world occurs. In these terms it is worth asking which approach to the appearance/reality issue might matter most in specific circumstances. Why does it seem so easy to persuade people in complex modern societies, where reliable information about 'reality' is generally available, to prefer 'appearance'? One way Adorno considers this question is via the Freudian notion of projection. The key here is that projection and the desire for metaphysical certainty may be significantly connected. In both cases the subject can be seen as imposing its own structure of thought onto the world: in the former to displace its own negative feelings onto an external object; in the latter to gain what the history of metaphysics tells us is likely to be an illusory control of the world. Once the issues raised by Kant become central to philosophy, this version of the question of appearance and reality becomes in some respects inescapable. It is not, then, that Adorno is offering a rigid alternative between abstract philosophical reflection and getting your hands dirty by seeing how a conceptual distinction plays out in concrete historical circumstances. His point is both that the former can contribute to the latter, and that the latter should also inform the former. How this occurs cannot be mapped out via a general philosophical method, and can only be achieved in specific investigations. This dialectical approach is the source both of some of Adorno's most important insights, and of what can for many be a frustrating sense that no defined position can emerge from it, because it seems constitutively to force one to sit on the fence.

The preceding discussion will appear from the perspective of many ways of doing philosophy as hopelessly generalized. Without a precise theoretical determination of which version of the appearance/reality distinction is being worked with one cannot hope to come up with a clear position on the issue. This objection, which assumes that the road to philosophical salvation depends almost completely on clear specification of the meaning of key terms, too often goes by default. Questioning it does *not* mean that one therefore advocates a lack of clarity: Adorno himself despairs of issues being forced into this kind of false alternative. Sometimes clarity based on clear conceptual definition is itself an illusion, because the definition obscures links of the issue to other issues. Adorno suggests the reasons for vigilance in this respect when he reflects on the dilemmas of philosophy in relation to the modern natural sciences. In the wake of Max Weber he sees the fate of modern societies in terms of the growing specialization occasioned by rationalization, which 'reifies' each area by giving it its own procedures that differentiate it from other activities.[4] This specialization occurs in philosophy too, which means that it loses touch with many of the motivations which gave rise to the need for it in the first place, a process which has been very clear in the way some analytical (and European) philosophy has lost touch with the concerns of non-philosophers. As such, for Adorno, 'organized science', which he uses here in its wider sense, therefore including philosophy, 'is really nothing but such a social network which prevents us as people who experience and think in a living way from really finding in science what we actually want to have from this science' (ibid., p. 4842). Adorno is not naïvely critical of this process, which he sees as leading to the defining modern 'split' (*Bruch*) between subject and object, and thus to the modern versions of the question of appearance and reality: '[I]t will not be possible, say by conceiving of a philosophy, now to leap over this split, because this split is not just one of our thought and reflection, but is one of a reified reality, thus of a world which is alienated from us for very real reasons' (ibid., p. 4843). The task of philosophy is to reflect on this split itself, in a 'self-reflection of science'.[5]

The difficulty of such a self-reflection of science lies in the fact that the 'sphere of objective necessities' has clear dominance over the 'sphere of the spiritual self-determination of humankind' (ibid., p. 4845). This is already a source of the likelihood of deception, including self-deception, gaining the upper hand over a rational grasp of the essence of a problem. The dominating pressure of socially created objective constraints creates a new version of the sort of natural constraints which were responded to by imaginary, mythological forms of control in traditional societies. This is a central theme of Adorno's work, and is most familiar from *Dialectic of Enlightenment*, though the extreme ways in which it is articulated in that text have obscured its more differentiated implications.

Adorno's stance with respect to the relationship between subject and object is not, then, primarily determined by the attempt to overcome what has been the main focus of modern philosophical debate in many areas, namely the kinds of epistemological scepticism which lead to the search for a way of reconnecting mind and world after their Cartesian divorce. While thinking, like Merleau-Ponty and others, that the epistemological version of that divorce can involve the myth of disembodied consciousness, Adorno also reflects on what underlies that divorce, which he sees in connection with 'the reflection of the *ratio* on itself' and with the break from 'religious dogmatism' (ibid., p. 4845). He thereby combines reflection on the philosophical problem of how subjectivity can give an objective account of itself with reflection on the process of secularization. The latter is not explicable simply in terms of the failure of arguments proving the existence of God, because it also depends on changes in the economic and social spheres. Rather than opting either for a sceptical position or for a philosophical response to scepticism, Adorno is interested in how the issue illuminates what determines the course of modernity.

Talk of modernity as 'reified' by processes of rationalization often provokes the justified response that modernity offers a very great deal which is undeniably an advance on what preceded the supposed reification. Adorno responds to this kind of objection in two main ways. He is, first of all, in no doubt that advances in medicine, social welfare, and so on, are just that, but the decisive question is why, when the benefits of these could be universal, they are denied to large parts of the world. Second, what makes these advances possible is involved in a 'dialectic of enlightenment', because the same processes can produce catastrophic results. The key to this much more problematic conception is the 'exchange relation', which gives rise to the commodity structure: '[T]his exchange relation extends into every conceivable relationship between people and also into the psychology of people' (ibid., p. 4848).

The objectifying process present in the commodity form, which enables wholly different things to be made commensurate and exchangeable, is also present in 'organized science', such that the 'rationality of science [. . .] is external to us' (ibid., p. 4849). The problem is that it is precisely this externality which is the foundation of the success of modern science, because the formulation of predictive laws depends on the contingent differences between subjective perceptions of actual things being excluded in the name of what they have in common. The internal response is, in contrast, essentially arbitrary (ibid., p. 4852). If philosophy is not to either seek, as it unsuccessfully did in some of the systems of the late eighteenth and early nineteenth centuries, to incorporate the sciences into itself, or to become merely subjective '*Weltanschauung*', its legitimacy is in question. Adorno's decisive dialectical move is to claim that the objectification constitutive of the commodity and of modern natural science is in fact a manifestation of *subjectivity*. Modernity is therefore based on the fact that the 'real root of all objectivity is subject' (ibid., p. 4887). But how can we make sense of this?

The first thing to say here is that one has to get used to the idea in Adorno, which is derived from Hegel, that the notion of a subjective and an objective pole, of a mind and a world that are somehow separate from each other, leads to a failure to understand the nature of subjectivity. This much is already apparent in his remark that the exchange relation becomes something internal to people, changing how they see the world in the most intimate ways. Think how object-relations theories in psychoanalysis can be connected to the nature of people's relationship to commodity ownership: why do motorists sometimes get violent if a cyclist inadvertently damages their car, even if it is insured?[6] The idea can also be understood by the fact that the language in which subjects articulate and express themselves is part of the objective world and can be affected by the functioning of commodity exchange. This is evident, for example, in how the language of emotion becomes reified by clichés from commercial films. From his early work on Kierkegaard and Husserl onwards, Adorno refuses to accept the idea of a pure interiority of consciousness, because subjectivity is always formed by 'external' pressures and influences.

The other main, related, source of Adorno's dialectical reversal is the Kantian revolution. Kant is not to be assessed here in terms of the supposed ultimate defensibility, or lack of it, of his philosophical arguments. The attitude behind Jonathan Bennett's notorious assertion about Kant's first *Critique* that it 'is wrong on nearly every page' (Bennett 1966, p. viii) is precisely what Adorno rejects: 'In the face of the evident enormously elevated status of Kant, it is always better if one tries to grasp obvious peculiarities, deficiencies, insufficiencies through [. . .] the difficulty of the matter in hand (*Sache*), than to want to understand them as merely subjective insufficiencies of the author'

(Adorno 1959–60, p. 4909). He thinks this stance should be valid for all understanding of significant philosophical texts. The alternative is that Kant, purged of his egregious errors, turns out to think the same as, for example, Peter Strawson (Andrews 1997). If one assumes, as the history of philosophy shows, that Strawson will only find a limited number of defenders, it becomes hard to know why such a fuss is made about Kant at all. If Kant was already 'wrong', and those who demonstrate this in a manner which supposedly leaves one with no further reason to read Kant are themselves 'wrong', the temptation is towards a kind of nihilistic scepticism, in which the history of philosophy is a history of irredeemable error. This might make the stance of many philosophers who still advance their truths in the usual apparently confident manner seem rather heroic, but a better way to see what is at issue here is that there must be something wrong with this way of doing philosophy.

Adorno thinks not that one cannot or should not show deficiencies in Kant and his interpreters, but rather that exclusive concentration on doing this means that one fails to engage with the 'matter in hand'. In this case the matter is precisely the issue of the root of objectivity in modernity being 'the subject'. But what is the alternative to the approach that involves seeing which arguments of Kant's hold water, and which do not, and replacing the latter with whatever happen to be the current analytical arguments?[7] It is important to remember here that Kant almost disappeared from American philosophy after the replacement of pragmatism with the analytical philosophy of Carnap and others, until the massive revival of interest in Kant beginning in the 1970s, which continues to this day.

We need here to consider a further key conception of Adorno's before looking in more detail at his understanding of Kant in the next chapter. Adorno derives a conception of what he terms the 'content' (*Gehalt*) and the 'truth-content' (*Wahrheitsgehalt*) of philosophy from aspects of work by Walter Benjamin, whose esoteric nature defies easy summary (see Bowie 1997, Chapter 8 for an attempt).[8] One way to grasp what Adorno means is precisely apparent in the fact that Kant disappeared and then reappeared in American philosophy. A basic reason for his reappearance, as suggested by John McDowell's *Mind and World* (1994), is that questions asked by Kant can show the indefensibility of reductionist scientific approaches in philosophy, which McDowell terms 'bald naturalism'. Even if one has justified doubts about the synthetic a priori or the table of categories – in Adorno's lectures on Kant's first Critique he warns his audience not to expect any convincing proofs from the Critique – the 'truth-content' of Kant lies in what he offers for a critique of a wholly objectifying approach to understanding the world. Crucially, how this critique is manifested in different historical circumstances – which requires detailed reflection on the contrasting understandings of science in those circumstances – is also part of the truth-content.

The last aspect of this example of Adorno's assimilation of Benjamin's ideas suggests why he connects the understanding of philosophy to the understanding of art. Adorno insists that the 'notion of content is alien to the positive individual sciences in their usual form' (Adorno 1959–60, p. 4863). 'Content' is the 'object of the criticism of works of art' (ibid.) and is 'what is communicated by this work of art' (ibid., p. 4864), which cannot just be communicated by concepts. Adorno takes the example of 'hope', which is central to Benjamin's essay on Goethe's *Elective Affinities*, seeing it as part of the content of Beethoven's piano sonata Opus 31 Number 2, the so-called 'Tempest'.[9] The music cannot be understood via the concept of hope, in the sense that the classifying term does not convey what the music conveys – which does not mean that the concept is irrelevant. Only by grasping the music itself can the 'idea' of hope emerge.[10] It does so from the 'constellation of a whole sequence of moments' (ibid., p. 4866), rather than being something which can be immediately identified. Just over two minutes into the sonata's slow middle movement, a sublimely simple melody rises up from a passage imbued with yearning and tension. Without an understanding of the emergence of the melody at that point in the movement, and of the forms of expression which Beethoven was transforming by this passage, one cannot grasp the 'truth-content' of the work.

It is easy to suggest that the sequence of 'moments' is actually indeterminately large, such that we have to include ourselves as contemporary listeners, or aspects of Viennese history in the post-Napoleonic era of political disappointment, as part of the constellation, and so on, and so forth, to the point of deconstructive absurdity. However, this criticism would miss the point of 'truth-content': it is not just any work which creates a constellation in which such content can become manifest, and engagement with art is not merely arbitrary.[11] As we shall see in Chapter 6, Adorno's resistance to relativism is based on the fact that in real engagement with culture nobody actually accepts that judgement is arbitrary. Were they to do so, they would have no grounds ever to defend their evaluations at all, when much of social communication is precisely based around such evaluation. Above all, truth-content is not something which is identified via the constellation, as it is thoroughly temporalized and does not remain the same, and the content can also 'die', as the work ceases to connect to other 'moments'.

Truth-content therefore has to 'happen' via the continuing critical engagement with the matter in hand, because it has to do with how a certain constellation manifested through the work can lead to a critical perspective on an established conception. In *Aesthetic Theory* Adorno gives the example of why the classical idea that artworks integrate diverse material into a unity, which is most notably achieved in some works of the middle Beethoven, can cease to be the truth-content of significant modern art. In modern music attempts simply to go back to an earlier, conventionally more 'beautiful' style rarely succeed in producing anything but kitsch: 'The most extreme integration is an extreme of illusion (*Schein*), and that leads to its transformation: since the late Beethoven, the artists who achieved the integration mobilize disintegration. The truth-content of art, whose organ was integration, turns against art, and in this turn art achieves its emphatic moments' (Adorno 1997, 7, pp. 73–4). Adorno is thinking of the way that Beethoven's late quartets incorporate abrupt changes of mood, no longer seek to balance the parts in relation to the whole, have passages of striking repetitiveness, and at times get close to expressive breakdown. How, though, is philosophy's truth-content to be grasped?

The simple answer is that Kant's truth-content may lie precisely in how, in varying contexts, his work can reveal what has been forgotten or repressed by established modes of thought. However problematic this conception may be, it does address the fact that the reception of Kant cannot be adequately understood if his ideas are judged solely in terms of whatever happens to be the dominant philosophical manner of arguing at a particular time: that is, the issue raised above with regard to Bennett and Strawson. The content is dependent not on what Kant himself may contingently have thought, but on what 'expresses itself objectively in his thought, what its truth-content is, what meaning it has beyond what is meant in a particular place' (Adorno 1995, p. 123).

Let us look in the next chapter, therefore, at how Adorno's approach works in relation to the idea that 'real root of all objectivity is subject' in relation to Kant. As we saw, Adorno is not interested in labelling his philosophy as idealist, materialist, and so on. He will, though, use a specific notion of 'Idealism' as the object of his criticism of philosophy, and advocate a certain kind of 'materialism'. The former, he maintains, seeks a definitive way of thinking, which appears possible because thought is supposedly determined only by itself; the latter rejects this, because thought cannot be fully transparent to itself, emerging rather from dynamic historical tensions between the subjective and the objective. The fact that these alternatives cannot be characterized in the standard form of a definition that specifies their response to basic philosophical questions, such as the 'mind/body problem', has to do precisely with the approach we are considering here. Adorno will, for example, be happy to talk about the truth in the 'Idealism' he makes his main object of criticism.

Before moving on I want to cite a remark from a very helpful and acute reader's report on the first draft of the present book that brings a vital issue into focus. The reader is concerned that Adorno's 'practice (of referring philosophical problems to social problems)' may be either 'too weak (it shows mere contingent associations) or too strong (it amounts to reduction)'. If Adorno is proposing a method of overcoming philosophy by referring philosophical problems to social problems, he is open to this criticism, and at times this seems to be the case. At the same time, the alternative suggested by the reader itself involves a tension of the kind which Adorno sees as a means of understanding the historical situation of philosophy. If one renounces traditional metaphysical goals in philosophy, one alternative is to look to understand in historical and social terms how those goals came to be what they were (part of the non-metaphysical interpretation of Hegel we shall look at later essentially suggests this). In doing so one is, though, open to the accusation of making mere contingent associations. If one then tries to ground those associations in a justificatory theory, one either heads in the direction of reducing philosophy to sociology or history, or returns to the idea that philosophical problems, which themselves include explaining the genesis of philosophical questions, have precisely the status that the renunciation of traditional metaphysics seeks to move beyond. It is the fact that none of these options seems satisfactory that is crucial: all involve something we cannot do without, but none avoids the danger of hiding something that may be decisive. Adorno tries to negotiate the tensions here by the kind of specific engagements with key thinkers and issues we are about to examine. Whether he succeeds depends for him on the degree of insight generated into the matters he thinks are most important. What this tells us about the ends of contemporary philosophy is the theme of the present book.

2
Contradiction as Truth-Content: Adorno and Kant

Subjectivity and truth

An essential feature of modernity is revealed for Adorno by the problematic relationship between subject and object in Kant.[1] The 'turn' from ancient to modern 'lies in the fact that the concept of the idea, which in Plato is opposed as something objective to subjectivity, is equated in the whole of modern philosophy precisely with subjectivity' (Adorno 1959–60, p. 4879). However, although Kant is often read in terms of subjectivism, his real concern in the first Critique is clearly objectivity. Adorno sees the form of the subject/object relationship as a 'relationship of tension between the moment [...] that something is thought, and the something *which* is thought'; this is 'the relationship of tension in which the movement of philosophy, the movement of thought is played out at all' (ibid., p. 4892). Clearly 'these two moments in Kantian philosophy are in continual friction with each other', and Adorno's interest lies in '*How* they are in friction with each other, what constellations they enter into with each other, what difficulties result from this' (Adorno 1995, p. 10). Kant's philosophy is itself to be regarded as a 'force-field', where 'behind the most abstract concepts which come into conflict with each other [...] stand what are in reality extraordinarily vivid forces of experience' (ibid., p. 13).

But is this version of 'experience' sufficiently robust to make much sense? The Adornian response to this worry is that without the experience that informs Kant's philosophy it is hard to explain how it has come to play a role in the most diverse attempts to comprehend modernity. Only by engaging with the contradictions that are played out in Kant can this conception of experience be concretized. Adorno's stance towards Kant is perhaps best captured by his remark that 'the power of the *Critique of Pure Reason* does not at all really lie so much in the answer which he gives to the so-called metaphysical questions, as it does in the very heroic, very stoical refusal to give an answer to these questions at all' (ibid., p. 17). That refusal is precisely part of the truth-content of Kant's philosophy, and is integral to the experience from which it arises. Only if one construes the task of philosophy in terms of what the history of philosophy shows is never achieved, namely definitive answers to metaphysical questions, would this perhaps rather startling view of Kant be indefensible.

Adorno argues that an exaggerated demand for metaphysical certainty can lead to a legitimate 'mistrust of philosophy', because 'philosophy generally really does behave as if this concept of a timeless truth valid for all future experience is the only one worthy of humankind' (ibid., p. 41). In fact, though, we live with a much more mobile relationship to truth, largely based on successfully coping with the pressures of our existence. A key tension in Kant is, then, precisely between the metaphysical demand and the ways in which it is contradicted by modern experience. Large parts of modern philosophy, as the idea of the 'end of philosophy' suggests, have been concerned to invalidate the metaphysical demand and replace it with what can be empirically proven and with the explication of what legitimates such proof. Adorno, however, thinks that the attitudes in such philosophy fail to understand that, without what gives rise to the metaphysical impulse, philosophy's ability to articulate ways beyond a given state of society may be lost. The substance of Adorno's interpretation has, then, to do with the meanings of the contradictions in Kant with regard to metaphysics.

The tension at issue here appears in Kant's 'idea' of 'an objective truth' that is achieved 'precisely through the subject', a subject which 'could guarantee everything' (Adorno 1959–60, p. 4911), but which is at the same time inherently finite. The dual status of the subject in Kant, remarked upon by Foucault and others, who argue that the subject is both something empirical and yet is the transcendental condition of objectivity, creates the problem of how to connect the contingent and the necessary sides of the subject. Adorno's response to this dilemma is that philosophizing in the light of this issue

> is really grasping constellations of subject and object [. . .] what appears to us as object almost always reveals itself as something which has come into being ['*ein Gewordenes*', in the sense of something that becomes itself, rather than having a static essence], and what appears to us as autonomous, powerful subject keeps on revealing itself as conditioned, as dependent on what there is. (Ibid., p. 4893)

The dialectical implications of this view are in one sense Hegelian. Adorno does not regard the basis of the autonomy of the subject (Kant's 'spontaneity') as a wholly internal attribute of subjectivity, because exercises of spontaneity occur in never fully transparent objective contexts; the pure moment of spontaneity is therefore impossible to specify. Adorno will, though, question the Hegelian way out of the Kantian dilemmas, because it does not take sufficient account of how objective pressures can mean that supposed self-determination via norms may be either illusory or a form of self-deception, rather than a rational accommodation with necessity.

The reason why the 'real root of all objectivity is subject' in modernity is, then, evident for Adorno in the idea that '[t]he *Critique of Pure Reason* really is the greatest attempt at the salvation of ontology on a subjectivist basis' (Adorno 1995, p. 54). It is not that the subject therefore really has sovereign command over the order of the world. Instead, the lack of an apparent alternative after the disintegration of a theologically founded objective world-order means that, as Kant shows, the subject now necessarily plays a role in how the world comes to be constituted. It is when this role becomes absolutized (in the form of what Adorno terms 'Idealism') that what can be self-determination turns into something analogous to the power of nature over the subject before the rise of modern science and technology. This reversal then leads to modern forms of thinking which can become as irrational as the myths of pre-modern societies: '[E]specially the mind which forgets its own origin in nature [. . .] more than ever falls prey to its origin in nature; i.e. is only able to perpetuate blind conditions like those which arise in nature' (ibid., p. 118).

Because Kant both suggests why the mediation of objectivity through the subject seems to be the only way in which metaphysics can be salvaged, and yet reveals the limitations of the subject, he makes apparent an essential contradiction in modernity. The power of the subject seems to lie in its self-determining reflective capacity to reveal what necessities are inherent in objective knowledge.[2] Only such necessities can give unity to the apprehension of the objective world, once dogmatic metaphysical assumptions can no longer be defended. However, this systematic unity comes up against what Adorno terms the Kantian 'block', the fact that the world is never reducible to the ways in which the subject conceptualizes it. It is precisely by refusing to give up on either of these positions that Kant is caught in contradictions that generate the truth-content of his work. Subsequent construals of Kant tend to fall on either side of this opposition between rational self-determination of thought and the sense of the limits of the subject. Compare, for example, McDowell's neo-Hegelian concentration on self-determination and the unboundedness of the conceptual (McDowell 1994) with Rae Langton's defence of the idea of the unknowability of intrinsic properties (Langton 1998). Adorno draws a more general conclusion from Kant's attempt to combine incompatible positions: '[T]he depth of a philosophy does not lie in the extent to which this philosophy can reconcile contradictions, but rather in the extent to which it is able to make contradictions manifest which are inherent in the matter [*Sache*] itself' (Adorno 1995, p. 128). Given that modern philosophy cannot be regarded as self-legitimating, its importance should lie in how it allows us to respond to the world, even though it may not offer answers to the questions it forces us to ask.

Unlike many commentators on Kant, Adorno is not primarily concerned with epistemology, in the sense of developing arguments that refute the sceptic. His concern is rather with what forces Kant beyond an epistemological agenda, even as he seeks to limit objectivity to what can be dealt with in terms of that agenda. Kant himself may have been 'awakened from his dogmatic slumbers' by Hume, but in seeking an alternative to the sceptical implications of Hume's empiricism more is at stake than the explanation of the conditions of possibility of reliable scientific laws. Kant, as Adorno insists, *presupposes* the truth of Newtonian mechanics, so basing his thought on a specific kind of warranted knowledge that developed at a particular time, and his concern is with what *legitimates* that truth. A key element here is how the modern sciences reduce the scope of what can justifiably be dealt with in philosophical terms: 'On the one hand philosophy would like to say the absolute [. . .] it would like really to say how it really is, what the *essence* is that lies behind all things. But on the other hand the positive sciences wrest from philosophy ever more of the questions which aim at this absolute' (ibid., p. 65). The result is what Adorno terms the 'residual character of truth' (ibid., p. 67) which philosophy like Kant's is left with 'when one has stripped away the apparently ephemeral, transient, historical' (ibid.), from it.

Kant is left, Adorno maintains, with just the issue of how synthetic a priori propositions are possible, as the core of the first Critique's account of epistemology, an issue which many of the subsequent philosophical attacks on Kant regarded as the source of his failure. The logical positivists think, for example, that mathematics must be a priori, because it is, like logic, 'contentless'. One might, therefore, as the analytical tradition did for a long time, just see the problem of the synthetic a priori as signalling the fact that one could effectively ignore Kant. Adorno, in contrast, thinks that the appropriate reading of Kant should not be in terms of a failure which seems to be the fate of virtually all positive arguments in modern philosophy. Kant's problem is precisely an expression of a historical tension. In order to isolate the supposedly truly philosophical questions, Kant is forced into trying to exclude the side of the object, because that is what is dealt with by the reliable scientific laws whose subjective 'conditions of possibility' he is investigating. The problem is, though, that the subject is reduced by this to being the repository of a series of logical rules whose provenance is mysterious, and it is this kind of reduction which Adorno reads as a sign of something important concerning the real fate of subjects in modernity.

When, in *Dialectic of Enlightenment*, Adorno argues that Kant's 'schematism', which is intended to build a bridge between the material and the form of cognition, is 'the interest of industrial society' (Adorno 1997, 3, p. 103), because it reduces everything to the ways in which it can be made identical with other things, the point is obviously wildly exaggerated. However, read in conjunction with the more cautious manner of arguing of the lectures, something more interesting appears, namely an account of why modern philosophy has such problems dealing with questions of subjectivity. The more the explanation of the subject concentrates on what can be objectified, the more is missed out by the approach in question, hence Adorno's interest in 'experience' and 'the apparently ephemeral, transient, historical', which forms the substance of individual subjective lives, and which is effectively absent from so much modern philosophy. This absence is one of the reasons why Adorno gives such philosophical weight to modern art: 'the apparently ephemeral' is central to the novel, for example. The contradictions in Kant's account of the subject are, then, an expression of a truth about subjectivity which can only emerge through those contradictions, and they push Kant's argument beyond its self-imposed limitations.

The consequence of what Adorno exemplifies via Kant is that 'the content of every metaphysics that can be thought at all and that concretely exists is after all again and again a content of experience' (Adorno 1995, p. 85), rather than a timeless true account of the world. The value of this approach lies in the way it no longer sees the history of metaphysics as a history of error, and yet does not incorporate the whole of that history into the kind of redemptive narrative characteristic of certain interpretations of Hegel. The challenge is to counter the accusation that the position entails a self-undermining relativism. Adorno's answer to this accusation has to do with the notions of experience and of truth-content, and with his suspicion of the demand for a definitive answer in such questions. He acknowledges that 'without the hope for the whole truth [. . .] something like philosophy cannot be thought at all' (Adorno 1959–60, p. 4913). But when philosophy concretely lays claim to such truth it results in the abstractions of the 'residual character' of truth. Only a combination, which is precisely the combination characteristic of the 'early German Romantic' philosophy of Friedrich Schlegel and Novalis (see Bowie 1997; Frank 1997), of the 'utopian' striving for 'the whole truth' with 'the unfathomable and melancholic knowledge of the vanity' (Adorno 1959–60, p. 4913) of the striving seems adequate to the modern philosophical situation. The different ways in which this combination is negotiated manifest 'the concreteness which really lies in the concept of philosophy, namely that of human circumstances' (ibid., p. 4927), where the demand for philosophical truth is ineluctable, and yet, while seeming always doomed to disappointment, can be the source of vital insights.

Adorno sums up the contradictions involved in Kant's first Critique as follows: '[I]t is at the same time a philosophy of identity – i.e. a philosophy which attempts finally to ground being in the subject – and a philosophy of non-identity insofar as it tries to limit this claim to identity through that which the subject comes up against, through the *block* that the subject encounters in its cognition' (Adorno 1995, p. 105). The Kantian division between the spontaneity required for judgement and the receptivity required for the provision of the material of judgement reflects this contradiction. German Idealism from Fichte to Hegel is predicated on questioning the division between spontaneity and receptivity, because the connection between the two seemed to be lacking (this problem was what led Kant to the notion of the schema), and this apparent lack leads back to older sceptical worries.[3] Adorno begins from this perspective, because of the implausibility of the idea that the synthesizing activity of the subject and the nature of the objective world given in perception are wholly distinct. However, he thinks that the German Idealist response leads to a 'philosophy of identity', of the kind entailed by the one-sided view of Kant's grounding of cognition in the subject, whilst conjuring away the contradiction between this conception and the 'block'. Adorno's concern is therefore with the 'tension between the interest in the objectivity of truth, on the one hand, and the reflection on the knowing subject as that which constitutes such truth, on the other' (Adorno 1959–60, p. 4930).

These days this tension appears most evidently in reflections on the relationship between causally based naturalistic explanations and the insistence that explanation itself has an irreducibly normative element. In the terms of the latter, one falls prey to the 'myth of the given' if knowledge is to be justified by some kind of direct evidence, rather than by the exercise of conceptual capacities which are in some measure spontaneous. The debate on this issue that has gone on between Robert Pippin and John McDowell (see McDowell 2008) has largely concerned itself with seeking the correct characterization of the relationship between the normative and the natural. While Adorno does offer some interesting material for such debates, his concern is more with what is expressed by them, their truth-content. Given the ever more differentiated attempts in the debates to determine the role of the spontaneous and the receptive, and so on, one can justifiably carry on the debate wherever it may lead, but one can also ask metaphilosophical questions about why this issue has come to form a focus of philosophy when it disappeared from Anglo-American debate for so long.

Adorno's approach is concerned not solely with the legitimacy of the arguments – even though he is quite clear that, as a philosopher, 'by making any assertion the claim is present in the assertion, whether I want it or not, even if I relativize it in whatever manner, that it is absolute, that it is absolutely true' (Adorno 1959–60, p. 4946) – but with what happens when we explore the contradictions which emerge from having to measure specific claims against an absolute standard. McDowell concludes his response to Pippin, for example, by questioning the idea that objectivity is 'socially bestowed' by intentional acts of individuals, because such an idea would make it unclear how the individual could get others to acknowledge their authority: 'That objects are authoritative over thought – certainly over its expression – is a feature of a social practice that has evolved into being as it is. The authority is genuine, because we can freely acknowledge it. But the idea of bestowing it on objects does not apply to anything we do, or anything any of our predecessors did' (McDowell 2008, p. 203). McDowell sees his comments as Hegelian in spirit – suggesting the need to be careful over how Hegel is interpreted. McDowell wants to correct what would, in Adorno's terms, be a view which weights things too far towards the spontaneity of the subject; Pippin, after all, wishes to 'leave nature behind' and just talk about our self-legislation, and the social bestowing of cognitive authority.

Like Adorno, McDowell follows Hegel in claiming that 'the idea of a sensuous manifold which is itself completely abstract' is a 'myth' (Adorno 1959–60, p. 4933). This claim precisely involves questioning a strict line between spontaneity and receptivity, because if the latter only received something wholly indeterminate the subject would have to project all its determinacy onto it. This would make it unclear how the subject could give any content to experience without having already acquired what makes experience be about the complex, differentiated world we are actually confronted with. McDowell's aims are, though, still determined by the analytical obsession with overcoming scepticism. This means that he then has to give an account of how we really 'have the world in view', committing himself to a defence of a version of 'direct realism' that says that our everyday perception of objects really is of those objects. Such moves have tended to lead to a to and fro between various, changing versions, both from McDowell himself and from his critics, of how the spontaneous and the receptive are to be characterized, and how they relate.

This debate clearly is important in combating causal accounts of perception which are part of the reductionist naturalism that accompanies the incursion of representationalist neuroscience into philosophical debate.[4] At this point, though, the Adornian stance on contradiction can take one in a different direction. Although McDowell sees himself as exorcizing philosophical anxieties (e.g. that of scepticism) in a Wittgensteinian manner, he does lay claim to a version of 'Absolute

Idealism': '[I]t is central to Absolute Idealism to reject the idea that the conceptual realm has an outer boundary' (McDowell 1994, p. 44). He argues this so as to escape a model in which there is a gap between the causal effects of the world on the subject and the way the subject conceptualizes those effects, because what is doing the causing lies beyond that boundary as a brute causal impact. However, if one looks at the examples McDowell discusses, they almost all concern perception of 'medium size dry goods', and this fails to give much purchase on the kind of real-world experience that cannot be understood as an agglomeration of small-scale objective perceptions.[5] In Adorno's terms the danger here is that one is landed again with the 'residual character' of philosophical truth. The argument that one has to start at this epistemological level has at some point to confront the fact that the debate never seems to get beyond it, to 'a full, objective and complete world' (Adorno 1959–60, p. 4933): that is, the world of 'experience'. The determination of the thought/reality relationship seems to be unavoidably contested at the abstract subject/object level. It is therefore 'contradictory' in the sense Adorno is stressing, where the contradictions are indicative of real historical contradictions with regard to the modern problem of how freedom fits into a world which the sciences show to be more and more subsumable into explanatory laws.

McDowell says, in a manner which echoes Adorno's accounts of Kant: 'If the forms of thought have their source in the pure understanding, but objects are given to us only through the senses, it is a substantive task to argue that the forms of thought are the forms of reality' (McDowell 2008, p. 197), and he claims that Kant's attempted solution dissolves into 'subjective idealism'. McDowell thinks this identity is ultimately a 'platitude', because, in Hegelian fashion, '[t]here is no way to conceive reality except in terms of what is the case', which has to coincide 'with the idea of what can truly thought to be the case' (ibid.). The Hegelian solution is arrived at by the revelation of how apparent immediacy (unconceptualized sense-data, etc.) is in fact mediated, because it cannot be made intelligible unless it is informed by concepts (hence the unboundedness of the conceptual). This view is, though, clearly at odds with what Adorno intends with his notion of the Kantian 'block'.

Adorno is not, as we saw, primarily concerned with objections to 'the idea of what can truly thought to be the case' with respect to the world of everyday objects. Instead he wants to investigate what is expressed about the modern world by the inability to reach an agreed end-point to the argument about scepticism. This has to do with a different sense in which subject and object in the modern world are in contradiction with each other. The very focus on the cognitive relation to the object, and on whether the concept can be said truly to convey the truth of the object, means that philosophy's job is the justification of identification. Adorno's alternative view, which doubts the usefulness of a philosophical reconciliation of the kind sought in epistemology, is that philosophy's 'content would be to express what is missed or excised by science, the division of labour, the forms of reflection of the business of self-preservation' (Adorno 2001, p. 235). This approach does not entail that Adorno thinks there is a philosophical way of disputing the well-warranted results of science; the question is what the exclusive concentration on such results may produce.

The preceding reflections can make more plausible a controversial reversal which is vital to Adorno's philosophy (and is present in a different form in the later Heidegger). The idea derives from Max Weber: 'The more the world is emptied of an objective meaning and is completely resolved into our categories, so completely becomes *our* world, the more meaning is removed from the world at the same time' (Adorno 1995, p. 168). Weber's idea of the 'disenchantment of the world' through modern science and bureaucratic rationality means that 'with, as it were, the familiarity of our world the metaphysical despair increases' (ibid., p. 169). Here Adorno's difference of focus from the (post-)analytical reception of Kant is most striking. Rather than being concerned with whether the Copernican turn really answers the sceptic, Adorno concentrates on the fact that modern science possesses an authority which the success of its technological applications makes undeniable. By making the world fit 'our categories', thus by rendering it the object of subjectivity, we gain control of it, but – and this is the decisive point – at the expense of the loss of 'objective' meaning, which does not depend on how the subject comes to constitute the world. This might seem like of piece of theological nostalgia – as Pippin (2005) suggests, when he maintains Adorno wants to 're-enchant' nature – but just claiming that is too easy, given that so many secular ways of making sense have theological roots and can survive the destruction by the natural sciences of their theological support (see Taylor 2011). As Adorno contends, the shift to the subject as that which constitutes the intelligibility of the world associated with Kant is a key source of the existentialist view of the 'absurdity' of existence that develops out of the decline of German Idealism's attempt to develop a modern metaphysics. The need to come to terms with the 'fall of metaphysics' is therefore generated by what in one respect is a massive increase in rational control, but some of the results of that control – and here Adorno's assumption is that the Holocaust is the key to modernity – are anything but rational.

At this point we come to a further controversial aspect of Adorno's thought. Adorno agrees that Kant's separation of the world of appearance and the world in itself is 'inconsistent' for all the reasons that have been given by commentators starting with Jacobi (who first asked how a thing in itself could cause an appearance if the category of cause only applied to appearances). However, 'this inconsistency is precisely the expression for the fact that we are admittedly reasonable and rational beings, but that, the more reasonable and rational we become, we must at the same time assure ourselves of the objective unreason, of the alienation of the world in an ever-increasing measure' (Adorno 1995, p. 173). Adorno reads this situation in the light of the theory of 'reification' which Georg Lukács developed from Marx in *History and Class Consciousness*, written in 1923, a book which also influenced Heidegger. The term 'reification' had until recently largely disappeared from wider discussion of the problems of modernity. Let us, though, look at what Adorno says in relation to Kant, as there are reasons for suggesting that the idea of reification might not be as dead as many had assumed.

Adorno's idea is that 'it is not that there is no opposition between subjectification of philosophy and reification, but rather that reification is a function of subjectification; that there is all the more reification as there is also subjectification in philosophy' (ibid., p. 174). Why is this so? The answer has to do with the processes analysed by Weber, in which the sciences and capitalism make more and more of the world identifiable in standardized ways. The attempt 'to relate everything that appears at all to a unified point of reference', namely the categories of the transcendental subject, has 'a tendency to reification' (ibid.). Adorno then makes a characteristic connection of the unified point of reference of the transcendental subject to the commodity form as it is understood in Lukács' interpretation of Marx. The subject's 'spontaneity [. . .] is really nothing but labour'; it is what we do in relation to the world. As the world comes more and more under human control, it 'becomes more and more just the result of labour, one could say it becomes congealed labour [. . .] and it becomes – by the fact that what is alive is always only on the side of the subject – [. . .] more and more something dead. One could say: the "commodity character" of the world, its rigidification always increases thereby' (ibid., p. 175). Here we enter important but problematic territory, where one needs to differentiate between Adorno's more and less successful approaches.[6]

In *Negative Dialectics*, for example, Adorno argues that 'the transcendental subject can be deciphered as the society which is unconscious of itself' (Adorno 1997, 6, p. 179), and that '[t]he universality of the transcendental subject is [. . .] the functional context of society' (ibid., p. 180). At one level this is a significant contention. The problem of the relationship between the individual empirical subject and the transcendental subject in Kant can be made sense of if one sees the transcendental subject's ways of processing the impact of the world as an abstraction from the real ways in which modern societies generate forms of identity and explanation which individuals internalize in order successfully to achieve instrumental goals.

The continuation of the passage in *Negative Dialectics*, however, excludes the possibility that such socialization can, depending on the historical and social context, be both repressive and enabling: 'The universal domination of exchange value over people, which a priori stops subjects from being subjects, debases subjectivity itself to a mere object, relegates that principle of universality, which maintains that it institutes the supremacy of the subject, to untruth' (ibid.). This sort of passage puts many people off bothering to engage with Adorno at all. The idea that the domination of exchange value means subjects stop being subjects is mere assertion, the product of precisely the sort of either/or thinking that Adorno attacks elsewhere. Clearly, modern forms of identity do influence the most intimate aspects of subjective life, but the ability to become critically aware of the fact of reification means that there is inherently more to subjective self-determination than the passage cited allows. There is admittedly a more complex issue here: reification must in some sense be 'unconscious', otherwise it would merely involve a moral failing on the part of the subject, and would have no real explanatory value, but that is not how Adorno makes the main point. Attempts to defend such passages by citing his dictum that 'today only exaggeration is the medium of truth' (Adorno 1997, 10.2, p. 568), and similar remarks, have to be confronted with the fact that when Adorno makes his case in a less exaggerated manner, there is something to the ideas about subjective domination and reification that he derives from Kant's contradictions. The problem lies not in the sense that the modern world produces the threat of reification, but in trying, as Adorno sometimes does, to give a unitary explanation of why this is the case, based on the category of identity.

Lukács' book makes links between Kant and Idealist philosophy and Marx's theory of commodity, links which Adorno often too uncritically adopts. The reason the book had such an impact on critical intellectuals in the 1920s was that it offered a productive framework for grasping how it was that so many people were spectacularly mistaken about the First World War and its aftermath, and for understanding what this meant about the possibilities for rational action in the modern period.[7] The questions the book provoked are part of what led to the foundation of the project of Frankfurt School 'Critical Theory'. The 'congealed labour' of modern technology and the social forms in which that labour was located (above all the commodity form), which not long before the war had seemed to promise growing prosperity and well-being (even as it gave rise in some areas to growing divisions between social classes), produced a catastrophe which still affects the nature of history today. This combination of the effects of the technologies which enable a greater control of nature with the irrationality of what that technology produces in certain social and historical circumstances is the key to the contradictions Adorno sees in Kant's rationalism. A key element in the Holocaust was the way in which people could come to be seen as mere things to be manipulated in terms of rules of the same kind as are used in forms of benign bureaucratic and technological rationality (see Bauman 1991).

However, as Axel Honneth argues in his book on reification, the atrocities of that period also had their roots in forms of hatred which denied human status to the Other, of a kind which sometimes develop over centuries (Honneth 2005).[8] Whereas aspects of the German genocide in particular may be related to the link between bureaucratic objectification and the objectification characteristic of the levelling of difference by the commodity form, some of what went on in other parts of Europe (and in Germany) often took far less 'rationalized' forms, and may be better explained in psychoanalytical terms. But in suggesting that the mechanisms of fear and rejection of the Other that psychoanalysis sees as lying behind racist violence have to do with bureaucracy and the commodity form, and thence to do with the forms of order of the transcendental subject, Adorno sometimes makes the same mistake that he criticizes in ways of thinking which seek a foundational principle that will give a unitary explanation of a phenomenon. The commodification process may well feed into the identification of the Other as a threat that has to be objectified because of the perceived need to defend against it, but commodification is not part of one overall process. By seeing any kind of identification, be it of the commodity in the economic sphere, of the natural object in scientific research, or of the Other in the social sphere, as a form of exclusion or repression, and underplaying the harmlessness of many forms of identification, Adorno brings together phenomena that need differentiating. As Herbert Schnädelbach (1987) has pointed out, it is vital, for example, to distinguish 'identification as', without which, as Adorno himself insists, coherent thought is impossible, from 'identification with', which can render things indifferently the same. Rather than see how Adorno at times falls prey to this trap, it is more interesting to look at the ways he suggests we may be able to avoid it.

Adorno does not advocate abandoning modern forms of rationality: 'identification with', though also part of the subject's drive for self-preservation with the potential for being employed repressively, is inescapable. Forms of rationality are inherently dialectical, both enabling much that we could not seriously wish to do without, and at the same time producing effects that almost nobody wants. If, as Adorno maintains, Kant's dualism of 'form and content admittedly must be mediated, but [...] cannot simply be abolished' (Adorno 1995, p. 352), and this dualism relates to how modern philosophy can inform us about reification, what are the consequences for the aims of philosophy? Adorno claims that 'every epistemology necessarily gets into such aporetic concepts' (ibid., p. 330) as Kant's, so the question is how this claim about the fate of epistemology relates to reification. As we have seen, the central issue is the status of objectivity in the light of the demise of the idea of a metaphysical world-order. Why, given the way that the sciences occupy much of what used to be the territory of philosophy, does Adorno suggest that 'epistemology always takes the path of the one who opens one hole and stops up another' (ibid., p. 331), because it cannot resolve the problem of the 'share of the object in cognition' (ibid.)? In order to resolve it one can, he says, only offer 'another moment of cognition' (ibid.), so remaining on the subject side of the duality, because there is nothing which can make this moment of cognition into the ground of the others.[9]

What, though, of the kind of contemporary materialism that tries to obviate the subject side altogether by reducing it to what will eventually be explicable in causal terms? Adorno's answer would be, rightly, that this is a manifestly metaphysical position which relies on a founding principle (whichever version of materialism is proposed), and so only offers a 'moment of cognition' which in no way can overcome the issues raised by Kant. It is only by accepting the fact that the epistemological problematic necessarily gives rise to contradictions between subject and object which are not amenable to philosophical resolution that one can begin to see a philosophical alternative that can offer a critical perspective on reification. What this can entail appears in Adorno's relationship to Hegel.

The Hegelian point is that the notional line between the subjective and the objective is not a fixed one, and that it changes in relation to historical developments. The forms the subject requires for cognition, which Kant regarded as somehow removed from contingency, are affected by the nature of the relationship to the object at different times; indeed, they could not have developed at all without contact with the world. In the modern situation, where there is a greater prevalence of 'congealed labour' in the form of scientific and other forms of warranted knowledge, more can be in one sense located on the object side, as we, for example, discover causal processes which determine and influence the subject. At the same time, though, the discovery of such processes may also make it possible for subjects to become more self-determining, because they can gain insight into what determines them, and seek to overcome it.

What determines us can, therefore, function as a form of reification, but this can itself lead to the possibility of overcoming reification, if we can become aware of the objective factors which had become part of ourselves as subjects. Adorno sometimes locates this dialectic too far on the object side (e.g. in the remarks cited from *Negative Dialectics*, above), though his reasons can be persuasive in specific contexts, like the Holocaust. If the subject/object relationship cannot be defined by an epistemological explanation of the mind/world relationship, this can mean that the dominant agenda for much modern philosophy is, as

Deweyan and Rortyan pragmatism claims, simply mistaken. However, that is not what Adorno primarily argues with respect to the significant philosophers, like Kant, because he sees 'mistakes' at this level as pointing to the need to read such philosophy in a different perspective, even as he accepts that it may no longer be a viable option for the present.

Honneth maintains that what links Lukács, Adorno, Heidegger, and Dewey is precisely their seeking an alternative to the epistemological model of philosophy based on the search for scientific objectivity, a model that privileges the 'ruling idea, according to which an epistemic subject stands opposite the world in a neutral manner' (Honneth 2005, p. 31). What is questioned in this alternative is the cognitivist assumption that our essential relationship to the world is of a subject seeking objective knowledge, including of itself, and that philosophy's task is to find a way of saying how that knowledge can be legitimated. This assumption lies at the heart of Adorno's linking the transcendental subject to reification, and suggests why, because the epistemological account seems constitutively to fail in its intentions, scepticism plays such a dominant role in much modern philosophy. Reification is, though, difficult to characterize, because an objectifying stance *is* a vital part of what makes possible both scientific knowledge and technical control, in medicine and elsewhere, and institutional structures that can make our world more tolerable. As such, critical perspectives which include all forms of objectification are implausible: they raise the same kind of problem as did the early Marx's view that all labour whose product is sold to another person is 'alienated'. A better way of approaching the root of reification is to ask whether the objectifying stance required for legitimate scientific knowledge can be applied to the capacity for achieving scientific knowledge itself. This is a version of the question which Adorno thinks leads Kant to the contradictions examined above.

The hermeneutic view common in some measure to Lukács, Adorno, Heidegger, and Dewey is that taking the stance required for scientific objectivity as the founding philosophical assumption is a mistake, because our primary relationship to the world is not cognitive at all, but rather – and here there are differences between the thinkers – practical, mimetic, or affective. Modern philosophy oriented towards the scheme of subject and object produces contradictions precisely because it seeks to ground our relationship to the world in a derivative mode of access to the world, in which the subject takes a neutral stance towards the object. This stance can, in the hermeneutic view, only develop from a prior non-objectifying stance, which Heidegger terms 'being in the world'. We have to 'understand' the world, in the sense of be motivated by and cope with it in a practical manner, and this depends on it making sense to us, before we can abstract from that understanding in the form of objective explanation. Honneth argues that the idea of a motivating concern with the world, which he sees in terms of the necessity of fundamental forms of 'acknowledgement' (*Anerkennung*), of other subjects and of the natural world, is genetically and methodologically prior to the abstraction that leads to the objectifications which form the focus of philosophy oriented towards epistemology. Reification results when this motivating concern becomes forgotten or lost via the growing domination of practices which begin from the assumptions that inform a cognitivist stance. Honneth makes some important differentiations in order to avoid the problem from which Lukács, almost invariably, and Adorno, sometimes, suffer, of equating all forms of objectification as forms of reification. Even the natural sciences depend on the prior social acknowledgement that something is a matter of human concern, which cannot be established by a cognitive argument. This is because arguments about knowledge can have no grip without a prior acknowledgement of the significance of the matter at hand that can be shared with others. Consequently it cannot be right to regard scientific objectifications as inherently reifying.

Honneth sums up Adorno's most defensible conception of reification as follows: 'Above all Theodor W. Adorno repeatedly emphasized that the appropriateness and quality of our conceptual thinking is dependent on the extent to which it can remain aware of its original bond with the object of a drive, thus with persons and things that are loved' (ibid., p. 69). The loss of the awareness of this kind of relation to the world can become systemic within modern societies – though aspects of modernity can also be said to allow such relations, particularly in the sphere of intimacy, to develop in ways that they may not in traditional societies. The possibility of such a loss of awareness is what takes the issue of reification out of the realm of individual moral failing and shows how objective factors in society, like commodification, can lead to distorted subjective responses. Adorno's focus on the centrality of aesthetics for rethinking the ends of contemporary philosophy becomes crucial here. Rather than adopting the epistemological perspective, which fails to lead to the kind of results that the natural sciences produce, Adorno thinks philosophy should take a critical stance with regard to the kinds of relations to the world which dominate at particular times in history. The difficulty lies in doing this without the philosophy attributing to itself a position which claims the kind of objectivity that the approach is concerned to question. Such a position is precisely what Adorno thinks is characteristic of 'identity thinking', which can lead to reification.

Adorno's concluding reflections on Kant in the lectures on the *Critique of Pure Reason* suggest that much depends on how one characterizes the relationship between form and content in Kant, where form is dependent on the transcendental subject, and where what content is depends on the historically changing nature of the subject's relation to the world.[10] Were Kant to be just an 'Idealist' he would fall prey to the stance Honneth shows to be the target of the alternative mode of philosophizing suggested by Adorno, Heidegger, Dewey, and others. He would resolve the contradiction between form and content, rather than revealing what the contradiction tells us about the modern situation of the subject. Adorno sees this situation in terms of the Hegelian notion of 'mediation', and in the following passage on Kant he already suggests why he will be critical of Hegel:

> It is not the same to say that forms are mediated by the contents to which they relate as it is to say that the contents are mediated by the forms to which they relate. Forms are actually *essentially* mediated by contents and cannot be thought at all without contents. There is always also something in the contents akin to the indication of what does not completely resolve into form, of what is not really exhausted in form. (Adorno 1995, p. 353)

The consequences of this rejection of a relationship in which thought and the content of thought are resolved into each other become apparent in Adorno's responses to Hegel, to which we turn next.

3

Immediacy and Mediation: Hegelian and Adornian Dialectics

The new Hegel

There has been a remarkable revival of interest in Hegel since the 1970s, which has now even become part of the debate in some areas of analytical philosophy (see Redding 2007). Hegel had largely disappeared from Anglo-American philosophy in the wake of the early twentieth-century criticisms by Bertrand Russell and others of an idealist holism (which was arguably not really Hegelian at all), for which things are only comprehensible via their relations to other things, in the name of analytical, 'logical' atomism, for which the world is conceived of as consisting of discrete atomic facts. The Hegel revival in the Anglo-Saxon world was fuelled by the idea of a 'non-metaphysical' Hegel, associated with Klaus Hartmann, Terry Pinkard, and Robert Pippin, and is summed up in Pinkard's idea that the 'sociality of reason' forms the core of Hegel's thought. In the metaphysical interpretation of Hegel he is the philosopher of 'absolute spirit', of which particular, historically situated, human thinking constitutes the relative manifestation, which can be transcended by philosophical reflection.[1] In the non-metaphysical interpretation Hegel's key idea is seen instead as his demonstration that reason is a social achievement that arises from people's historical encounters with the world and each other, there being no location outside these encounters from which reason could be judged. Hegel can be seen in both approaches as filling the gap left by Kant when he failed to give a genetic account of how the forms of thought of the transcendental subject could develop at all. For Hegel these forms emerge via the necessities generated by the growing differentiation of the ways subjects relate to things in the world and to other subjects. The question which divides the metaphysical and non-metaphysical interpretations is how this process is to be philosophically articulated.

Adorno's attitude to Hegel is in one respect a response to the metaphysical Hegel, who is seen as embodying the 'hubris of philosophy' (Adorno 1959–60, p. 4940) by seeking to dissolve the real into what can be articulated in concepts. At the same time, though, Adorno adopts much of the dialectical manner of his thinking from Hegel's insights into the necessity of contradiction. This would seem to bring Adorno close to the non-metaphysical interpretations, because he sees contradictions as arising through social interaction. It is therefore important to assess the extent to which what Adorno adopts and rejects in Hegel is compatible with the contemporary appropriation of Hegel as the philosopher who reveals the failings of the assumptions that inform much of the history of analytical philosophy. If the 'new Hegelian' approach is significant for the way that it reorients the agenda of philosophy away from the dead-ends of the analytical tradition, Adorno's philosophy can be examined in terms of what it can contribute to a critical evaluation of that reorientation.

In the light of Adorno's interpretation of Kant, the conflict between the metaphysical and non-metaphysical interpretations of Hegel need not result in a definitive resolution concerning which interpretation is correct. Looked at philologically, there is much to be said for the metaphysical interpretation, and it takes some effort to make the many passages in Hegel that are couched in theological terms into something non-metaphysical. Adorno also cites passages from Hegel's *Philosophy of Right* which point in the direction of a glorification of the state, suggesting ironically that 'it's no coincidence that military images occur to one if talking of the *Philosophy of Right*' (Adorno 2001a, p. 64). Conversely, Hegel's relevance to contemporary philosophical issues can be readily established in terms of his accounts of the inadequacies of empiricism, or of the constitution of 'mindedness' through interaction between subjects. In Adornian terms these conflicting approaches should tell us something about the reality in which they emerge, where a concern for adequate contextual understanding of the thought of the past cannot simply be reconciled with the idea that texts from the past have a philosophical life in the present.[2] Adorno's responses to Hegel should be read in the light of these realities, as much as in the light of competing arguments about and interpretations of Hegel's texts.

Adorno summarizes a crucial aspect of his view of Hegel when he characterizes Hegel's relationship to Kant as follows: 'By taking over from Kant the thesis of the unknowability of the infinite in a certain sense, he at the same time makes this thesis itself the vehicle of knowledge of the infinite' (Adorno 1959–60, p. 4946). This characterization involves another way of looking at scepticism, the issue which haunts German Idealism. Hegel's strategy is to turn scepticism against itself. The fact that 'finite', particular knowledge of things and the laws that govern them is – as the progress of modern science shows – 'negated' by being refuted by subsequent knowledge is often taken as the basis for a sceptical position. Kant was construed by some as contributing to the sceptical problem by separating knowledge of appearances from things in themselves. Hegel argues, though, that the process of negation itself is what leads to the 'infinite', rather than the infinite involving the Kantian 'block', because it allows us to see that the truth about truth is that it depends on contradiction. The logic of the movement from one theory to the next needs to be grasped as a whole from within, there being no extra-mundane location from which to assess the movement, and so no initial founding form of knowledge, no 'immediate' given, that philosophy has to explain by seeking a perspective from outside the process of negation. This is what Hegel means by 'absolute knowing'. Paul Redding contrasts the metaphysical and non-metaphysical construals of this idea: 'Rather than understand "absolute knowing" as the achievement of some ultimate "God's-eye view" of everything, the philosophical analogue to the connection with God sought in religion, non-metaphysical interpreters see it as the accession to a mode of self-critical thought that has finally abandoned all non-questionable mythical "givens", and which will only countenance reason-giving argument as justification' (Redding 2012).

This latter stance, as Robert Brandom has shown, can make Hegel part of what leads to an 'analytical pragmatist' approach to philosophy, in which the 'game of giving and asking for reasons' is 'privileged among the games we play with words. For it is the one in virtue of which they mean anything at all – the one presupposed and built upon by all the other uses we can then put these meanings to, once they are available' (Brandom 2009, p. 176). Giving and asking for reasons 'is the practice that institutes *meanings* in the first place' (ibid.). The decisive issue here is how the notion of 'meaning' is understood, and this has wide-ranging consequences for how Adorno's ideas relate to contemporary philosophy. The narrow construal of meaning characteristic of much modern philosophy can be seen as Adorno's main target. How this is the case can be shown by looking at some of the contradictions involved in Hegel's philosophy.

Adorno's critical response to Hegel does depend on the idea that Hegel lays claim to a modern version of a God's-eye view, and that this is the epitome of 'identity thinking', for which the 'real root of all objectivity is subject'. However, he also adopts many of those aspects of Hegel which do not entail the totalizing claims associated with the metaphysical interpretation of Hegel. In the lectures 'Introduction to Dialectics' of 1958, Adorno sums up his dual response to Hegel:

> [A]dmittedly [Hegel] was the first really to carry out a radical critique of the concept of a first philosophy, at the same time, however, as in a certain sense sustaining the pretension to such a philosophy, insofar as

he equated the culmination of the carrying out of the movement of the concept with precisely that origin ['*jenem Ersten*', in the sense of the foundation for philosophy, of the kind Descartes saw in the *cogito*]. (Adorno 2010, p. 30)

Hegel, then, makes the end of the process of mediation between subject and object the foundation of philosophy, rather than beginning with the assumption of their identity as the foundation. Adorno always argues against a foundational given (such as 'sense data' as the foundation of cognition in empiricism, or the idea of 'atomic facts' from which 'elementary propositions' are built in the *Tractatus*). He maintains that 'there is no such last thing, nothing absolutely given and purified of all mediations, be it [Husserlian] pure consciousness or [empiricist] pure sensuous datum' (ibid., p. 149). But does his criticism of first philosophy apply to Hegel's account of the 'movement of the concept'?

Criticism of a foundationalist 'given' has, as we have seen, recently been revived as part of the pragmatist and neo-Hegelian critique of the founding assumptions of analytical philosophy. These assumptions have fallen prey to the argument that they involve what Wilfrid Sellars calls the 'myth of the given', the idea that there are 'immediate', sensory data that lie outside the 'space of reasons', which are the basis of knowledge. In opposition to this idea, the Hegelian view is that knowledge is only intelligible in terms of the way concepts gain their determinacy via their relation to other concepts, not by 'immediate' grasping of irreducible facts. How do we discriminate between what constitutes a fact and what doesn't, without already relating it to other things? However, in his *Science of Logic* Hegel then seeks to give a complete systematic account of the ways in which the relations between concepts become determinate, thus suggesting that the subject can map out in advance the structure of all the ways in which the world could be intelligible. For Adorno this exemplifies the problematic aspect of how the modern root of objectivity is subjectivity, and so constitutes 'philosophical hubris'.

Adorno points to the historical reason for his criticism of the Hegelian notion that mind can delineate the ultimate dynamic structures of reality, when he refers to the idea that 'the impotence of spirit [*Geist*] in relation to reality was demonstrated in a probably unparalleled manner' by the events of the Hitler era (Adorno 1959–60, p. 5061). This might, though, again sound like a complete change of subject, from an epistemological question to an empirical question about something contingent and historical. It is therefore important to see how Adorno's criticisms of 'Idealism' insist on more than is usually dealt with in the recent Hegel revival, because this illuminates his dialectical treatment of the 'fall' of metaphysics. The non-metaphysical interpretation of Hegel sees the social progress of rationality as manifesting itself in the ways that certain historical practices and claims cease to be defensible. Nobody can now legitimate an argument for the oppression of women or ethnic minorities, or defend child labour. This stance, argues Robert Pippin, relies on our being able to give 'a narrative account of why we have come to regard some set of rules or a practice as authoritative' (Pippin 1999, p. 68), there being no other court of appeal which is not either merely abstract or metaphysical. This is a powerful and important argument, but it is not clear how much philosophical back-up it provides for a strictly Hegelian stance, or needs from Hegel's philosophy; the point might also be made from a pragmatist point of view.

Rather than think that Adorno would regard Pippin's idea of authoritative narratives as being rendered merely illusory when it is confronted with the Holocaust, he should be seen as regarding the narrative as insufficiently dialectical, because it does not take sufficient account of the contradictory aspect of all forms of progress. The point for an Adornian approach is that the advances that Pippin registers are also predicated on repression and suffering that cannot be redeemed by those advances, even as they may reduce future suffering.[3] If the truth for philosophy lies in the articulation of the progress of reason in Pippin's manner, it may neglect the suffering and destruction which underlie such progress, and which can still, in a perhaps unrecognized form, be a repressed part of each new situation: '[T]he reasonableness of history can only prove itself in terms of *for whom* history really is reasonable' (Adorno 2001a, p. 62). The philosophical task in the latter case is therefore to articulate or express what is ignored when a certain conception of rationality comes to dominate. There are in this view no metaphysical criteria for legitimating what is rational, because modern history involves so many reasons to doubt whether there really is universal progress in rationality, as opposed to rationality within specific areas of human activity. Adorno asks one to think in terms of what happens to that which is excluded from what comes to be seen as 'authoritative', and not to do so as though one is engaged in a continuous narrative of developing rationality, because such a narrative can itself become a means of obscuring what has been repressed.

One should also take account of historical context here: the background for Adorno is the Nazi period and the Stalinist terror, whereas Pippin may be thinking more in terms of the successes of post-war democracy. These successes are, though, beginning to look increasingly fragile in the face of rapacious global capitalism and ecological devastation, which fit more with Adorno's account of modernity. Even if some of Adorno's criticisms are more apt for the metaphysical interpretation of Hegel, there are dimensions of the Hegel revival which are open to his critique. The philosophical point here will be that the neo-Hegelian approach fails to deal adequately with aspects of human existence which are articulated and expressed in non-conceptual forms. This is a result of the sometimes too restrictive conception of sense-making in the approach, which can be seen both on a more historical level, and on a more specific argumentative level, through the crucial issue of immediacy and mediation.[4] What this difference signifies has to do with conflicts over the understanding of the tasks of philosophy in modernity.

One reason Adorno does not adopt a directly anti-metaphysical stance is that the meaning of metaphysics in the history of philosophy is itself contradictory. On the one hand metaphysics can involve the repression of suffering, by seeing it as overcome by some higher purpose: in the face of the Holocaust, Adorno thinks that metaphysics that tries to make sense of history in this way can only be ideological. On the other hand the significance of metaphysics also lay in its attempts to respond to suffering, rather than in trying to ground the legitimacy of knowledge or morality: 'The need to give a voice to suffering is the condition of all truth. For suffering is objectivity which weighs on the subject; what it experiences as most subjective to it, its expression, is objectively mediated' (Adorno 1997, 6, p. 29). Adorno regards Hegel's attempts to see the rationality even in the most appalling developments as a repression of suffering in the name of 'optimism about history [*Geschichtsoptimismus*]' (Adorno 1997, 5, p. 320). If metaphysical attempts to respond to suffering generated nothing but illusion, then metaphysics would indeed be merely ideology, or a function of Nietzschean *ressentiment*. However, like Marx's religion as the opium of the people, metaphysics has at times also played a real role in mitigating suffering by offering it forms of expression. The challenge is therefore for philosophy that ensues from the fall of traditional metaphysics to play this role in the face of Weberian disenchantment and reification, without merely creating new illusions, of the kind which formed the target of Marx's critique of religion. The very ambivalence in the German word *'Schein'* suggests one key direction here: Adorno's concern with aesthetic appearance is evidently part of his attempt to explore ways of making sense of suffering that are not merely illusory, even if they cannot be redemptive. If suffering can, in Hegelian terms, only be dealt with at the level of seeking a rational understanding of the necessities that led to it and overcoming them in the name of the advance of reason, one is left with a sense of something missing.

The neo-Hegelian account of the sociality of reason is often presented in a way which takes too little account of how social relations specific to modernity produce disaster. This can be suggested via one of Axel Honneth's concluding remarks in his book on reification. Honneth is not specifically referring to neo-Hegelianism, but the focus on socially negotiated normativity is central to Pippin, Pinkard, and others. Pippin says that the core of his Hegelianism is the idea that 'to live freely' is to lead a 'life commonly and justifiably measured by some norm' (Pippin 1997, p. 409). Honneth remarks:

> Social criticism has essentially limited itself in the last three decades to assessing the normative order of societies in terms of whether they satisfy certain principles of justice; in the process, despite all the successes in grounding such standards, despite all the differentiation of the underlying perspectives, it lost sight of the fact that societies can also normatively fail in another sense than in the infringement of generally valid principles of justice. (Honneth 2005, p. 106)[5]

The kind of normative failure Adorno is concerned with can be suggested if one thinks about the example of 'mourning' as a response to loss. Other examples, to which we will come in later chapters, have to do with expressive responses to suffering and destruction in art, and the centrality of music in Adorno's thinking has much to do with its relationship to mourning.

Mourning is not a cognitive process or part of the game of giving and asking for reasons. It is rather the search for ways of making sense of loss which do not, as Freud suggests of 'melancholy', just involve repetition. Repetition can be a form of reification, in the sense Honneth derives from Adorno, because it involves a failure to acknowledge what has been lost. Adorno is, for example, very aware of how the economic and political success of post-war Germany, where new rules and practices became 'authoritative', also masked what Alexander and Margarete Mitscherlich called 'the inability to mourn' (Mitscherlich and Mitscherlich 1967). Successful mourning must find its own form of expression and articulation, which cannot simply be measured by a norm, though changes in the norms governing social practices can play a role in the search for such expression. The need for more than the normative involves areas of culture where freedom cannot be understood in terms of measurement against a norm, but has rather to do with the ability to develop expressive responses, and so emancipate oneself from the past, whilst still acknowledging it.

One challenge for philosophy in Adorno's terms can, then, be said to lie in finding ways, in the wake of the Holocaust, to mourn the loss of traditional metaphysics as a response to suffering. In this respect Hegelian conceptions may contribute to a failure adequately to acknowledge that every change in the normative order of society can be seen as being shadowed by irreducibly individual painful experiences which cannot always be responded to in terms of socially agreed norms. Hegelianism can here encourage a kind of forgetting which does not do justice to the experience of individual suffering. If the Hegelian subject reaches maturity by realizing the necessity of saying farewell to childhood and binding itself to the norms of adult society, the Adornian subject realizes that the losses a farewell to the magical aspects of childhood entails will affect the attempt to reach maturity, and will need their own forms of expression if they are not to have pathological effects. As John Dewey puts it: '[A] man is not an adult until after he has been a boy, but childhood does not exist for the sake of maturity' (Dewey 1958, p. 99). The underlying issue here has, then, again to do with questions of meaning and making sense.

Immediacy and meaning

Robert Brandom restricts meaning to what can be normatively constituted in the game of giving and asking for reasons, and he derives his grounds for doing so from his interpretation of Hegel. Seeing the implications of Brandom's appropriation of Hegel tells us a lot about Adorno's philosophical ideas. The metaphysical and non-metaphysical approaches to Hegel are connected by the question of 'immediacy' and 'mediation', because both approaches agree that Hegel's philosophy can only work by showing that intelligibility only arises through mediation. It is, however, important here to make a distinction between the empiricist sense of immediacy, where – immediate – 'sense-data' are construed as arising from direct causal impacts on the organism and are used as the foundation of cognitive claims, and the sense that arose in Schelling and early Romantic philosophy that is associated with the word '*Anschauung*', 'intuition', which has to do with the ways in which we are always already in contact with an intelligible world even before we conceptualize it. This latter sense leads in the direction of what we looked at in relation to Honneth's account of reification, namely Heidegger's 'being in the world', and so on (to which one might add Merleau-Ponty's insistence on the embodiment of mind), which, as Honneth suggests, are the basis of the non-epistemic stance needed for the criticism of reification. Hegel shares something with this stance, insofar as there is no Cartesian gap between subject and object, but the ultimate truth of their relationship is arrived at for him when the content of intuition is mediated in a philosophical system.

Adorno agrees that the account of cognition in empiricism is based on false immediacy, but does not agree that the second sense of immediacy is also always susceptible to the Hegelian critique. Brandom and Pippin, however, see both understandings of immediacy as invoking something which is only really intelligible through mediation. The danger of the idea of immediacy does lie in appeals to something which is not rationally available. Schopenhauer, for instance, seeks to establish that the ground of appearing reality can be described as the 'Will': that is, as something which is only accessible through immediate experiences such as pain, sexual urges, and so on. This sort of thinking is the source of 'vitalism', the current of philosophical thought that crystallizes around the end of the nineteenth century, which contends that our conceptual appraisals of the way things are fail to capture their real essence, which must be accessed by some special kind of experience: for instance, in religious, sexual, or aesthetic forms of ecstasy. This idea is what appealed to Wagner in *Tristan and Isolde*, where the true nature of things is ultimately revealed in the *Liebestod* ('love-death'), when rational consciousness gives way to dissolution into the 'All'. Adorno attacks such versions of immediacy, whilst recognizing that they can be a sign of something that needs to be understood in a more defensible way. The side of Hegel's dialectic he wishes to sustain 'takes the moment of irrationality into thought, into the *ratio* itself as something which immanently contradicts it' (Adorno 2010, p. 65), rather than being something wholly external that is only accessible by renouncing reason. How, then, is the moment of irrationality to be incorporated into rational thinking without repressing its essential content?

Hegel's objection to what became vitalism is famously expressed in his opposition to the 'night in which all cows are black', which he sees as the way the absolute appears in philosophies that rely on an immediate sense of contact with the world in 'intuition'. Pippin couches the Hegelian objection in normative terms, by asking how the view based on immediacy could be legitimated. The appeal to a different kind of justification from a mediated one that employs the justificatory norms developed in a self-determining community is, he thinks, a form of dogmatism. The appeal needs justification by means of norms whose legitimacy is established via a narrative of how they became binding. The subject's capacity for self-determined critical reflection through the adoption of such norms cannot be assumed to be determined by something else, because this would require an appeal to something that cannot be justified by giving reasons. Pippin is thinking, for example, of Nietzsche's idea of the 'Will to Power' as the ground of the subject's self-determination, where apparently rational justification is really grounded in the urge to overcome the Other. Any claim to have access to this ground brings the person making the claim into the 'space of reasons', and so negates the basis of the claim. How can the space of reasons be questioned, apart from giving *reasons* why it is based on something else? Once again, these are in many respects compelling arguments. So how can Adorno avoid such objections?

If meaning is only conceived of in terms of what Brandom specifies via a contrast between 'sapience' and 'sentience', the Hegelian position is very plausible. Sapience is precisely what is required to play the game of giving and asking for reasons. The decisive factor, Brandom argues, is the ability to make commitments to claims, on the basis that these can be inferentially justified to others. Whereas a parrot may be able to be trained reliably to respond to the presence of red things (in sentience) by squawking 'Red!', it does not *know* what it is doing because it cannot commit itself to what follows from the claim that something is red; lacking sapience, it does not know what 'red' *means*. What follows from the claim is what allows one to justify the claim, on the basis that, say, it rules out its being green, entails its being coloured, means it is the same colour as my favourite sweet, and so on. In Hegelian terms, meaning, then, here depends on mediation. As long as one stays at the semantic level, at least with regard to reference to perceivable objects in the world, this seems pretty convincing: without the ability to make inferences you cannot claim to understand the entailments of verbal assertions. However, there are forms of understanding and expression which do not work in this manner, and here we have a version of the repression I suggested can be present in the idea of progressing rationality. Sapience is clearly an advance in control of the world, but it may also produce needs arising from what can be lost in such advances. As I have argued elsewhere (Bowie 2007), the change in the status of music from the end of the eighteenth century onwards has in part to do with the sense that rational control couched in verbal language loses sight of essential ways of making sense which demand other forms of expression.

It is not fully clear in Brandom's account how one gets from the immediate content of sentience to the mediated content of sapience, and whether the latter exhausts how the former can be understood. This is where Adorno's discussion of immediacy and mediation becomes important. One can, for example, tell stories about the initiation of children into forms of inference during language acquisition, but there are so many other dimensions in play in such processes that singling out this one dimension is precisely what raises Adornian suspicions about 'Idealism'. Without rhythm, tone, and other, what Adorno terms, 'mimetic' dimensions of language-use, which are not directly semantic (though they can play a role in semantic content), the motivation for language acquisition (and the content of many utterances) would be missing in key respects. Do we really just learn to communicate because we are learning to justify what we say about things (which we evidently can also do), as opposed to expressing how we feel about them or making sense of them in some other non-propositional manner?

Aesthetic issues are important here. David Cooper argues that models of meaning based on the justification of assertions 'lose their *prima facie* plausibility when attention is paid to the meaning belonging to activities less commonly subjected to rational appraisal than the making of assertions. (To ask about the meaning of a painting would not, typically, involve asking about the artist's entitlement to express what he did.)' (Cooper 2003, p. 5). What Adorno intends has to do with these very concrete aspects of non-semantic meaning. To understand why his approach has philosophical substance that is not open the accusation of invoking immediacy as the 'night in which all cows are black', we need to look at the lectures on 'Questions of the Dialectic' (Adorno 1963–4). The basic issue, then, is how immediacy and mediation are understood, and how this relates to philosophical accounts of meaning.

Adorno begins by arguing that there can be no mediation without something immediate that is to be mediated. The Hegelian concern is that this presupposition is precisely what leads to the night in which all cows are black: it is only by determining it that the immediate can be spoken of at all. At the beginning of Hegel's *Logic*, 'being' has to be opposed to something else for it to be thinkable at all – and so brought into the space of reasons. Adorno insists, though, that 'it is not now a matter of restoring immediacy as something absolute' (ibid., p. 8945), which would indeed make it the indeterminate One that Hegel criticizes. His question to Hegel is 'whether [...] it is not the case that the concept of mediation differentiates itself in itself; whether one can still without differentiation speak at all of mediation as a kind of invariant, as of a kind of basic category which has to be retained all the time' (ibid., p. 8946). The remark is explicated in the following, where he picks up the idea we saw at the end of Chapter 2, concerning the asymmetry between the mediation of the object by the forms of the subject's thought, and what mediates the subject: 'There is always also something in the content akin to the indication of what does not completely resolve into form' (Adorno 1995, p. 353). This 'something' involves what Adorno means by 'non-identity'.

Adorno asks 'whether the thought that every subject is mediated by its content doesn't have a different meaning, whether mediation here does not mean something completely different from what it means when I say that every content is mediated by subject' (Adorno 1963–4, p. 8947). The idea of the subject being mediated by 'content' brings Adorno close to the Heidegger of *Being and Time*, and he distinguishes between Heidegger's 'pluralistic, antisystematic motivation in the approach of the ontology', which 'was very clearly to be felt in the doctrine of the existentials, the ways of finding oneself [*Befindlichkeiten*]' (ibid., p. 8965), and the later Heidegger, where he thinks (very questionably) that Being takes over the 'Idealist' function of the system in German Idealism. What is meant by the subject being mediated by the content is clarified in the following:

> [T]he side of the content is, of course, mediated; I just want to say with this that this mediation is in principle of a different nature, is differently structured from formal mediation; one might call the latter a cognitive mediation, while the first mediation, through the content, relates to a sphere which precedes all cognitive function, all mere cognition [...]

in order that something such as cognition can be thought at all, because otherwise there would be no cognition of anything at all. (Ibid., p. 8948)

In the lectures on *History and Freedom*, he formulates the point like this: '[T]hrough this relation to its determinants, which shows immediacy to be mediated, immediacy is admittedly broken, but at the same time still sustains itself. For only insofar as there is such immediacy, there is such a primary experience, only to this extent can one talk of mediation at all' (Adorno 2001a, p. 32). Adorno is interested here in 'ontological difference', in what Heidegger explores via the idea that a prior non-cognitive understanding of Being (which can be practical, emotional, etc.) is the necessary condition of all cognitive explanation.

Charles Taylor, following Heidegger and Merleau-Ponty, characterizes this immediate understanding as follows: 'We are able to form conceptual beliefs guided by our surroundings, because we live in a pre-conceptual engagement with these that involves understanding' (Taylor 2002, p. 114). Hegelian and other Idealism ends up, despite itself, with a formal system of categories of thought that determine each other, and rejects the notion of ontological difference, precisely because it sees it as appealing to something immediate. This opens Idealism to the danger of reification, because non-cognitive forms of acknowledgement of the natural world and other subjects can thereby be neglected. In relation to the terms Brandom employs, one might say that Adorno is deconstructing the distinction between sapience and sentience, because the latter does not merely entail a 'reliable differential responsive disposition' of the kind that animals can be trained to have, but can involve the ability to produce appropriate expressive or symbolic sense-making responses to the world and other people whose content is not essentially cognitive, but may also form a crucial part of verbal communication. Taylor talks in this context of 'disclosive' forms of articulation.

Richard Bernstein suggests that Brandom favours his version of a Hegelian 'rationalist pragmatism' of the game of giving and asking for reasons over '"conceptual assimilationism", where the emphasis is placed on the continuities between discursive and non-discursive creatures' (Bernstein 2010, p. 226), and the latter is a version of precisely what concerns Adorno. Bernstein contends that one can combine these positions, for reasons he shows were proposed by C.S. Peirce. Peirce delineates 'grades of self-control', beginning with those shared with animals: 'There are inhibitions and coordinations that entirely escape consciousness. These are, in the next place, modes of control which seem quite instinctive' (ibid.). These modes then develop to the point where man can sapiently 'control his self-control', which takes one into the moral sphere, where he can then 'exercise a control over his control of control' (ibid., p. 227). The point is that '[t]he brutes are certainly capable of more than one grade of control; but it seems to me our superiority to them is due to our greater number of grades of self-control than it is to our versatility' (ibid.). The discursive game of giving and asking for reasons is therefore not topically different from other forms of accepting and rejecting which are characteristic of the interactions with the world of all conscious beings, but is, rather, a specific kind of more differentiated form of control, albeit a hugely important one. Dewey makes a similar point in *Experience and Nature*: 'If [...] language [...] is recognized as the instrument of social cooperation and mutual participation, continuity is established between natural events (animal sound, cries, etc.) and the origin and development of meanings' (Dewey 1958, p. xiii). Adorno is also 'deeply convinced that the difference between human beings and animals is not to be taken as emphatically as idealist philosophy wishes to persuade us it should be' (Adorno 2010, p. 139).

Adorno specifies his philosophical criticism of Hegel by looking at the issue of 'being' at the beginning of Hegel's *Logic*. Hegel says that just talking of 'being' is talking of the 'indeterminate immediate', which is the same as 'nothing', because there is no articulated content in the notion of 'being'. Hegel then goes on to say that this leads to the mediated idea of 'becoming', which combines being and non-being, as something ceases to be in one sense, and comes into being in another. This establishes the basic pattern of how his system is constituted. Adorno objects to this use of 'nothing': '[B]ut in this little nuance, in which he has equated the indeterminate something, because of its absolute indeterminacy, with nothing, in this little nuance precisely that prior decision in favour of absolute Idealism seems to me to lie, which is to be eliminated in a new review of questions of the dialectic' (Adorno 1963–4, p. 9001). The problem was apparent in the contradictions in Kant's view of the relationship between receptivity and spontaneity: '[O]n the one side [is] something completely indeterminate, about which one can say nothing, so that it is the same as nothing, and on the other side forms which for their part only have a sense if they relate to something, namely to something specific' (ibid., p. 9001). In this form, as we saw, Adorno thinks the problem is not philosophically resolvable. Hegel seeks to resolve it in the idea of absolute Idealism, which puts all the determinacy on the side of the mediating forms of the subject, so leaving the problem of the 'share of the object in cognition' that cannot, on pain of Idealism, be just 'another moment of cognition'.

Dialectic and non-identity

The alternative to a dialectic which absolutizes the concept is, however, hard to explicate, precisely because of the danger of certain versions of immediacy suggested above: '[T]he intention is directed towards the non-identical [. . .] but in a completely strict sense, this non-identical cannot be attained, except through identity' (ibid., p. 9058). It would otherwise be unintelligible, language and thought depending precisely on identity. But if the relation of thought to its object did not involve an aspect of non-identity in the object, thought would be empty, because it would not be directed at something other than itself. This was Adorno's point about Kant sustaining the contradiction between form and content, which leads him to favour Kant's unresolved contradictions over Hegel's resolution, and this approach can point to the ongoing conflicts over the interpretation of Kant as evidence for its plausibility.

Adorno distinguishes, therefore, between a trivial sense of non-identity, in which 'every single object that is subsumed under a class also has determinations which are not contained in the definition of that class' (ibid., pp. 9053–4), and the 'emphatic concept', which leads to the following exemplification of his non-Hegelian version of dialectic: 'Here it is therefore not only a question of the particular [. . .] being more than its concept [. . .] but also [. . .] the opposite, namely that the concept, the emphatic concept, is always more than the particular thing that is included under it' (ibid., p. 9054).[6] Adorno does not think that a philosophical explanation of the relationship between the subjective and the objective – of the kind present, say, in the correspondence theory of truth, or in Brandom's inferentialist account of sapience – is adequate to the ways in which concepts function in real historical circumstances. Concepts can cut off dimensions of the object that do not accord with a dominant ideology, but they can also keep alive what is missing in a given state of understanding of the object. How they do the latter is, though, not just a function of inferentialist sapience, because it can have to do with expressive modes of articulation, where giving reasons is not adequate to what is at issue. The obvious examples here can once again be found in the aesthetic sphere, and the crucial point, as we will see in Chapter 6, will be the centrality of aesthetic issues to wider questions about the ends of philosophy.

Adorno uses 'freedom' as an example of what he means by an emphatic concept. Freedom is not adequately understood if one thinks of it just in terms of Kantian or Hegelian individual self-determination in accordance with norms. Such a view of freedom seeks to reconcile it with necessity by seeing the subject as freely constraining itself in the name of Pippin's 'life commonly and justifiably measured by some norm' (Pippin 1997, p. 409). However, for Adorno, self-determination – which he in no way rejects as the core social goal, though he does think freedom has to be thought of in more than these terms – can easily produce oppression, given that in real situations the norms it involves have generally developed in unjust social conditions. Hegel would evidently agree at one level, given that he bases the history of self-determination on the development of mutual recognition. However, Adorno sees this as too abstract, because it does not show how, in the real circumstances of modern capitalism, self-determination is possible without obstructing or damaging the other. This damage is not necessarily intentional (though it can be), but structurally inevitable: the complexity of modern socio-economic arrangements makes one's control over the effects of one's norm-governed actions at best limited. This lack of control of the effects of one's actions is one reason why Kant ends up making good-will the only thing which is good in itself, but this, for Adorno, is another version of Idealism, of seeking a pure solution on the subjective side of a contradiction.[7]

Adorno's problematic dictum in *Minima Moralia* that '[t]here is no true life in the false' (Adorno 1997, 4, p. 43) can be understood, then, in relation to the difficulties of self-determination in complex, commodity-dominated societies, where a trip to the supermarket can oppress a third-world farmer without one realizing it. Balzac already captured the essence of this issue in *Le père Goriot*, with the hypothetical story which asks whether, if the hero could kill someone in China without anyone knowing, in order to become rich, he would do it. The point is that this is what the development of capital at the time was making possible, whilst also concealing that this was what one was doing. Just saying that it may often be possible in principle, so there is no philosophical reason to make anything of such an example, is precisely the kind of thinking which Adorno's manner of doing philosophy is intended to oppose, because the ways in which the object side influences the transparency or even the possibility of self-determination are for him often decisive.

A further – extreme – example of the issue Adorno is concerned with appears if one tries to understand the situation of the pilots who dropped the bombs on Hiroshima and Nagasaki, or on Dresden. They may have been shortening the war by incinerating countless people, but it is probably impossible to know if that is what they achieved. That they sincerely believed they were shortening the war in a justified manner – that is, that they took a self-determined stance on their action – seems to be the only way of bringing what they did into the space of reasons, but they may also have been unconsciously acquiescing to the pressures of their training, or led by a false sense of 'patriotism', and so on. There is no final answer to this possibility either, though there have been some empirical attempts to get one (e.g. by Günther Anders [Jungk 1961]). In Adornian terms the indeterminacy here with regard to the ethical content of the situation shows how far the 'primacy of the objective' can make established ways of looking at moral issues in modernity problematic.[8] If all we can do is say that they did their best, as self-determining actors, the philosophical point of saying this at all is hard to see, because saying they were sincere does nothing to illuminate the objective moral enormity of what happened. Conversely, Adorno's stance can be seen as utopian: what he means is that until society is organized in such ways that people do not end up in the situation of the pilots, there can be no unproblematic sense to self-determination. However, this latter stance, which suggests directions for political action that can be sought in concrete situations, arguably gives more content to the notion of self-determination than assertions about what distinguishes us from merely sentient beings. If we take the more pragmatic side of Adorno suggested by this latter version of what he is saying, we avoid the sense of paralysis associated with the dictum from *Minima Moralia*.

The sociality of reason may be harder to realize than is suggested by the idea of self-determination through norms, because self-determination is not always something transparent. Adorno, as we shall see in Chapter 5, uses aspects of psychoanalysis to question the transparency of self-determination. History shows that the conditions for self-determination are inherently fragile because the pressure of accumulated 'congealed labour' affects how subjects apprehend the world at every level. This might sound as if freedom therefore becomes something utopian, which, when Adorno suggests that it can only really exist in a just society, it does. However, as we just saw, there is a more pragmatic dimension to Adorno's explorations of the notion. Freedom for Adorno must be dialectically understood, via what contradicts it in real situations, rather than, say, in terms of an definitive philosophical proof of the existence of free-will (on this, see Chapter 5). The latter would just be another resolution of the relationship between subjective and objective on the subjective side.

Adorno elsewhere gives the example of the liberal norm of free and fair exchange, which is 'universally developed' and thereby 'becomes its own opposite' (Adorno 2008, p. 47). He is clear that nobody could justifiably argue against the norm of free and fair exchange, and that we cannot do without exchange as the 'measure of comparability' (Adorno 1963–4, p. 9056). However, when that exchange is located in the reality of reified social conditions it easily becomes an excuse for oppression. In the world of the globalized economy this has become very evident in the way that the 'liberation of trade' too rarely functions to the advantage of economically under-developed countries. Just saying that globalization therefore does not involve real free and fair trade obscures the way in which concepts work in real situations. In the dominant terms what is happening may be termed free and fair, because it is often within an agreed legal framework, but the point is that this framework rests on accumulated past coercion and injustice.

Constellations

Rather than seeking a reconciliation by working through the contradictions between thought and reality to a philosophical conclusion in the manner of Hegel, then, Adorno thinks that the claim to resolve such contradictions in philosophy will mask real contradictions, whose solution does not lie within philosophy: the 'production of a state of reality free of contradiction is a matter for human practice and not a matter for philosophy' (Adorno 2010, p. 125). The analyses Adorno proposes work with the idea that concepts form 'constellations' in particular circumstances, which he distinguishes from what happens in 'system': 'Constellation is not system. It is not that things are reconciled, that everything is resolved in the constellation, but one thing throws light on the other, and the figures which the individual moments form together are determinate signs and a legible writing' (Adorno 1997, 5, p. 343).[9] Rather than philosophy offering a definitive account of the relationship between the subjective and the objective – and this includes a dynamic account like Hegel's, which does not set them up as opposed quantities – 'philosophizing is really grasping constellations of subject and object [. . .] the concrete determination of the moments of subject and object is always also the determination of the historical form which they have actually taken on in history' (Adorno 1959–60, p. 4893). This might sound rather vague, but is an apt description of how the contingency and partiality inherent in all engagement with a serious issue can be acknowledged without this leading in a sceptical direction.

Things become 'legible' when the connection of 'moments' begins to reveal what is otherwise hidden. There is no method which can fully control and predict how this happens, but that does not mean that the investigation has to be arbitrary. The role of a specific understanding of language is crucial here: the real use of language is equally resistant to analysis in terms of a definitive method, but that does not mean that it is somehow deficient in the way it was thought to be by some of the founders of analytical philosophy. The reduction of the use of language in the presentation of an issue to being a series of propositional claims fails to appreciate the 'mimetic' aspect of communication. This is most obviously apparent in literary texts. What Proust's *À la recherche du temps perdu* conveys about love is not best understood in terms of it stating a claim that love rests on the inability of projection to be satisfied by reality (which is broadly true of what the novel says about love), because this fails to convey the experience that is only available via the novel's complex dynamic presentation of the nature of love.

Rather than involving a method in which one 'progresses from the concepts step by step to the universal genus', the concepts move into a constellation. That illuminates what is specific about the object which is indifferent or a burden to the classificatory procedure. The model for this is language. It does not just offer a sign system for the cognitive functions. Where it appears essentially as language, becomes presentation [*Darstellung*], it does not define its concepts. It provides the concepts with their objectivity via the relationship into which it puts the concepts centred about an issue [*Sache*]. (Adorno 1997, 6, pp. 164–5)

This description could be applied to the texts of the later Wittgenstein, which cannot be understood just as a series of arguments – there is, for example, no 'private language argument', but rather a series of explorations where 'one thing throws light on the other' – and can be seen as very precise 'presentations' of issues which leave open space for further development (see Eldridge 1997). The close relationship of the two thinkers here is not surprising, given Adorno's and Wittgenstein's shared sense of the centrality of music for philosophy (see Bowie 2007). Adorno also cites Max Weber's idea of 'composing' sociological concepts from accumulations of information.[10] The point is that there is no priority of logic before the actual practices in question.[11] Logic may help clarify what results – Adorno insists that one cannot do without formal logic in classifying things (Adorno 2010, p. 62) – but it can also become an obstacle if the only form of valid response to an issue is seen as building in logical steps according to agreed systematic premises, as opposed to composing the elements in response to the contingencies of the reality in question.

Adorno discusses the philosophy of the earlier Edmund Husserl in relation to the subject/object issues we have been considering: 'Husserl sees only the rigid alternative between the empirical contingent subject – and the absolutely necessary ideal law which is pure of all facticity: but he does not see that truth is not resolved in either of these, but is rather a constellation of moments which cannot be apportioned as a "residue" of the subjective or the objective side' (Adorno 1997, 5, p. 79).[12] The issue then becomes the historical constellation which led Husserl to this rigid alternative, which leads to questions about the success of the natural sciences and the problematic status of the individual subject's understanding of the world in relation to this success. This was a major theme in the debates in Germany from the later part of the nineteenth century onwards over the relationship between the natural and the human sciences, and the issue is very much alive in the contemporary debate over 'naturalism' and 'scientism'.

Later, in *The Crisis of European Sciences and Transcendental Phenomenology* (1976), Husserl would abandon much of the stance Adorno criticizes. Empirical historical contingencies led him to rethink the implications of the idealization involved in scientific laws in terms of the cultural effects of the 'mathematization of the cosmos', which excludes qualitative 'subjective' human relations to the life-world. In Adorno's terms Husserl's move is the source of greater philosophical insight than either of his positions on their own. Adorno talks, in a manner which again echoes early German Romantic philosophy, of 'a dialectic, thus a thinking, which has to do with the constellation, with the whole, with the context, and at the same time knows it is not assured of such a whole' (Adorno 2010, p. 319). Dialectical thinking is, he suggests, perhaps only possible if it has 'the character of being fragmentary' (ibid., p. 320). This means not that it gives up trying to grasp the whole of what determines us – that would be a surrender to the systemic pressures of modernity – but that it remains aware that the claim to have succeeded can itself be part of the problem philosophy has to confront in the face of the fall of metaphysics: '[P]recisely because our whole logic and our whole scientific thought is [. . .] one which knocks the world into shape according to our purposes, it at the same time does not do justice to the world which does not fit that thought' (Adorno 1963–4, p. 9050). The question is the status of this world, and how justice could be done to it. The deficit Adorno sees in Hegelian rationalism has to do with a failure to take sufficient account of the dialectical nature of instrumental rationality, which can mutilate the natural and human worlds, while also shaping them according to our purposes. How, then, does this deficit appear in a contemporary philosophical perspective?

The connection of Adorno's critical interpretations of a Hegel who is construed in predominantly metaphysical terms to the nonmetaphysical versions of Hegel has, as we saw, to be made in terms of the implications of the issue of immediacy and mediation. Brandom's drawing of the line between sapience and sentience is a way of arguing for the necessity of mediation if sentience is to be rationally intelligible. Another way of couching this issue is in terms of culture's relationship to nature. Brandom thinks a line can be drawn between the two, because all discussion of nature must belong in the cultural space that is constituted in the game of giving and asking for reasons. Any theoretical alternative to this, as we also saw in relation to Pippin, must legitimate itself via the same game, on pain of undermining its own stance, or of dogmatism. The questions posed in this respect by Adorno can be seen as follows. The drawing of the line between nature and culture is the core of large parts of the Western intellectual tradition, not just in philosophy. The success of the natural sciences seems, though, to bring more and more of what the subject is onto the side of nature, by bringing it under natural laws. However, that success is at the same time a cultural achievement, and in this sense an achievement of subjectivity. Given the success of the sciences in this respect, why, though, is the cumulative social and political effect of sapience in the modern period so often catastrophic?

Whatever may be wrong with Adorno's attempts to address the catastrophes of modernity, he makes us aware that the freedom which is the basis of modernity is inherently contradictory, and that there are no easy ways out of the dilemmas it throws up. The new Hegelians can here seem rather limited in comparison, because they rarely address the extremes of the history in which they seek to explore the sociality of reason. Brandom's approach looks in this perspective rather like another version of what Adorno saw in terms of Kant's being left with a philosophical 'residual character of truth'. Instead of the question of how synthetic a priori propositions are possible, there is the question of inferential justification as what is left as the philosophical basis of human culture.[13] This view of justification in some respects offers a great deal, and is a considerable advance on much that characterized the analytical tradition (such as being left with logic and observation statements as the basis of the only strictly meaningful forms of language). Without what Brandom seeks to render convincing, we are, as Rorty has suggested, returned to the sterility of scepticism-inspired questions about subject/object epistemology or the correspondence theory of truth. But it remains unclear what the pay-off of Brandom's remarkable technical labours could be beyond the bounds of academic philosophy. Adorno's ideas are important, then, because he offers a way of moving beyond the idea of drawing a nature/culture line, in the direction of rethinking the very ways in which we conceive of nature in relation to humankind.

Adorno suggests resources for confronting crises – from those created by technological and economic developments, to those created by the myths that emerge in the attempt to make sense of the cumulative pressures that result from these developments – which, it is more and more apparent, we lack adequate resources for comprehending. His basic thought, as we have seen, is that the objectifications of the sciences are both an achievement of subjectivity and yet can also take on the objective power of the nature which the subject sought to control by those objectifications. Stated this abstractly, this does not mean a great deal, but the idea can generate genuine insights when it is specified in real situations. The weight of Adorno's arguments derives from the fact that the progress of scientific rationality is too rarely adequately matched by advances in the social forms of organization in which that progress is located. As *Dialectic of Enlightenment* suggests: '[R]eal history is woven from real suffering, which does not at all diminish in proportion with the growth in the means of abolishing it' (Adorno 1997, 3, p. 58). The basis of such statements is that what is epitomized by the Holocaust should not be regarded as the exception, but as the universal warning about how subjectivity can take the form of domination. In this perspective the grotesque inequalities of the contemporary world and its ever-increasing destruction of nature should form the focus of philosophical criticism of forms of rationality, rather than the search for the essential principle of rationality.

While making justified criticisms of Adorno's tendency to reduce the sources of all the ills of modernity to a unitary notion of identity and reification which spans the sciences, the commodity form, and so on, Pippin claims that all Adorno really offers is therefore an illusory re-enchantment of nature. Some of the passages he cites from *Negative Dialectics* are indeed open to this criticism, but there is more to the issue than these questionable formulations. The story Pippin tells is that the modern sciences led to the collapse of 'the teleological, scholastic view of nature' (Pippin 2005, p. 116), which revealed the 'really disenchanted character of nature' and was 'a great liberation'. He continues: 'Once the problem of nature as whole is simply left behind, the incompatible commitments of bourgeois society with respect to freedom can be seen more clearly and subject to critique much more effectively' (ibid.). From an Adornian perspective Pippin makes the error of thinking that one can obviate one side of the dialectic of subject and object, on the basis of the supposed transparency of self-determination. Pippin's version of Brandom's sapience suggests the problem: he summarizes the way German Idealism, using 'extraordinary language', sees self-determination: '[T]he I's relation to itself is "the Absolute", the unconditioned possibility of which explains the possible intelligibility of all else' (Pippin 1997, p. 404). If that relation has not in fact 'left nature behind', Adorno's concern with nature will not be simply a manifestation of the desire to re-enchant nature. Adorno's post-Holocaust challenge to philosophical thinking which seeks to do what metaphysics sought to do is that 'it should think against itself; and that means that it must measure itself by what is most extreme, by what is most inconceivable if it is still to have a justification as thought' (Adorno 1998, p. 181). How this idea relates to 'nature' and to Pippin's tendency to over-extend the idea that self-determination is an adequate response to the horrors of modernity will concern us in the next chapters.

4
Nature

Why 'nature'?

Discussion of 'nature' in metaphysical terms became an increasing problem in the twentieth century, because the functioning of the objective – and some aspects of the subjective – world was explained ever more successfully by the natural sciences. These rendered many philosophical accounts of nature redundant, because they lacked empirical confirmation and overtly or covertly sought to restore teleological assumptions that were contradicted by non-teleological forms of scientific explanation. However, the contemporary sense that the relationship of humankind to the non-human world is in crisis has increasingly revived philosophical concern with 'nature' and our place within it. The assumption that scientific discovery of nature's laws should be the main focus of philosophical attention here gives way to questions about science's relationship to the rest of human culture. The obvious problem in all this is, of course, what is actually meant by the term 'nature'.

In his discussion of the subject's self-determination that we considered at the end of the last chapter, Robert Pippin refers to one way in which the term 'nature' is employed in modernity when he says with regard to the idea that there is a prior 'source' to the subject's self-determination: 'Except insofar as such a "source" or "origin" or [Heideggerian] finitude is self-consciously determined as such, it is nothing; it is the "night in which all cows are black"' (Pippin 1997, p. 405). Calling the source 'nature' makes no difference in these terms, as the designation would still have to be legitimated in the space of reasons. We can only do this via sapience, which requires inferential justification of the content of the term – nature must in this case be opposed to sapience for it to have any determinate content (e.g. as that which Pippin thinks we can 'leave behind') – but this undermines the attempt to claim that nature is the source of sapience in any specifiable sense. Saying that our thought depends, for example, on what Schelling called the 'unconscious productivity' of nature is, Pippin claims, therefore dogmatic, another version of immediacy.[1] Now Adorno insists that appeals to an 'origin' of any kind contradict the whole aim of his thinking – he sees the 'question of nature as something absolutely primary, as absolutely immediate in relation to its mediations', for example, as 'deceptive' (Adorno 1997, 6, p. 353) – so how can 'nature' play such an important role in what he has to say?[2]

Pippin's attention to Adorno's apparent desire to re-enchant nature neglects one way in which Adorno takes account of nature, namely in terms of what he calls 'materialism'. This is not a metaphysical thesis of the kind that is opposed to 'idealism' as a characterization of the true essence of being, but is rather to be understood via Adorno's post-Holocaust assertion that 'the basis of morality today rests, I would almost like to say: in the feeling of the body, in the identification with unbearable pain [...] morality, what one can call moral, thus the demand for life that is right, survives in unadornedly materialist motives' (Adorno 1998, p. 182). Importantly, this conception includes non-human animals, which only those terminally infected by Cartesianism think cannot suffer unbearable pain. Far from re-enchanting nature, this serves as a Feuerbachian reminder of sensuous 'natural' being in a way we will see developed by Albrecht Wellmer. As the extensive discussion of pain in philosophy suggests, pain cannot be understood simply in terms of the concept of pain. For Adorno, pain demands a kind of understanding that has to be based on a sense of affinity to the other that is prior to discursive interchange. The perceived philosophical difficulty in the discussion of pain is that, on the one hand, pain seems to be something irreducibly private and subjective – only I can feel my pain – but, on the other, is something which is locatable and has degrees of intensity, which suggests that it is 'objective', in the sense of belonging in the causal nexus of the objective world. This is yet another case where a subjective/objective dualism gives rise to endless philosophical contradictions.

In the terms of the analytical debate, which oscillates between a subjective and an objective account of pain, the issue raised by Adorno does not even register, so concerned are those involved with the epistemological issues.[3] The key here lies in how one thinks about 'objectivity', which can in some contexts be equated with 'nature'. For thinkers like Fichte and Schelling, following the etymology of the German word *'Gegenstand'*, the objective 'stands against the subject', rather than just being what is true, though it can also be that. Adorno follows this meaning, insofar as pain is 'objective': '[S]uffering is objectivity which weighs on the subject' (Adorno, 1997, 6, p. 29). This suffering is inherent in our biological make-up and can be explained in part by evolutionary theory. However, the matter is clearly not so simple, because the way objectivity which 'stands against' the subject is manifested depends on history, and Adorno cites historical examples, such as a visit to his own family from the Gestapo, of how one can experience the immediacy of this kind of objectivity (see Adorno 2001a). Such an event is, as he makes clear, the result of thoroughly mediated historical developments, but these can produce the same kind of immediate threat as one can encounter in relation to the natural world.

The worst historical manifestations of suffering in the Holocaust, which epitomize for Adorno what sustains the demand for morality, underline why there can be no redemptive metaphysics. The subject can be literally destroyed by this objectivity, and those who survive or who come after are faced with the realization that life can take on humanly created forms which are worse than death. Our fears about mortality and our susceptibility to pain, which society and culture can in some measure render more tolerable, can also be intensified by social developments like the Holocaust. The Lisbon earthquake may have destroyed the idea of Providence for many during the Enlightenment, but natural contingency, of the kind we now know will destroy the earth and eventually the rest of the universe as we know it, is qualitatively different from the human production of something appalling that does not result from ineluctable necessity. Adorno sees Idealist metaphysics, which before this kind of humanly created catastrophe might still hold out the hope of showing why life had a transcendent meaning, as the attempt, by showing how the objectivity of pain can be transcended, to escape the realization that there can be worse than death. The denial of the reality of the temporal body in the name of a timeless philosophical truth, which had been part of metaphysics since Plato, becomes a piece of ideology because of the historical disasters of modernity: '[T]he metaphysical thesis of the meaningfulness of the world or even of a world-plan which is the basis of everything that happens protests at the moment at which the production of a connection of meaning between what has happened and the ideas is lacking' (Adorno 1998, p. 189).[4]

So what does a philosophical response to the relationship between history and nature look like in Adorno's perspective? The contrast between a causal, objective account of pain (irritation of C-fibres, etc.) and the subjective experience of pain involves the kind of contradictions between subjective and objective that we looked at in Adorno's responses to Kant. One way to see why is to ask whether pain, *qua* subjective experience, is part of nature or not. No decision on this could be made unless one had a settled definition of the meaning of 'nature'. The point from an Adornian perspective will be that there can be no such definition, given the issues concerning subjective and objective, but that will not mean that one cannot talk of nature. One highly influential way to specify nature is apparent when Kant describes nature in the 'formal' sense as 'the lawfulness of appearances in space and time' (Kant 1968, B, p. 165). What is natural is therefore that which is subject to deterministic causal laws, as opposed to that which 'gives the law to itself' in self-determination. In some still disputed sense, this involves a separation of ourselves as self-determining beings from nature, but it also leads to problems of dualism, and thence to the attempts to resolve the contradiction on the subjective or the objective side. Adorno can, in contrast, be seen as deconstructing the difference between self-determination and nature. This means not abolishing the difference, but rather seeing how the strict division breaks down, and seeing what is expressed by the philosophically important conflicting responses to the issue of nature and its other.

In contemporary reductive naturalist terms, which miss out the contradictions and tensions we saw in Kant, the truth about pain is what is discovered by establishing the laws under which the neurological data can be subsumed, anything else belonging to 'folk psychology', or whatever candidate is chosen as the target of the reduction. In Adornian terms such a position can itself, despite its aim of eliminating anything which smacks of the merely subjective, be considered as another version of Idealism, because it actually presupposes a unity that can only be based on subjectivity. Kant maintained that we could not *know* that the whole of nature was deterministic, and only presupposed universal determinism for the realm of appearance as a regulative idea that guides scientific inquiry. For reductive naturalism, universal determinism has to be the founding postulate. But what grounds the postulate, apart from the arbitrary stipulation that the real is what can be discovered in terms of laws of nature, a stipulation which cannot be grounded in its own terms? Is the postulate itself real, and how would the claim that it is avoid vicious circularity? This position can go as far as arguing that pain is therefore not real, which borders on the offensive. As John McDowell suggests: 'When we ask the metaphysical question whether reality is what science can find out about, we cannot, without begging the question, restrict the materials for an answer to those that science can countenance' (McDowell 1998, p. 72).

John Dewey suggests that thinking which proceeds from a Cartesian subject/object split leads to the situation where '[o]ne thinker turns metaphysical materialist and denies reality to the mental; another turns psychological idealist, and holds that matter and force are merely disguised psychical events' (Dewey 1958, p. 10).[5] This bad alternative is why Adorno sees all such positions as Idealist: the 'idealistic basic motive' lies in 'the opposition of unity as the unity of subjectivity [the unity of everything as subject to deterministic laws or the unity of everything as dependent on the mental] in relation to the multiplicity of diffuse and divergent nature' (Adorno 1998, p. 142). Adorno does think that something like Kant's transcendental unity of apperception (the 'I think' which 'must be able to accompany all my representations' [Kant 1968, p. B 131]) is vital to the constitution of knowledge, but it does not serve as the foundation of a metaphysical position, whereas the postulate of reductive naturalism must.

Reductive naturalism's apparent lack of interest in the experience of pain, the experience which for Adorno leads to a way of sustaining morality, means that naturalism now plays an analogous role to the metaphysics which tried to justify pain as a part of a meaningful world-order. More critically, the reductive, eliminativist perspective shares with the objectifications which produce human cruelty the objectification of something whose meaning lies precisely in its subjective nature. The proof of the ultimately metaphysical thesis that the truth about pain is really neurological involves pretending that the historical world – where the nature and significance of pain have been shown to change, because socially influenced reactions to pain change how it manifests itself and how subjects respond – does not 'really' exist either. As Albrecht Wellmer puts it, a purely nomological scientific perspective 'rests on a blocking out of everything which is constitutive of what makes the social and historical world what it is *as* a social and historical world' (Wellmer 2009, p. 218).[6] None of what I say here, it should be added, is directed against well-warranted science, such as neurological pain research. The target is rather the philosophical appropriation of causally based theories, which can be used to offer ways of alleviating suffering, for a metaphysical point of view about what is 'really real'.

What emerges here is a conflict over how nature is understood which is not just a philosophical dispute about a contested concept. Wellmer makes the decisive point: 'The nature which we, as acting and deliberating creatures, are *aware of* as our own nature – the nature Adorno speaks of – is not the nature of scientifically objectified brain processes, but the living nature of our body with its neediness, its impulses, its potentials and its vulnerability' (ibid., p. 220). Nature is both the 'the lawfulness of appearances in space and time' of natural science, and what, even from a post-metaphysical, Darwin-informed point of view, we know or feel ourselves to be, independently of however much science we also happen to know. I may think my depression has to do with serotonin levels, but that is not how I experience it: depression can only be properly understood *as* depression via its phenomenology, not by putative physical causes and states whose alteration may alleviate it. From Adorno's perspective, the main philosophical issue is not a decision on whether the reductive naturalist position is defensible (which, given his arguments about Idealism and metaphysics, it cannot be), but what the emergence of such a position means.

The idea that the objectifying view of nature is not adequate to the

Feuerbachian living nature in which people, including reductive materialist metaphysicians, are motivated to do what they do in the most diverse ways is the issue that will really affect the cultural responses to how to reduce suffering, not an unlikely victory in reducing the second idea of nature to the first, or vice versa. The differences in responses to depression between those who think taking the right pill is what matters and those who think talking to the right therapist is the answer, and the political ramifications of such differences, show why this is not an abstract issue. Moreover, the tension between the two senses of nature involved here is itself part of the history of modernity, and this tension is inherent in ideas which Adorno developed very early in his philosophical career and continued to elaborate throughout his life.

'Nature-history'

The discussion so far may trouble those who assume that definitions are required if discussion of a philosophical issue is not to become arbitrary. The problem is, as became apparent in German Idealism, that finding a definition of nature actually entails trying to solve the main philosophical problems of modernity. A great deal of Adorno's philosophy derives from thinking about the relationship of nature to history. In one sense nature is just 'the universe', everything, including consciousness. Reductionists can jump in at this point by saying consciousness is a brain-state, brain states are physical, and, hey presto, one solves the problem: everything is physical and deterministic. As we saw, this is about as metaphysical as it can get, as well as being largely useless with respect to the understanding of actual human life, where even reductionists hopefully don't think of their child's depression as just a brain-state. However, if one then insists on the autonomy of the mental, leaving nature as the 'realm of law', worries of the kind that ensued from Descartes and Kant force one into trying to explain how the two are connected, and thence into the subject/object dialectic.

German Idealism is precisely concerned with the problem of trying to explain how subjective and objective relate, without falling prey to either dogmatism, Berkeleyan idealism, or some kind of materialist reductionism. German Idealism begins when, following Kant, Fichte makes self-determination the core of philosophy by seeing both cognitive and practical relations to the world as grounded in human activity, in opposition to what is seen as the determinism of Spinozism (see Bowie 1993, 1997, 2003b). The power of the Fichtean position lies in the idea that if one seeks to ground self-determination in something notionally 'objective', be it brain processes, or Schelling's 'productivity' of nature, one ends up either in the situation where the grounding principle must itself be absolute, which is equivalent to making it God, or in a regress of explanations of the grounding principle.[7] There are, however, grounds for questioning the absolutizing of subjective spontaneity, even in the attenuated version suggested by Pippin, which is why Schelling's position, for example, is more complex than his critics make out (see Bowie 2010). Kant is forced to locate self-determination in a sphere outside of space and time, the realm of universal determinism, which makes it unclear how the intelligible can be manifested in the form of empirical actions. The demand therefore seems to be to locate self-determination as somehow part of nature itself. This is clearly impossible for nature in the formal sense, but it was not for nothing that Kant wrote the *Critique of Judgement*, where nature is more than nature in the formal sense. He did so not least to come to terms with the idea that we are connected to nature in more than cognitive ways.

Schelling suggests the importance of this kind of connection when, in an anticipation of Adorno, he argues in 1806 that self-determination which is seen as in opposition to 'nature' may not be the unquestionable endowment which Fichte seems to think it is: '[I]n the last analysis what is the essence of [Fichte's] whole opinion of nature? It is this: that nature should be used [. . .] and that it is there for nothing more than to be used; his principle, according to which he looks at nature, is the economic teleological principle' (Schelling, 1856, p. 17). Here nature becomes that which can be misused by a mind which sees the object as simply something to be overcome, in the name of self-determination. Is this, then, how one should define nature, namely as the 'Other' which mind seeks to dominate? The key point is that such a conception only emerges at a specific point in history, when systematic human control of nature starts to become possible because of the advances of the sciences, and theological ideas of nature as Creation go into decline. The further point derives in part from psychoanalysis, though it is already implicit in Schelling. The idea, which suggests the core dialectic in Adorno, is that domination of objective nature is not all that is in play here, because the subject comes to dominate its *own* nature, in the name of preserving its natural existence. Without the repression of the nature of 'our body with its neediness, its impulses, its potentials and its vulnerability', self-preservation through social organization of the control of the external nature that can destroy us is threatened, but that very domination produces threats in its turn.

An account of this kind might seem to rely on just changing the sense of 'nature', but if one does not make a dogmatic grounding assumption about what counts as nature the logic of the argument leads to dialectical shifts in the meaning of nature, which have real effects. Adorno often sees this situation in terms of what he terms '*Naturgeschichte*'. The term is difficult to translate because 'natural history' has come to mean the study of natural phenomena. Adorno's employment of the notion, for want of a better translation, of 'nature-history' is based on the idea that in modernity the opposition between the terms, where nature is history-less, and history, which is sometimes seen as the realm of freedom, is opposed to the static world of natural laws, breaks down.

A further element in what Adorno means by nature-history lies in the notion of 'second nature'. This notion became important around the end of the eighteenth century in Europe as a response to the changing status of nature that is most obvious in the revaluation of wild nature from being a threat to being something to be valued for its own sake. This revaluation leads to the rise of philosophical aesthetics, one of whose founding concerns is the relationship between the beauty of nature and the beauty of art, which is already an indication of what is meant by nature-history. On the one hand, second nature means what it means in everyday parlance, namely what 'becomes second nature' because it happens without one reflecting on it – the idea goes back to St Augustine's 'Custom is second nature'. In a recent interpretation, John McDowell (1994), via Gadamer, links this idea to the notion of *Bildung*, thus to the development of cultural habits that sustain social intercourse in the 'space of reasons', which are not reducible to what governs the 'space of causes'. On the other hand, in certain areas of Romanticism at the end of the eighteenth century, the idea of second nature also starts to be related to the idea that humankind needs to re-establish contact with nature by achieving a new kind of relationship to it, after a 'fall' from a preceding kind of contact to first nature leads to 'alienation'. In *The German Ideology* Marx and Engels claim, in a passage cited by Adorno in *Negative Dialectics*, that '[h]istory can be considered from two sides, be divided into the history of nature and the history of humankind. But the two sides cannot be separated; as long as people exist the history of nature and the history of people condition each other' (cited in Adorno 1997, 6, p. 351). The idea of second nature is here used to characterize the development of capitalist society. Social second nature, in the form of practices and institutions involving established power structures, is both what protects us against threats from first nature and what threatens us in a similar manner to first nature – or can be an even greater threat, as the Holocaust will show.

Adorno adopts elements both of a Romantic view, in which we destroy the natural world at our peril, and of the Marxian view, in which society can become 'nature', in the sense of that which can dominate or destroy us. His first development of the notion of nature-history, which is heavily reliant on Walter Benjamin's *Origin of the German Play of Mourning*, is a lecture, 'The Idea of Nature-History', given in 1932. Adorno continued to use ideas from this text throughout his career, and his later versions of the ideas are less arcane than the often obscure formulations of the lecture. In order to find a way into what he intends with his reflections on this issue, I want first to look briefly at another attempt to work out the contradictions in the notion of nature which we have encountered so far, that of Dewey in *Experience and Nature* (first published in 1925). Consideration of Dewey's ideas can elucidate what is behind Adorno's reflections, and suggests a neglected strand of thinking about nature which is relevant, for example, to McDowell's Hegel-inspired reflections in *Mind and World*.

What these days is generally termed the 'metaphysical realist' conception of nature claims that what is true of nature is true independently of whatever anybody thinks is true of nature. The problem with this position, as has often been argued, is that it leads straight to scepticism. How would we ever know we had reached the truth about an aspect of nature, given that this would have to be the truth as articulated in thought? In one sense (though specifying this sense proves remarkably difficult) it is, of course, rational to assume that the true laws governing the physical world are 'always already there', even if we don't ever know when we have access to them. Moreover, it is implausible to think that what contemporary science tells us in most domains is not better warranted than what was previously thought. One might make exceptions here, of course, such as evolutionary psychology, when it seeks to explain socially influenced behaviour involving the 'space of reasons' in purely biological terms. It is nearly always in the social domain that the idea of unidirectional scientific progress in history starts to falter. This latter issue has precisely to do with the idea of nature-history, one of whose aims is to show how history can come to be seen as nature for ideological reasons.

The point about the metaphysical realist assumption is that in it truth can only be a 'regulative' idea, whose aim is presumably to guide or motivate *practice* in relation to an issue where any definitive assumptions necessarily presuppose what is to be established. Kant's 'ideas of reason', such as the notion of the thoroughgoing lawfulness of the realm of appearances, do not play a 'constitutive' role. From a Nietzschean perspective, of a kind which appears in aspects of Adorno, the realist regulative idea is, though, likely to be a version of 'God', as the timeless essence of the real that we may hope to reach, but which may just be our projection. Orientation to such a goal is, in this respect, likely to be at the cost of attention to all the other factors involved in cognition. From another perspective, the true world in the metaphysical realist sense might also be considered a prime case of the 'night in which all cows are black': nothing can be articulated about it in thought, except the claim that the way it is is independent of thought, which cannot strictly be known. There is not even the suggestion in metaphysical realism that there may be some other way of understanding the real, of the kind suggested by theories involving 'intuition' – Dewey regards the aesthetic as crucial here – the metaphysical realist line is instead relentlessly cognitivist. Dewey thinks the whole cognitivist picture, which is still involved in what underpins many debates between realists, anti-realists, and so on, is faulty, precisely because it fails adequately to understand how nature and history relate.

From a Deweyan perspective the metaphysical realist idea of nature is basically vacuous, because it says nothing substantive with regard to science as a social practice. You can do good science without wondering about the metaphysical realist's 'true world', and the metaphysical concern can easily mask repression of reflection on the aims of science, which are far more essential to the reality of what science *is* than a constitutively disputed metaphysical goal. Underlying Dewey's approach is the awareness that we cannot say what nature 'really is', because that involves a reification, in which what nature really is is presupposed as what the natural sciences would find out if inquiry were complete. Such a conception presupposes the actual history of science, only then to regard it as merely contingent in the face of the truth it is supposed eventually to reveal. If we take history seriously, though, the obvious fact is that nature is not a historical constant and goes through radical transformations, for example, from being God's creation, to being what is at stake in contemporary debates between naturalist and other positions. These debates, crucially, feed into philosophical and political arguments about the aims of human society. The ideas involved in this history are only to be regarded as mere contingent additions to what nature really is if we presuppose a God's-eye view of the totality of the laws of nature. Now the standard fear in this context is of relativism, but, as German Idealism realized, that depends very much on how the absolute is conceived. As Hilary Putnam puts it against Bernard Williams' idea of the 'absolute conception': 'It cannot be the case that scientific knowledge (future fundamental physics) is absolute and nothing else is; for fundamental physics cannot explain the possibility of referring to or stating anything, including fundamental physics itself' (Putnam 1990, p. 176). In Dewey's pragmatist terms: 'Without the uniformities, science would be impossible. But if they alone existed, thought and knowledge would be impossible and meaningless. The incomplete and uncertain gives point and application to ascertainment of regular relations and orders' (Dewey 1958, p. 160).

Rather than assume the standard philosophical contrast between timeless laws of nature and the temporality of history, Dewey prefers to couch the issue in terms of differing forms of temporality:

> Events change; one individual gives place to another. But individually qualified things have some qualities which are pervasive, common, stable. They are out of time in the sense that a particular temporal quality is irrelevant to them. If anybody feels relieved by calling them eternal, let them be called eternal. But let not 'eternal' be then conceived as a kind of absolute perduring existence or Being. It denotes just what it denotes:

irrelevance to existence in its temporal quality. These non-temporal, mathematical or logical qualities are capable of abstraction, and of conversion into relations, into temporal, numerical and spatial *order*. (Ibid., p. 148)

The dualisms that constitute the substance of much post-Cartesian philosophy

> have a single origin in the dogma which denies temporal quality to reality as such. Such a theory is bound to regard things which are causally explanatory as superior to results and outcomes; for the temporal dependence of the latter cannot be disguised, while 'causes' can be plausibly converted into independent beings, or laws, or other non-temporal forms. (Ibid., p. 149)

The real process of investigation into nature is, then, inherently temporal, and the mistake is to assume that the result of the inquiry 'is already there in fully fledged being and that we just run across it. [...] That there is existence antecedent to search and discovery is of course admitted; but it is denied that as such, as other than the conclusion of the historical event of inquiry in its connection to other histories, it is already the object of knowledge' (ibid., p. 156). In consequence: 'In some degree, every genuine discovery creates some transformation of both the meanings and the existences of nature' (ibid., p. 157), because what nature is is indissolubly linked to the nature which investigates it, namely us. A version of what is entailed by this thought underlies Adorno's reflections on first and second nature, and on nature-history.

Dewey rejects an idealist construal of the transformation involved in successful scientific inquiry. While idealism is right that recognition of the active role of mind in cognition means that 'the found rather than the given is the proper subject matter of science', it misunderstands the role of mind: '[A]n office of transformation was converted into an act of original and final creation. A conversion of actual immediate objects into *better*, into more secure and significant, objects was treated as a movement from merely apparent and phenomenal Being to the truly Real' (ibid., p. 158). This criticism is already close to Adorno's criticisms of Idealism, and Dewey continues: 'In short, idealism is guilty of neglect that thought and knowledge are histories' (ibid.). Against the idea that nature is complete in itself as the 'truly Real', Dewey insists that nature and history cannot be separated, and that the idea of a completed system of nature is just a projection of a particular assumption about the timeless truth of mathematics onto nature, so 'attributing all qualities inconsistent with nature thus defined to "finite" mind, in order to account for ignorance, doubt, error and the need of inference and inquiry' (ibid., p. 160). The key to what both Dewey and Adorno oppose in traditional philosophy is the way in which dynamic aspects of existence are relegated to a secondary status, in the name of philosophy and science making 'nature', as the truly Real, into what can be definitively conceptualized.

Their opposition to such thinking can help reframe many philosophical issues. For example, much energy still goes into the attempt to specify the relationship between causes and reasons ('Can reasons be causes?', etc.), and this relationship often depends on the assumption that nature is the realm of necessity, the 'space of causes', and that history opens up the 'space of reasons' based on self-determination. The difficulty is that history, as was already a core theme in Greek tragedy, is also a realm of necessity, which means that people's reasons for doing things can be caused by *social* pressures, or simply imposed. Moreover, if one does not think of nature just in Kant's formal sense, it is also that which can be despoiled by human action, leading to the mass mistreatment of factory-farmed animals, destruction of habitats, and so on. While the harm to animals may not be an assault on their 'freedom', a merely causal account of such harm is not an account of the harm at all. As Wellmer suggests: 'It appears that for a description of the behaviour of more highly organized animals we are dependent on a vocabulary which has its origins in the experience of ourselves as a part of living nature, that is to say in our "participant's" perspective as a part of living nature' (Wellmer 2009, p. 222). It is not that the tension between causes and reasons is some kind of mistake, but an abstract philosophical specification of their difference fails to be adequate to the relationship of nature and freedom. First nature's causality and the causality of second nature differ, but they both entail questions about how freedom is to be conceived, beyond the specification of it as self-determination.

One way to see what Adorno means in this area is to look at what he says about music. Music cannot be understood as wholly belonging to the 'space of reasons', depending as it does on the capacity for 'mimetic', gestural, and other kinds of responses, which are part of the living nature that we share with animals. Tonality is a key example of 'second nature' for Adorno, not least because it was (and is) argued that it has its roots in first nature, via a supposed 'natural' connection of what is actually a historically developed harmonic system to our responses. The turn away from tonality in the 'new music', particularly of the Second Viennese School, involves moving away from a 'form of reaction' which 'through the generations has, as second nature, instilled itself in people. It determines musical behaviour largely independently of their consciousness and their intention' (Adorno 1997, 15, p. 193). Moving away from this second nature involves 'conscious control' in order to escape that 'form of reaction' (ibid.). Whatever one thinks of the case which Adorno makes here,[8] the phenomenon is clearly part of what is involved in musical innovation, and is a metaphor of a wider issue, namely of how something humanly created becomes 'nature-history'.

In his account of Hegelian practical philosophy, Pippin cites the case of the development of opera, whose norms have an objective status for those engaged in it, even though their emergence is not the result of any individual's intention (Pippin 2008, p. 75). Opera is in this respect an analogous phenomenon to the one Adorno cites, but Pippin's account generally does not share Adorno's critical sense that such norms can become ideological. One can, at the same time, question the rather schematic way in which Adorno sees tonality, whose resilience in music is not easily explained as just a piece of unconscious determination relating to other forms of social domination by convention. When Adorno says, 'In the musical pre-conscious and in the collective unconscious tonality appears, although it is for its part a historical product, to have become something like second nature' (Adorno 1997, 17, p. 277), the use of the indefensible Jungian notion of the collective unconscious suggests the problem. Musically competent people can give good reasons why they accept tonality, despite the dangers Adorno suggests.[9] The initial point here is that 'second nature' is itself contradictory, whence its link to the idea of nature-history. It can be a source of ideological responses, which seek to deny the possibility of change, so making social reality function like the reality governed by natural causality. Ideology results from the attempt to legitimate the social as the natural: 'Precisely because the nation is not nature, it must continually announce to itself that it really *is* something like proximity to nature, immediacy, community of the people' (Adorno 2001a, p. 156). Second nature can, however, also be the basis of social and cultural cohesion, by establishing space in which self-determined innovation is possible. It is arguable that Pippin trusts too much in second nature, and Adorno too little, and the reasons have to do with what Adorno thinks of in terms of nature-history.

Adorno gives a further indication of why art offers a way of understanding nature-history when he says: 'Every art contains elements which seem natural, self-evident at the moment of their production. Only in the course of the further development do they become evident as themselves something which has become and which is transient, does what is natural about them become evident as "second nature"' (Adorno 1997, 16, p. 499). Similarly, he maintains with regard to the unreflective idea of first nature: '[W]hat we encounter as nature is in truth second nature and not first, and [. . .] we, in order to give abused and oppressed nature its due, must not allow ourselves to be blinded precisely by that appearance of the natural' (Adorno 2010, pp. 166–7). Nature in the formal sense is a manifestation of a historically developed stance towards the physical universe, not something that is simply given. Taking these two remarks together explains the cryptic assertion in the lecture on nature-history that 'all being [*Sein*] or all entities [*Seiende* – the terms come from Heidegger] can only be grasped as an entanglement of historical and natural being' (Adorno 1997, 1, p. 360). It is not only that cultural products which give the appearance of being natural (such as the diatonic harmonic system) can be shown by reflection to be historically produced, but also that any way in which nature is articulated in society is not to be regarded as expressing something 'purely natural'.

The consequence is not that theories in the sciences, for example, are to be regarded as somehow *per se* questionable, *qua* explanations or predictive laws, but that the claim that they are expressing what nature 'really is' cannot be sustained, because what the sciences reveal is inextricably bound up with other forms of historical human activity. Only, as we saw in Dewey, if one stipulates that the natural is really just what can be expressed in timeless mathematical form can one exclude history from nature. Wellmer makes the key point that emerges from the rejection of the reduction of nature to nature in the formal sense:

> It seems that we cannot reconstruct the history of nature, part of which is the emergence of human forms of life and of the spheres of subjective and objective spirit, in terms of a nomological physical theory, precisely because to describe what is essentially *new* in the process of evolution we need categories beyond those of physics and not reducible to them. (Wellmer 2009, p. 222)

What we have seen so far should make Adorno's somewhat opaque, proto-deconstructive formulations in the seminal lecture more transparent: '[S]o everywhere that I operate with the concepts of nature and history, definitive determinations of essence are not meant, instead I am following the intention to drive these two concepts to a point at which their pure falling apart is abolished [*aufgehoben*]' (Adorno 1997, 1, p. 346). The concept of nature Adorno rejects is one 'that could be most readily translated by the concept of the mythical', by which he means 'that which has always been there, which, as being which has been established by fate, appears in history, is what is substantial in history' (ibid.). Elsewhere he says that he means by 'nature [. . .] the history-less, Platonically ontological' (ibid., p. 349), which is also what was opposed by Dewey.

The target of Adorno's lecture is in certain respects the Heidegger of *Being and Time*, whom Adorno sees as making the notion of 'historicity' into the essence of being, so remaining within a philosophical or metaphysical framework which seeks founding categories into which the real can be fitted.[10] Adorno, while seeking to avoid relativism, understands the truth of the issue in question as having a 'temporal core' that demands a particular mode of inquiry. The alternative is what he sees, in the light of his understanding of the history of philosophy, as the vain attempt to establish philosophical founding ideas. Philosophical understanding does not always depend on the analytical isolation of some aspect of the issue, but sometimes also depends on what was suggested by the idea of the constellation. In a constellation a combination of elements provides the illumination which obviates the assumption that foundational philosophical questions must be answered before an issue can be understood. As we shall see in the next chapter, this means that an issue like freedom can be seen as in key respects an empirical question because it can only be grasped by its emerging in a specific context and by finding a way of articulating that specificity.

The seminal lecture's best points are made a bit more clearly in the 1964–5 lectures on *History and Freedom*, where Adorno uses the original lecture as the basis of further reflections. He suggests that, for Hegel, nature is just the 'natural basis of history' (Adorno 2001a, p. 168), such as geographical conditions. This means that history's 'blindly natural character' in its most emphatic manifestations – it confronts people with a second nature that can be more of a threat than first nature (ibid., p. 169) – is neglected in favour of the story of developing rationality. Defences of unjust political conditions in modernity are, as Adorno, following Marx, points out, often couched in terms of what is 'natural', such as 'It's human nature' in defence of socially produced greed. These days, supposedly neutral genetic data are used to legitimate views on matters where the relationship between social and natural causality cannot be neatly separated. At the same time as seeing that all conceptions of nature are historically mediated, the opposite should also be seen, namely 'everything historical as nature, precisely because it still remains, by dint of its own violent fixity [*Gesetztheit*: the sense is not wholly clear, "*gesetzt*" generally meaning "staid", but also having the sense in Kant and Fichte of what is "posited"], under the spell of the blind context of the nature which it pushes away from itself' (ibid., p. 179). The history of the species' self-preservation against the threat of nature involves seeking to dominate nature, and so produces its own forms of domination, which can then result in precisely what self-preservation sought to avoid.

The philosophical task is to find a way beyond this dialectic without falling prey to the illusion that there is a final way out of it. The problem is that, unlike Marx, who thinks that praxis is the answer to philosophy's failure to resolve contradictions, Adorno's historical experience is that praxis too often involves other versions of the same problems. This stance has led some critics on the Left to accuse Adorno of producing an essentially aporetic position, which gives too few indications of how theory can lead to better practice. However, although it is clear that Adorno does often argue as though all political practice is undermined by nature-history, his conception of the tasks of philosophy does not preclude it playing a role in progressive social change. Philosophy can, for example, undermine dogmatic assumptions about the legitimation of social practices. Were this not the case it becomes hard to explain why contemporary thinkers, like Wellmer, are convinced that Adorno has decisive things to say about the relationship between nomological and other accounts of what we are.

The difficult and more questionable part of Adorno's conception of nature-history lies in his appropriation of Benjamin's ideas for the question of nature and temporality, which Adorno regards as decisive for the understanding of the fate of metaphysics in modernity. The basic idea again involves the rejection of a philosophical method which relies on the idea of the transcendence of temporality. As we saw in Dewey, this idea is associated with regarding nature in mathematical terms, in a way which excludes the fact that nature is in certain respects inherently temporal. Nature's causal laws are indeed not expressed in temporal terms, but the laws are manifest in a temporal world, which is where they can mean anything, by affecting what people do with respect to how they conceive of nature. Benjamin's account of the seventeenth-century baroque 'play of mourning' (*Trauerspiel*, as opposed to tragedy, which Benjamin sees as an expression of a timeless, mythical world-order) underlines how the baroque writers saw nature 'as eternal transience in which only the saturnine gaze of those generations recognized history' (cited in Adorno 2001a, p. 180). Rather than nature being eternal, then, it is what becomes the reminder of transience, hence its becoming history. Instead of looking to nature for symbols of the eternal essence of things, nature in modernity offers allegories of transience, for instance in the image of the death's head.

The problem here is that Adorno loads a huge amount of significance onto what is in many respects a very circumscribed historical phenomenon. His wider point involves a specific understanding of modernity that raises some difficult questions. The other main source of Adorno's reflections (and Benjamin's) is Georg Lukács' *Theory of the Novel*, written in 1914–15, first published 1916, which is concerned with the novel as the form of what Lukács calls 'transcendental homelessness'. The novel articulates the conviction that meaning is no longer immanent within the world and that we are faced with a search for meaning which can never restore a timeless whole that makes sense. This situation comes to be seen as the split between 'facts' and 'values' that is manifested in the conflicts which characters in the novel face over how they should act. What Adorno is interested in here is 'the transmutation of metaphysics into history', which 'secularizes metaphysics in the absolutely secular category, that of disintegration/decay [*des Verfalls*]' (ibid., p. 181). Rather than hoping for a restoration of a world which makes sense as a whole, philosophy should be concerned with the 'fragments which the disintegration brings about [*zeitigt*]' (ibid.), so that '[t]here is more hope for metaphysics in the finite [. . .]

than in the abstract form of eternity which in vain seeks to wrest itself from transience' (ibid., p. 182).

The last remark can be seen as pointing in the direction of art, which can illuminate the transient in ways which make sense of life, even though the illumination is itself transient. For Adorno, art succeeds best via the development of a particular form, rather than being a direct response to philosophical, social, or political issues. Significant art may therefore not be prey to the subject's domination of the object, which he sees as characteristic of modernity, because art is expressly 'appearance', in contrast to metaphysical claims to express the truth of being. The conclusion of Adorno's reflections on nature-history in the lectures on *History and Freedom* is that philosophy should, in the face of the disintegration of metaphysics, become – and here Adorno uses a term he generally, because of its association with Heidegger, avoids – 'hermeneutics', by interpreting 'the particular, the specific' (ibid., p. 186). The particular cannot be grasped in terms of systematic philosophy and is manifest in historical constellations. Interpretation (*Deutung*) 'elicits from the phenomena, from second nature, from the mediated, from what has been mediated by history and society that surrounds us, its having-become' (ibid., p. 189). The 'having-become', the mediation, is, though, itself to be understood 'as an extended immediacy, as something natural [*als ein Naturverhältnis*]' (ibid.), because it arises not from real self-determination, but rather from the objective pressures of a society, in which people often reproduce what they try to escape. Unlike the Lukács of *History and Class-Consciousness*, Adorno does not think there is a political resolution of this contradiction, though he evidently does not reject a politics based on the need for social and economic change.

Adorno associates his approach to immediacy and mediation with philosophy's becoming 'critique'. This involves 'a secularization of melancholy' (ibid., p. 188) because, as we saw in relation to the idea of mourning in the last chapter, it takes place on the assumption of the loss of transcendence and of any hope for a redemptive metaphysics. A passage from *Against Epistemology/Towards a Meta-Critique of Epistemology*[11] captures something of Adorno's picture of what happens if philosophy ceases to try finally to resolve the relationship between subject and object, mind and nature:

> Seeing through the proposition of identity means, though, not letting oneself be persuaded that what has come into being cannot break the spell of its origin. All music was once a service to reduce the boredom of the rulers, but the Late Quartets are not table music; tenderness is, according to psychoanalysis, the formation of a reaction to barbaric sadism, but it became the model of humanity. The obsolete concepts of epistemology too point beyond themselves. In their most elevated

> formalisms and in anticipation of their failure they are a piece of unconscious historiography, which can be salvaged by helping them to self-consciousness against what they mean from their own point of view. This salvation, remembrance of the suffering that sedimented itself in the concepts, waits for the moment of their disintegration. It is the idea of philosophical critique. [...] The time has come not for First Philosophy, but for a last philosophy. (Adorno 1997, 5, p. 47)

This is another of those passages which makes those suspicious of Adorno despair. However, the core idea that one can 'break the spell of something's origin' has to be taken seriously in the light of the recurrent idea in modern philosophy that philosophy itself may have become the problem, rather than being a means for solving problems. This idea is apparent, for example, in Wittgenstein's 'therapeutic' approach to philosophical dilemmas, and in Adorno's rejection of the idea that there could be a resolution of the questions of epistemology that would not be just a version of 'Idealism'.

Adorno's stance here involves the kind of meta-philosophical reflection familiar from Richard Rorty, where episodes in the history of metaphysics need not be seen as part of a history of error, or as Hegelian stepping-stones to absolute knowledge, but rather as aspects of human self-understanding that are not fundamentally different from episodes in the history of literature or the sciences. The added critical dimension in Adorno derives from the idea of nature-history and its relationship to making sense of the temporality of modernity, which for him involves an inevitable sense of loss. Rather than make a judgement on the viability of his approach here – we will look at more aspects of the issues in the coming chapters – it is better to conclude the chapter by seeing more of what Adorno's approach means in relation to how contemporary thinking deals with the concept of nature.

Since Kant much Western philosophy has, as we have seen, tended to regard nature predominantly as the object of the natural sciences, and this has led to the sense that questions of subjectivity are somehow either radically different from questions in the physical sciences, or will eventually be reducible to physicalist forms of explanation. Neither position, though, is satisfactory, and what is needed are approaches which do not ignore what makes sapience different from instinct, but which do not create an uncrossable gap between them either. Adorno takes up a variation of the idea of the 'residual character of truth' we encountered in Chapter 2 when he discusses the 'theory of truth as residue' ('*Residualtheorie*'), according to which 'the objective is what remains after the crossing out of the so-called subjective factors' (ibid., p. 256). He thinks that this theory 'may be valid where the object is not itself a human one that is mediated through *Geist*' (Adorno 1997, 9.2, p. 138): that is, in the physical sciences' explanations of nature in the formal sense. He is, then, concerned not with an attempt to see truth claims in the natural sciences as inherently infected by ideology, but rather with the over-extension of scientific claims into what is in fact the realm of obsolete metaphysics.

The account of the theory of truth as residue, which is part of Adorno's positive assessment of what Hegel has brought to modern philosophy, continues:

> That in the realm of the so-called sciences of society, wherever the object itself is mediated by 'mind', the fruitfulness of cognition does not succeed by the exclusion of the subject, but rather through its most extreme exertion, through all its stimulations and experiences – this insight, which today is only wrested from the reluctant social sciences by self-reflection, derives from the system-context of Hegel. (Adorno 1997, 5, p. 257)

The essential core of Hegel which Adorno adopts, and which suggests why Hegel has become the focus of recent philosophy concerned to get away from re-runs of Cartesian and other problems of dualism in philosophy, lies in the way in which '[t]he poles which Kant opposed to each other, form and content, nature and mind, theory and praxis, freedom and necessity, thing in itself and phenomenon, are all penetrated by reflection in such a way that none of these determinations stands still as something final' (ibid.). The question is whether the reflection in question aims, as Hegel does, at fully overcoming the contradictions in philosophy, or whether, as it does for Adorno, it interprets the contradictions as expressing particular historical constellations whose resolution would require a change in historical reality.

The shifts in the sense of the concept of nature in Adorno can be seen as resulting from the avoidance of making nature into any kind of foundational concept that is defined by what it is not, thus in contrast to 'mind', in whatever sense it gets in philosophy. Such an approach not only avoids the need to define nature or mind in a true philosophical theory, but thinks that the very idea that one should is the mistake, which is why nature and history are inextricably linked. This does not mean that the terms do not have any clear sense; instead the senses are articulated via the tensions that arise in trying to explicate them. The senses of nature in Adorno range, then, from the 'objective', in the sense developed in German Idealism, which 'stands against' the subject as a threat to its self-preservation or self-realization – and so can also include society as oppressive second nature – to that which can be oppressed and mutilated by instrumental reason, to which philosophy – and art – should seek to give a voice. The former sense results from the demands of self-preservation, the latter from how those demands result in the opposite of self-preservation. How, though, can that which can destroy us if we don't control it also be something which itself needs preserving in what sounds like the same way as we ourselves do? For Adorno this contradiction between the senses of nature is precisely the reality which is manifest in the historical shifts in the sense of the term. There can be no definitive way out of the contradiction, so the key is to understand what makes second nature, without which we cannot survive, become catastrophic. In Adorno's view this danger is associated above all with the Holocaust. Such understanding has therefore to come about by detailed historical analysis and awareness, and cannot be solely an intra-philosophical matter. The urgency of the issue can be suggested by the following, which makes it clear why limiting philosophical debate about nature to the terms of the versions of the formal conception of nature in contemporary naturalism, or to the choice between free-will and determinism, is so mistaken.

Adorno's approach to nature is captured in the following striking remark from the lectures on *Problems of Moral Philosophy*: 'We are really no longer ourselves a piece of nature at the moment when we notice, when we recognize, that we are a piece of nature' (Adorno 1996, p. 154). This recognition is by no means something which the philosophical tradition has offered adequate means for achieving. Thought, as Adorno's criticisms of 'Idealism' suggest, has often been regarded as what separates us from nature, or, at the other extreme, as something which will eventually be incorporated as part of nature in the formal sense. Adorno rejects both alternatives in the name of relating to nature in ways which acknowledge that even what seems to separate us from nature depends on nature. The nature in question is, however, not the nature of causal laws, but rather the nature to which we have an affinity that is not captured by the ways in which we think of it conceptually, which is manifest in our 'mimetic' responses: 'Were this moment [of affinity] completely eradicated, the possibility that subject could know object would become completely incomprehensible, unleashed rationality would become irrational' (Adorno 1997, 6, p. 55). Reflection of this kind takes us beyond thinking which is unaware of how it can damage nature by regarding it merely as what can be objectified in the name of controlling it. This may sound as abstract as the reductionist assumptions I am using Adorno to query, or like a version of re-enchantment. Adorno's reflections are, though, predicated on the historical shift with which I began the chapter. They indicate what lies behind the growth of ecological awareness of the limits of the human capacity to exploit nature. Adorno reminds us of the perennial need to rethink the terms in which philosophy has dealt with nature and to understand how these terms can also be interpreted as an expression of what has led us to the present potentially disastrous situation.

These issues raise questions about how self-determination relates to natural necessity, and in order to lead into to the next chapter, where we will consider the issue of freedom, I want to conclude by looking at a passage where the contradictions Adorno identifies are starkly apparent, via the ambivalence inherent in the notion of nature:

> Subjects are free, according to the Kantian model, to the extent to which they are conscious of themselves, identical with themselves; and yet in such identity at the same time unfree, to the extent to which they are subject to its compulsion and perpetuate it. They are unfree as non-identical, as diffuse nature, and yet, as such, free, because in the impulses that overpower them – the non-identity of the subject with itself is nothing but this – they become free [*ledig*] of the coercive character of identity. (Ibid., p. 294)

The argument is a version of ideas deriving from psychoanalysis, but should be understood within the framework that we have been developing. The compulsion involved in identity in Kantian terms is the condition of self-determination according to norms. We are capable of rational self-limitation via the adoption across time of norms to control our differing impulses. This depends on the transcendental unity of apperception, as what constitutes our identity. Were our natural impulses just causal parts of our physical nature, one might then view self-determination as identical with freedom, in the tradition that follows from Rousseau's warning that identifying freedom with the following of impulses makes us slaves to our passions. However, in Adorno's view, this splits the subject in a manner which fails to acknowledge that we also are our impulses. These are not just random instincts and are capable of great differentiation, a fact which will be crucial to Adorno's ideas about art. Without ways of dealing with these impulses that are not just based on subjecting them to norms, our potential for fulfilment is diminished. As we saw, norms which concentrate on grounding social justice tend to neglect motivations and impulses which are not adequately grasped by the assumption that it is only when they are brought within the space of reasons that they make sense. The need for differentiated expressive resources for our 'diffuse nature' is central to Adorno's conception of freedom, even as he is aware that the development of real self-determination is essential to progressive social change. The point here is that ideas about self-determination which do not see the dialectic involved in the passage just cited can fail to appreciate difficulties involved in the understanding and realization of freedom. We shall explore these in the next chapter.

5
Freedom

The meanings of freedom

Adorno suggests how he understands freedom in a passage from *Negative Dialectics* which precedes the passage on Kant's idea of freedom cited at the end of Chapter 4: 'The contradiction between freedom and determinism is not, as the self-understanding of the Critique of reason would like it to be, one between the theoretical positions of dogmatism and scepticism, but one of the self-experience of subjects, sometimes free, sometimes unfree' (Adorno 1997, 6, p. 294). The implications of this compressed remark are vital for contemporary thinking about moral philosophy, where so many philosophical approaches lead to theoretical dead-ends that are too often of little use in dealing with concrete issues concerning human freedom in modernity. Adorno's point is that the issue of freedom is not to be settled by a philosophical resolution of whether there is free-will or not. His stance thus puts in question one focus of many versions of ethics. The question which has dominated much modern philosophical debate is the 'location problem': how is one to fit whatever is meant by freedom into a nature which is assumed to be thoroughly deterministic? A characteristic response to this problem is the thesis of 'compatibility' between a nature that is completely deterministic and our capacity for moral responsibility, though the complexity of the attempts to formulate just what this means keeps growing. Too often compatibilism seems to mean that it is OK to *think* that you are free, although, from an absolute scientific perspective on nature, you are actually wholly subject to natural laws, even if we don't know them all yet. The implicit assumptions here can be used to tell a history of modernity in which what makes sense of human lives ceases to be 'really real', and the objective course of events as seen by the physical sciences becomes the model of the real, often with very problematic consequences for the rest of culture.

Adorno's perspective emerges from the questions discussed in the preceding chapters concerning the concept of nature. If the thesis of universal determinism is considered in the light of the arguments from Dewey and Adorno that we saw in the last chapter, which regarded the idea that the truth about nature lay solely in what is expressed in timeless deterministic laws as an invalid metaphysical reduction, the attempt to deal with freedom by making compatibilism work will be based on an indefensible abstraction. Moreover, a philosophical account of freedom which does not take account of the experience of real people who have lost or gained freedom empties the debate about freedom of its point. It is highly contestable to assume that the philosophical debate about whether freedom really exists is the central issue in the question of human freedom. The suffering which deprivation of freedom can entail, or the existential challenge which freedom poses to people in post-traditional societies who seek orientation in the face of the loss of theologically grounded prohibitions, makes it clear that the question of whether freedom can really be explained by the correct physicalist account of the functioning of nature involves a 'grammatical' error, in Wittgenstein's sense.

One cannot understand people suffering from lack of freedom at all if one assumes that ultimately free-will is an illusion. If one cannot see the ethical problem in even seeking to argue that freedom is just an illusion, one is presumably also unable to understand what is at issue in the significance of lack of freedom – how does one even understand what is supposedly lacking? – hence the grammatical error. Adorno makes the crucial point: '[I]n the situation of a complete determinism with no gaps, criteria of good and evil would be just completely meaningless, you couldn't even ask about them' (Adorno 1996, p. 218), because there must be some sense of the alternative to complete determinism for freedom to be an issue at all. In Adornian terms it is vital to keep in mind the causes and consequences of seeking to base one's response to the question of deprivation of freedom on a scientistic metaphysical thesis concerning the reduction of the will to something to be explained by natural laws, rather than on the suffering of those who are deprived of freedom.[1]

It might, however, seem as though separate issues are being conflated here. Conceptual distinctions between questions of political freedom and questions about freedom of the will are, as Mill suggests in *On Liberty*, easy to make: 'The subject of this Essay is not the so-called Liberty of the Will, so unfortunately opposed to the misnamed doctrine of Philosophical Necessity; but Civil or Social Liberty: the nature and limits of the power which can be legitimately exercised by society over the individual' (Mill 2011, p. 1). Mill's remark also suggests another much-used distinction, namely between 'negative' freedom, freedom from external constraint, and 'positive' freedom, freedom as self-determination by norms. The conceptual distinctions can, though, actually obscure some key issues.

Adherence to the scientific reduction that seeks to deny freedom of the will ought itself presumably to have political and legal consequences. In its extreme form the scientific reduction should mean that there is no moral basis for sanctioning people's behaviour and that one should instead rely on present or future forms of chemical or other intervention to correct their deviations.[2] But whence would the *authority* for such intervention derive? Any answer to this question already presupposes more than can be legitimated in terms of a scientific explanation based on the assumption of the solidity of facts as opposed to the arbitrariness of values. Moreover, questions concerning self-determination in a deterministic universe only emerge in many of the ways which concern contemporary philosophers at a particular point in the development of modernity. Debates about freedom in the globalized world have also been complicated in recent times by the questioning of the focus on individual self-determination, in the name of ways in which the community may legitimately be said to possess priority over the individual by some thinkers from, for example, China and other areas of the Far East. Much of what is at issue here can be seen to be inherent in the tensions between a Kantian and a Hegelian conception of freedom and self-determination, and this tension will be the main conceptual source of Adorno's reflections.

Once again recent work on Hegel has revived issues concerning Hegel's conception of ethics which can change our response to what Adorno proposes, and which can in turn be questioned by some of Adorno's reflections. Robert Pippin's *Hegel's Practical Philosophy* presents a hugely insightful version of Hegelian ideas that moves in certain respects in similar directions to Adorno, though there are paradigmatic differences between their responses to Hegel. The differences arise again in relation to the understanding of self-determination in Hegel and in Adorno. One source of the differences is very straightforward. Adorno bases his final reflections on ethics in *Negative Dialectics* on the claim that 'Hitler enforced a new categorical imperative on humankind in the state of unfreedom: to organize their thinking and action in such a way that Auschwitz does not repeat itself, that nothing similar should happen. This imperative is just as resistant to being given a grounding as in its time the givenness of Kant's imperative' (Adorno 1997, 6, p. 358). Hegel criticizes Kant's categorical imperative for being empty and formalistic, because it offers an abstract criterion for judging how to act which fails to take into account that individual action is always situated, and so is always informed by the concrete, historically developed, ethical life of a community. Adorno's concern, which is epitomized by the Holocaust, is that in modernity concrete ethical life may be unavoidably bound up with distortions occasioned by the factors that we have considered in the preceding chapters. Any version of the Hegelian alternative to Kant's perceived failure to establish a concrete basis for his moral philosophy is therefore in danger of conspiring with what Adorno seeks to overcome by his very specific version of a moral imperative. By adhering to the norms of a community, we may well help produce something which leads to gross inhumanity.

In seeking to avoid this problem we seem, however, to be forced back in the direction of something like a Kantian universalist imperative, which Adorno will also give good reasons to question. But does Pippin's new version of Hegel's approach to ethical life offer ways beyond Adorno's suspicions of Hegel?[3] As we have repeatedly seen, Adorno's underlying thought is that the Holocaust is the manifestation of essential aspects of modernity. Pippin overstates what Adorno intends, however, when he claims that Adorno adheres to 'the thesis that National Socialism and the Holocaust were not aberrations in the development of Western Enlightenment, but the logical outcome' (Pippin 2011). If it were true that this outcome was the logical consequence of 'Western Enlightenment', Adorno would be rejecting any sense of modern rationality. What he is really concerned to show is that its development is nearly always two-edged, because what makes the modern world more inhabitable can also be what enables systematic inhumanity. Pippin, in contrast, thinks of modernity predominantly in terms of the development of the previously unavailable possibility of living a self-determined life in a community which acknowledges my self-determination. Pippin's judgement on Adorno is not adequate to Adorno's views developed in the lectures, and there are more points of convergence on some key issues than he appears to think. We seem in fact to need something of both conceptions to understand ethics in modernity. How, though, are we to respond to the contradictions between such positions, given that they also share a great deal? Both insist, for example, on the need for moral philosophy to take adequate account of the social and historical factors which form the content of moral life.

Pippin's account is an attempt both to reorient the direction of practical philosophy, and to change the interpretation of Hegel's philosophy. Both Pippin and Adorno offer ways of looking at moral philosophy that can move beyond the endless to and fro of the sort of analytical ethics that seeks, for example, definitively to adjudicate between consequentialist and deontological stances, or to give a definitive response to the 'location problem'.[4] Pippin's Hegel shares with Adorno the rejection of the idea that moral philosophy should consider 'the exercise of practical reason on the model of an individual reflectively deliberating over possible courses of action' (Pippin 2008, p. 19). Kant famously made the core question of moral philosophy 'What should I do?'[5] This question tends to load everything onto the issue of the spontaneity of a subject deciding between opposed courses of action, and thus onto a particular notion of the freedom of the will. In contrast, 'the issues that dominate so much of the modern post-Cartesian, post-Kantian discussion about nature and mentality do not ever arise for Hegel: subjective self-certainty, raw feels, intentional states, mental objects, and their possible or not possible reducibility, and the problem of spontaneous causation in action, or "could have done otherwise" issues' (ibid., p. 57). Hegel does not think he needs to 'establish some unique causal capacity [like Kant's 'causality of reasons'] in order to establish the possibility of freedom as he understands it' (ibid., p. 16). This means that Hegel does not separate social and political questions concerning freedom from the metaphysical question of the freedom of the will. Adorno, like Hegel, sees subjects of moral life as inherently constituted by the pressures and norms of the social and historical world which they inhabit, though his analysis is significantly different.

The central claim which underpins Pippin's version of Hegel is where some of the implications of the divergence become apparent: 'The essential desideratum for Hegel in any theory of freedom [. . .] is the possibility of an actual and experienced identification with one's deeds and practices and social roles, the conditions necessary for the deeds to be and to be experienced as my own [. . .] (such that I can stand behind, own up [sic] what I have done as truly mine)' (ibid., p. 6). My freedom can therefore only be realizd via my relation to others, who can acknowledge my commitments and hold me to them, as I can hold myself to them. The core elements of Hegel's account, Pippin contends, are the 'sources and nature of normativity, *how* we have come to hold each other to certain accounts [. . .] what goes wrong with certain ways of collectively doing so, what goes right with others' (ibid., p. 63). The radicality of Hegel's position lies in the fact that '(i) this is *all* an account of spirit amounts to and (ii), within that account he defends a sweeping claim: that the advent of modernity marks off a decisive and unsurpassable phase in this attempt, the "overcoming of and liberation from nature"' (ibid.). In a development of Kant, 'we are subject to no law or principle of action that we do not "legislate for ourselves"' (ibid., p. 65), and, against the metaphysical interpretations of Hegel, 'spirit is a self-imposed norm, a self-legislated realm that we institute and sustain, that exists only by being instituted and sustained' (ibid., p. 112).

Agency is 'as much, if not more, a matter of retrospective justification and understanding and mutual recognition than a matter of prior deliberation and the power to choose' (ibid., p. 146). The key here is the need for social acknowledgement if ethical life is to have any substance at all: whatever happens 'inside' me when I make a moral decision is only intelligible via norms which exist 'outside' me. These norms bring into existence the ethical realm in which my action is an action at all, rather than something caused or something unintelligible. (This is another kind of critique of a 'myth of the given', where the given would be the pure moment of subjective spontaneity in isolation from the world in which it occurs.) I may, though, in this view, still do something incomprehensible in terms of existing norms. This would not exclude what I do from having ethical value, if what I do comes to be seen as valuable and legitimate in the light of historical changes which my actions may help to initiate. Pippin cites Stanley Cavell: 'Intention is no more an efficient cause of an object of art than it is of a human action; in both cases it is a way of understanding the thing done, or describing what happens' (cited in ibid., p. 162). Pippin: 'The notion of rational agent [. . .] functions a bit like "being a speaker of a natural language"; where vocalizations count as speaking the language only within a language community that commits the speaker to various proprieties and entitlements' (ibid., p. 197).

These claims deserve sustained attention, but the difficulty we shall use Adorno to highlight begins to be apparent in the following summary, particularly the last part:

> To say everything at once: Hegel's eventual claim will be these three conditions of successful agency [recognition by others of my self-attributed social identity; recognition of 'the deed as falling under the act-description which I invoke'; and recognition of me 'as acting on the intention I ascribe to myself'] cannot be satisfied unless individuals are understood as participants in an ethical form of life, *Sittlichkeit*, and finally in a certain historical form of ethical life, in which such relations of recognition can be genuinely mutual, where that means that the recognizers are themselves actually free, where the intersubjective recognitional relation is sustained in a reciprocal way. (Ibid., pp. 220–1)

Although Adorno's lectures *Problems of Moral Philosophy* share certain aspects of such a conception, their essential starting point could not be more different. The difference will make clear a revealing split concerning the philosophical understanding of ethical life in modernity.

Pippin refers to 'what is at once one of the most noble and most abused notions of nineteenth-century thought. [. . .] The idea is that I cannot be properly said to be free ("actually" a free and self-determining agent) unless others are free, that my freedom depends on theirs reciprocally' (ibid., p. 214). Adorno makes similar claims: 'Freedom would be, as Kant says, literally and truly an idea. It necessarily presupposes the freedom of the whole, and cannot, as isolated freedom, thus without the freedom of the whole of society, even be thought' (Adorno 1996, pp. 261–2). As such, 'the question of the right life would be the question of the right politics' (ibid., p. 262), and this is precisely where the impossibility of 'thinking freedom' arises. It would be mistaken to reduce the difference I am concerned with here to political differences, given that Adorno's and Pippin's aims are in some respects similar. The decisive difference becomes obvious when Adorno says that 'the reason why the question of moral philosophy has become so problematic today is first of all that the substantiality of ethics [*Sitte*], thus the possibility that a right life was already given and present in the forms in which the community exists, has become radically obsolete' (ibid., p. 22). This is because 'the community has gained such a superiority over the individual, because we are forced so much into conformity at every moment by countless processes that that agreement of our own individual destiny [*Bestimmung*] with what is forced upon us by the objectivity of the context can no longer be produced' (ibid., p. 24). It is once more important to remember in relation to such remarks that Adorno's main assumption is that the Holocaust was not a unique aberration, but a product of factors in modernity to which we are all subject.

Part of what underlies the difference between Adorno and Pippin is suggested in the phrase, quoted from Pippin above, that modernity involves the 'overcoming of and liberation from nature'. In short, where Pippin thinks we can still justifiably think in terms of our acknowledgement of our actions as our own, Adorno thinks that our entanglement in 'nature-history' puts the transparency of this acknowledgement into question, because the causality of social pressure can take an analogous form to destructive natural events. Self-determination can be an illusion born of the failure to understand how one is determined, which can be 'natural' in the sense of what is given to us through biology – Adorno is clear that biology is always mediated by its relation to social forms – but can also be what determines us through the pressures of social existence in irrational and unjust circumstances. This is not simply a theoretical question: the centrality of the Holocaust for Adorno derives not least from its being perpetrated in the country from which the ideas underpinning Pippin's vision of modern ethical life emerged. There is no necessary connection between the context of the emergence of a conception and its validity, but Adorno does suggest there is a connection in this case. Given that both Pippin and Adorno refuse to separate the question of freedom from the contexts in which freedom is supposed to exist, a hasty judgement on the validity of their respective stances is likely to miss some vital issues. Pippin dismisses Adorno's most negative view of modernity, in which 'there is no right life in the wrong', but he does so largely on the basis of rhetorical and polemical exaggerations in *Negative Dialectics*. A more plausible version of Adorno's ideas can be found in the lectures just cited, and in the lectures translated as *History and Freedom*.[6]

Moral contradictions

In a discussion of Ibsen's *The Wild Duck* Adorno describes a situation which is paradigmatic for his reflections on moral philosophy. Neither the pragmatic, cynical character, Relling, who avoids acting in terms of the 'higher' moral ideals of life, because he sees ideals as illusions for coping with life rather than as absolute guiding principles, nor Gregers Werle, who seeks to follow idealized moral norms without being concerned about what concrete effects this may have in a difficult situation, can be seen to be justified by the drama. Adorno puts it like this: 'One has to keep hold of the normative, of self-criticism, of the question of the right and the wrong, and, at the same time, of the critique of the fallibility of the instance which thinks it is capable of such a self-criticism' (Adorno 1996, p. 250). He cites a comment by the theatre critic and director Paul Schlenther on *The Wild Duck*, according to which Ibsen, despite his attachment to aspects of Hegel, 'does not resolve the contradiction, but instead shapes the insolubility of the contradiction itself' (ibid., p. 238).

This view of the contradictions in self-determination makes it easier to see why Adorno is suspicious of a Hegelian view, and how he connects his suspicion to the dark side of modernity. Pippin's Hegel regards the core of practical philosophy as a harmonization of the individual with the norms of a community which can tell a story of their development that legitimates them, there being no other form of legitimation which would not entail indefensible metaphysical or other dogmatic claims. Individuals see the norms as allowing them to constitute themselves as moral subjects by regarding the norms as their own. Adorno argues that in the situations characteristic of modernity the subject's harmonization with communal norms cannot be as transparent or unproblematic as it seems to be for Pippin and Hegel. One obvious aspect of the difference here is the subordinate role of Freudian considerations in Pippin, as opposed to Adorno.[7] Pippin allows a role for cases where one is unaware of one's true intentions, but this does not adequately take into account how social norms may systematically facilitate blindness to the reality of one's deeds. This reality may not be immediately apparent, but it need not be a metaphysical postulate either.

Adorno arrives at his criticisms of Hegel via an extended exploration of Kant's moral philosophy. The underlying issue is the relationship between individual and universal in modern societies. Kant seeks to reconcile individual and universal via the categorical imperative, in which the demand made on the individual is to universalize the norm governing their action. Before he gets to Kant, Adorno makes a major point about action in modernity which already suggests a different perspective from the Hegelian one. In *Negative Dialectics*, during a discussion of *'das Hinzutretende'* ('that which is additional', which relates to the sources of moral motivation that are not captured by theoretical considerations), Adorno argues something that initially seems to coincide with Pippin's Hegel, but which then makes the distance clear:

> The self-experience of the moment of freedom is linked to consciousness; the subject only knows itself to be free to the extent that its action appears identical with it [this is the moment stressed by Pippin], and that is only the case with things that are conscious. In these alone does subjectivity painfully and ephemerally raise its head. But insistence on this narrows itself in a rationalistic manner. (Adorno 1997, 6, p. 226)

Adorno makes clear in *Problems of Moral Philosophy* what distances him from the rationalistic consequences of the consciousness of freedom. He thinks there is an 'a-theoretical' moment in morality – *'das Hinzutretende'* – which is apparent when someone decides to resist dominant norms.

Just as Pippin tends, in the face of modern history, to underestimate the dangers of the idea of ownership of communal norms, Adorno can too easily totalize the idea that norms in modern societies constitute a 'context of delusion' which makes moral action impossible. However, the power of the Adornian approach derives, as we saw, from the idea that Nazism expresses something perennial about what can go wrong with the ethical development of modernity, and Pippin reduces this to Adorno's thinking the Holocaust is the 'logical' result of the Enlightenment. The case that Adorno cites is of his meeting one of the members of the 20 July Plot to kill Hitler, who managed to escape the terrible fate of most of the conspirators. The man tells him that there are situations which are 'so unbearable' that one acts against them, even in the knowledge of what may well become of one (Adorno 1996, p. 19). Knowledge of the unbearable situation is clearly necessary, but is not what is decisive. Instead there is a 'moment of irrationality' (ibid.), of 'spontaneity' (ibid. p. 17 – this is not meant in the technical Kantian sense), that is vital in such situations: 'As such one could say that moral contemplation [. . .] to the extent to which the moral as action is always more than thinking, always comes into a certain contradiction with what is thought about' (ibid., p. 21). Instead, then, of proposing a concrete philosophical model of ethics, Adorno sees the task as bringing to light why thinking about freedom leads to contradictions. He also provides an account of motivation, but this involves an aspect which takes one outside the scope of theoretical reflection.

In contrast to Pippin's 'Goethean' notion of insight into the necessity of self-determination according to norms that one learns willingly to adopt, Adorno sides with Hamlet, with the sense that there is an inherent dissonance between my existence as individual and the norms with which I am confronted. Explaining moral action in terms of a reconciliation of the individual's impulses and motivations with communal norms can therefore fail to account for the manifestations of moral life in concrete situations. Hamlet illustrates the problem that 'people suffer from their knowledge, because they have the experience that there is no longer a direct way into practice from this knowledge, but that one needs a third thing, precisely that element of irrationality, of what is not purely reducible to reason' (ibid., p. 168). This element leads people like the July conspirators to act, even though rationally they know they are likely to be tortured to death, and might even do more to defeat Nazism by staying alive.

The problem in a Kantian conception is that in almost any concrete moral dilemma, especially in the interconnected world of modern capitalism, it is a question not just of one maxim that is to be universalized, such as 'Thou shalt not lie', but of competing maxims occasioned by competing demands. In discussion of the issue of lying, Kantians try all sorts of manoeuvres to suggest one cannot lie justifiably, rather than seeing, for example, that the imperative to save lives may be the more important one in some situations. The contingent fact, to which Kant himself points, that, by lying in order to save life, one may make something worse happen applies to anything else one might do, including telling the truth. Abstract being-right of the kind suggested by Kant's desire for moral purity in the prohibition on lying is a target of Adorno's approach, but he is equally sure that there is no easy alternative. The question of freedom of the will is central to modern philosophy, as Kant suggests, but in Kant (as in so many other philosophers) it seems to involve simply the idea that moral behaviour 'does not come under natural causality'. However, the real problem, Adorno contends, is 'the nature [*Bestimmung*] of this freedom, the nature of causality and the relation of freedom and causality to each other' (ibid., p. 47).

The remark from *Negative Dialectics* with which we began the chapter is elucidated when Adorno suggests that 'the highest foundation of morality, namely the categorical imperative, is really nothing more than subjective reason itself as something absolutely and objectively valid' (ibid., p. 53). The sceptical attempt to 'contest the universal necessity and obligation of moral laws by relating them to the subject' (ibid.) is thus reversed. It is precisely via the individual subject's adherence to a universal imperative that the 'dogmatic' objective necessity of pre-modern cultures is supposed to be restored. This leads to Kant's hybrid notion of a 'causality through freedom'. Adorno says in *History and Freedom* that '[t]he oxymoron "causality from freedom" rests on the equation of will and reason qua lawfulness' (Adorno 2001a, p. 345). The problem with grounding causal explanation is that it leads either to an infinite regress of causes or to an absolute origin, which is therefore not a cause in the initial sense, for which each cause is itself also an effect.

Freedom, seen as the capacity to initiate a new causal sequence, seems, therefore, and here lies the source of the emphatic versions of German Idealism, such as Fichte's, to be an 'absolute spontaneity'. There is something of this in Pippin's position (see Pippin 1997, p. 404, cited above in Chapter 3). This sense of absolute spontaneity is, though, also the source of Kant's dualisms, where the spontaneity of the intelligible subject is wholly separated from nature in the formal sense, in order for it not to be a determined part of the causal realm.

Adorno makes the problem with regard to moral philosophy in this respect very clear:

> [I]f one just insisted on saying: there is admittedly something like freedom in the absolute, but as soon as I move into the limited realm of experience [...] there is only causality and you can't find any freedom, then nothing at all would be done for practice itself with this announcement of this principle of freedom. For practice is always the practice of empirical human beings which relates to empirically given circumstances. (Adorno 1996, p. 82)

He argues that 'this double difficulty, that something like the sphere of the human can exist neither in absolute lawfulness nor in absolute freedom is really the most profound reason for Kant being forced into the paradoxical construction of a causality through freedom' (ibid., p. 84). This situation is the source of apparently (and sometimes actually) rather implausible construals by Adorno of what happens in Kant's moral philosophy.

Kant is, Adorno argues, caught between, in the realm of appearance, the absolutizing of causality – which is, though, in Kantian terms, itself the product of the *subject*'s spontaneous ordering of appearing nature, not an attribute of things in themselves – and, in the intelligible realm, absolutizing the subject's freedom. Absolute freedom lacks any limits; these would contradict the essence of freedom, which ceases in these terms to be freedom at all if it is limited by anything empirical. The result is an absolute which 'has the same character of blindness and externality' (ibid., p. 87) in both cases. Focusing moral philosophy exclusively on either side of this dichotomy makes concrete moral life impossible to understand. The dialectic of Enlightenment in Kant results from the fact that 'there is really only on the one side the sphere of cognition of nature in the sense of an uninhibited pragmatism "What can I do with it?", and on the other side the sphere of morality as the sphere of the absolute validity of laws of reason' (ibid., p. 95).

Now this may seem an extreme view, but Adorno, as we have seen, reads Kant's philosophy as an expression of contradictions in modernity, so its value may lie more in what it reveals in this respect than in the possible validity of its arguments. Reconciling how we come to control nature, including our own nature, through objectifying, causal explanation, on the one hand, with the idea that self-determination is the key to meaningful human life, on the other, is a problem that can be related to the contradictions Adorno sees as constitutive of modernity. In both cases there is the sense that these conflicting aspects can become dangerous if they are absolutized. Kant connects cognitive ordering by the subject and the subject's self-determination, because they both depend on spontaneity. There are, then, good grounds for seeing his philosophy precisely as an expression of the implications of the modern attempt to reconcile the ability to bring more and more of nature, including the nature that we are, under control, with the idea, crucial for Pippin, that the main way in which post-theological human life may make sense is in terms of our capacity for a norm-governed self-determination which 'leaves nature behind'. The question is how these two aspects are connected.

The basic Kantian problem which Adorno makes very clear is that 'even practical philosophy, which, by relating to our real actions, always has to do with the material of experience, cannot be absolutely separated from experience' (ibid., p. 103). Hegel sees this problem in his critique of the abstract nature of Kantian imperatives, but it is not certain he is able to resolve the problem it entails. The core of Kant's morality is autonomy, but this leads Adorno to the following reflection: '[E]verything that I do not know as a pure rational being and all lawfulness that I do not derive from my own reason, by the fact that they bind me to something which is not myself in this emphatic sense, but which is heteronomous, which I make myself dependent on, actually inhibits the principle of freedom' (ibid., p. 107). Kant's notorious rigorism, which, in the *Metaphysics of Morals*, dictates that even a society which was dissolving itself should execute the last murderer in its jails before doing so, in the name of justice – not in the name of protecting people from danger – suggests the worry.

Adorno shows how this worry goes very deep: '[I]n a certain sense the two contradictory moments of [Kantian] moral philosophy, namely the idea of freedom and the idea of, one has to say, suppression, above all of the suppression of any natural impulse – the suppression of inclination, the suppression of sympathy – both really only come about for the sake of freedom' (ibid., p. 108). If happiness has to a significant extent to do with how I deal with my natural impulses, it seems 'incompatible with reason as a universal principle' (ibid.). It therefore becomes unclear what the point of reason can be at all, given Kant's way of characterizing it. This is because Kant does not ask the question 'whether the absolute realization of reason would not mean something like the fulfilment of precisely everything that is suppressed by him' (ibid.) as being part of the determined world of appearance. Everything that is suppressed belongs in Kant's sense to the causal realm of nature, so freedom and the justified satisfaction of natural impulses are incompatible.

Kant seeks to bolster the idea of freedom by linking it to the ideas of God and immortality, but, in an echo of Schelling's criticisms of rational theology, this means philosophy makes 'the existence of the divinity [...] dependent on the principle of human reason' (ibid.), when reason itself presumably ought to be secondary to the divinity which makes reason possible at all. Despite Kant's insistence that theology is outside the scope of the understanding, he remains within the 'ontotheological' paradigm which is a version of what Adorno terms 'Idealism'. Consequently, philosophy

> makes its own First and Absolute once again dependent on something that, according to the meaning of this First and Absolute, really would be something secondary, for the reason in question [i.e. the reason of the philosopher] can again for its part only be thought if one thinks of it too as something abstracted from finite human beings and each time incorporated in them. (Ibid., p. 110)

Kant tries to make freedom the core of his philosophy at the same time as ensuring that his understanding of freedom is wholly separate from our relations to the empirical world and to our impulses. Here Adorno again reads the philosophical aporia as the expression of a real contradiction.

Kant does not legitimate the categorical imperative by an argument; it is 'a fact, the moral law is a given' (cited in ibid., p. 112), which means that 'in order to be valid it needs those three principles or entities: God, freedom, and immortality' (ibid.). The contradiction arises because, in Kantian terms, action has to be in accordance with the categorical imperative if it is to be morally justified. The problem is 'that between such a law, that between the idea of good and right action, and the possibility of following the law, there is a real contradiction' (ibid., p. 113). The contradiction is a result of the effects of modern rationality. Here the reasons for Adorno's distance from a Hegelian stance become very apparent. In Kant 'the possibility of absurdity does not appear: the absurdity that there is the idea of the Good and the obligation to do good and to fulfil the law, but that, at the same time, people are refused the possibility of fulfilling it, by the totality of the social context in which they are inserted' (ibid. p. 114). Kant thinks he can reconcile social necessities with the demand for freedom; Adorno's conception is predicated on the sense that this reconciliation has been rendered illusory by modernity. In Hegel's terms there has to be an inherent reconciliation of the individual and the social whole, because the individual only gains any kind of legal status via the development of mutual acknowledgement that is enshrined in the laws of the state.

It is not, though, that Adorno simply wishes to argue against Kant, or, for that matter, Hegel. He thinks that the way in which Kant's approach leads to necessary contradictions in thinking about freedom is more appropriate to the world that generates the Holocaust than is Hegel's insistence on mutual recognition as what resolves the tension between the individual and the social whole. However, Adorno's position itself involves its own rigorism: it relies on the unfulfilled utopian idea of a just social totality, in which people would be able to 'fulfil the law', and it can at times share the abstract status of Kant's moral philosophy. Without involving something of what Hegel means by *Sittlichkeit*, it is hard to see how even 'damaged life' would be possible at all without descending into a Hobbesian 'war of all against all'. Adorno presumably knows that the everyday observance of norms is what allows for the admittedly flawed functioning of any society not in a state of total disintegration, so the question is how to make sense of his position without it just becoming aporetic.

One of the Hegelian elements in Adorno is present in his insistence that the 'givenness' of reason in Kant's sense, which is a priori, because Kant must exclude it from the deterministic empirical realm, cannot be independent of some kind of 'experience', in which we are aware of reason as something that affects the world we inhabit. Otherwise there could be no connection of reason to what actually happens in moral life.[8] The contradiction involved here in Kant opens up precisely the space which Adorno thinks is the location of the problem of modern freedom. Many people find something intuitively convincing about the categorical imperative, because it involves the democratic injunction not to arrogate to oneself rights that one would not grant to others. Even without Kant's intelligible realm the idea of some such imperative is hard to dismiss. Adorno suggests that 'however much people are in opposition to certain moral ideas or orders, they orient themselves to some compulsions or other, they have respect for something (ibid., p. 121). The question is the content of that respect, and here Adorno makes a decisive move.

Adorno acknowledges that Kant is empirically right with respect to the imperative, insofar as 'something like conscience really exists' (ibid., p. 122). The problem is that the compulsion exercised on people by their conscience 'says nothing at all about the legitimacy of this instance as such' (ibid.). In one respect this is close to Pippin's contentions concerning the social content of norms, but Adorno's move beyond the individual conscience is in a different direction. Conscience is now, Adorno argues, an object of empirical research in psychoanalysis, and he thinks that Kant would acknowledge the advance this involves with respect to the awareness of the role of psychological factors in moral life. Given the bad press that psychoanalysis has often received, especially in recent years, it might seem that Adorno is on weak ground here, but his point is simple and plausible. The imperatives which drive conscience are 'internalizations of the dominant social norms in a given situation, which are transmitted to us by the nature of the family, and which we generally internalize by identification with father-figures' (ibid., p. 123).[9] Most crucially, the compulsion of the super-ego tends to 'transfer itself on to things which are no longer compatible with reason' (ibid.). The 'unity of moral compulsion with reason itself' (ibid.) is contradicted by the ways in which internalized moral compulsion can, as the Nazi period teaches, lead to irrational cruelty.

Any attempt to isolate the imperative from the empirical world has to admit that 'this formal, abstract form of the moral law is for its part again drawn from these actual compulsions' (ibid., pp. 123–4), not from some timeless intelligible realm. In consequence: 'If every relation to real forms of behaviour which are expressed by the ideal of duty were to be cancelled, then at the same time the substance of what Kant introduces under the conception of compulsion would also be cancelled' (ibid., p. 124). The notion of autonomy is necessarily infected with some measure of heteronomy, and the compulsion of duty therefore 'cannot be an absolute source of law for the ethical' (ibid.). Norms in real societies that give the content of duty have to be critically appraised, even if we lack a philosophical foundation for the location from which to appraise them, of the kind sought by Kant in the categorical imperative.

The question is, then, how to conceive of autonomy in a way which does not simply square the circle between being compelled and being free, by arguing that one should be willingly compelled by duty. This is arguably the position shared, despite their many differences, by Kant and Hegel. As Hegel puts it in the *Encyclopedia* § 513, in a remark which sums up Pippin's stance on the subject's identification with its normatively constituted actions:

> The *substance* that knows itself as *free*, in which absolute *ought* is just as much *being*, is real as the spirit of a people. [. . .] The person knows, as thinking intelligence, that substance as its own essence, and ceases in this conviction to be an accident of it. [. . .] [The person] does his duty, without selective reflection, as *his* duty and as something *real* [*als Seiendes*] and has in this necessity himself and his real freedom. (Hegel 1959, p. 402)

Adorno's refusal to accept this kind of harmonization in the face of the reality of modern history relates to aspects of his diagnosis of the sources of the ills of modernity. It is not, though, that Pippin thinks such a harmonization has been achieved. Hegel 'thought he saw coming into view a resolution of this social conception of rationality in institutions that embody mutuality of subjectivity, or genuine equality, in a way that rises to a general resolution of the problem of practical rationality. Today, I do not think anyone in his or her right mind would argue this is true' (Pippin 2011). The question is how to respond to the non-achievement of this harmonization.

Kant's notion of reason involves an essential contradiction, which Adorno suggests is revealed by Nietzsche's more insightful criticisms:

> [Kant] is profound and truthful enough to see that reason as a pure organ of truth and truth and as organ of our self-preservation are not two absolutely different media [...] but that reason which makes itself independent and directs itself towards truth is, so to speak, a dialectical product, so to speak the child of that self-preserving, in the normal sense, practical reason. (Adorno 1993, p. 131)

The instance that we require to survive, which Adorno characterizes in terms of 'instrumental reason', needs another kind of reason to limit its possible negative effects. The genesis of the latter is, though, inconceivable without the former. This is what leads to the contradictions in Kant, who seeks to separate the two, even as he is aware that they cannot be wholly separate. Kant is thereby also led to a contradictory view of nature, both as just the 'the lawfulness of appearances in space and time', and as something which is teleologically conceived as somehow harmonizing with the idea of reason. This is the source of the notion of a 'causality of reason' as a bridge between the contradictory senses of nature, and the attempts in the *Critique of Judgement* to understand the ways in which we may feel in harmony with nature.

It should be clear from this part of Adorno's analysis that the exaggerated story in *Dialectic of Enlightenment*, which led Habermas to his influential criticism that Adorno thinks solely in terms of instrumental reason (see Habermas 1981, 1985), does not straightforwardly apply here.[10] Adorno is aware that there is more to reason than instrumentality, but his claim is that instrumentality has become the dominant modern form of reason. The moment of 'non-identity' present in Kant's failure to give the moral law a philosophical grounding – Adorno talks of the way Kant just 'breaks off' the philosophical argument by seeing the law as 'given' – suggests to Adorno that 'right action is not to be purely resolved into theoretical requirements' (Adorno 1993, p. 144). The attempt to 'deduce from pure reason why there should be no torture in the world' (ibid.) is likely to lead to irresolvable theoretical difficulties of the kind that fill books on moral philosophy. Think of the 'trolley problem' we touched on in Chapter 1. The hope for a philosophical solution to the problem must be confronted with the fact that if, *per impossibile*, such a situation were really to arise, there would be a host of other factors in the situation that are not included in the original statement of the problem. The way the problem is initially formulated inherently pushes one towards a choice between consequentialist and deontological positions, but these other factors could quite possibly be decisive, making it clear that the apparent core choice is merely a questionable abstraction. Without the ultimately ungroundable sense that in concrete situations one has to do or not do certain things on the basis of one's moral experience, rather than on the basis of philosophically legitimated founding principles, theoretical reflection would never come to an end.

This may sound like a cop-out, but Adorno makes a telling point with regard to philosophy's role in the understanding of freedom: '[O]nly to the extent that the context [*Umwelt*] is limited does something like the famous Kantian freedom exist. [. . .] [E]ven if one were to live completely as an individual in the sense of the Kantian imperative, it is very undecided how far such a right life would touch the objectively entangled and enmeshed nature of existence today' (ibid., p. 147). The often badly framed claim that 'an ethics' is impossible in modernity makes sense in terms of the idea that philosophical reflection is not going to give theoretical criteria for right action which can just be applied in concrete situations to solve moral dilemmas. Rorty's idea that moral philosophy may be best understood via novels reminds us that moral life continues however much philosophy fails to arrive at theoretical answers to ethical questions. Something akin to this approach is present in Pippin's Hegelian stance, which sees moral life as embodied in the norms through which a society is constituted, rather than as something to be understood by a generalized philosophical theory. Both he and Adorno are part of a Hegelian alternative to most forms of practical philosophy, insofar as they reject theories which exclude experience, in the sense that we have seen in Adorno, from the substance of moral reflection.

However, Adorno does add the claim that the sedimented internal and external effects of instrumental reason are such that ethical transparency is effectively impossible. This is a kind of inverted image of Pippin's Hegelianism, where sedimented norms are the very condition of possibility of ethical life. Adorno maintains that it is often structurally impossible to do the right thing. In some circumstances this may well be the case, but one of Adorno's failings in this area lies in his totalization of the ways in which moral action may become impossible. Each position, then, needs an aspect of the other if it is not to be implausibly one-sided. Pippin sees the sedimentation of norms in terms of the liberation from nature, which makes sense both in terms of modernity's demand for liberation from 'dogmatic' appeals, in the manner characteristic of pre-modern law, to God and nature as a source of legitimation of norms in the social sphere, and in terms of a rejection of scientism for its involving attempts to reduce the space of reasons to the space of causes. This position depends, though, on an understanding of nature which Adorno regards as failing to take account of the contradictions in modern conceptions of nature, of the kind we have seen in his reading of Kant and in his reflections on 'nature-history'.

Nature and freedom

Kant's strict exclusion of freedom from causally determined nature gives rise to instructive contradictions, which will suggest that 'leaving nature behind' can be the source of an underestimation of major issues in modernity. We saw some of the arguments why in Chapter 4, and we now need to look more closely at Adorno's account of freedom. He does not have a 'heroic' conception of freedom, because he is so insistent on our natural, embodied form of existence. Mind, *'Geist'*, in a basic sense which is prior to any specific philosophical characterization, evidently emerges from nature, but 'despite this, mind will [. . .] project a tiny bit beyond the context of the natural' (ibid., p. 152). As such, outlining a version of the 'space of reasons', 'what we call nature in general itself defines itself only in opposition to what we possess in terms of mental/spiritual experience [*geistige Erfahrung*] [. . .] [A]lthough all our representations [*Vorstellungen*] [. . .] derive from the realm of nature as a whole, in their constellation they are not reducible to this context' (ibid., p. 153). We can change how we connect our ideas in a manner which is not fixed in the same way as what the ideas are about is fixed, such as when we imagine 'what is not already the case' (ibid.) by changing the constellation in which we think of things. This can, as we will see later, be thought of in terms of an understanding of the relationship between participation and observation which prevents the former being reducible to the latter. Adorno claims that this ability to connect ideas is really what Kant was thinking about with regard to nature and freedom, but that what is involved cannot be expressed 'in a logic of Either/Or' (ibid.), because it creates the split between empirical and intelligible, and thence the temptation of Idealism in the sense which Adorno rejects.

We already encountered Adorno's essential claim in Chapter 4, namely that '[w]e are really no longer ourselves a piece of nature at the moment when we notice, when we recognize, that we are a piece of nature' (ibid., p. 154), so that '[w]hat transcends nature is nature that has become aware of itself' (ibid., p. 155). This is not a transcendence which opens up a new realm of reason or freedom, of the kind present in the theologically inspired idea that humankind is elevated above the natural world by reason. Though he does not deny a certain kind of transcendence, Adorno is warning against what can lead to reason being really just disguised self-preservation, and to destructive nature-history. Instead it is a transcendence via which one 'recognizes oneself as a moment of what is blind, and by this gets beyond what is blind' (ibid.). This recognition is 'the self-reflection of nature in humankind' (ibid., p. 156). The dialectic involved here is explicitly different from a Hegelian self-recognition in otherness. Adorno sees this as in danger of being a form of narcissism, where the otherness of nature gets lost in the process of 'leaving nature behind'. Freedom here is the awareness that one cannot transcend one's natural being by wholly subjecting nature to one's ends, particularly the end of self-preservation. From a contemporary Hegelian perspective it could at this point be contended that such a claim is still located in the space of reasons, and, by invoking nature, involves an element of 'intuition', thus of dogmatism. However, what the Adornian perspective wishes to sustain is not a positive appeal to nature, but the awareness of the limits of how we seek to transcend nature by giving reasons. Such awareness is not just the result of arguments in the terms of the space of reasons but can also be arrived at through the kind of sense-making that Adorno sees as central to art.

The idea of 'the self-reflection of nature in humankind' echoes Schelling's account of freedom in his 'middle' philosophy from around 1809 onwards, particularly the essay 'Philosophical Investigations into the Essence of Human Freedom'. A central goal of Schelling's work is precisely to question the ways in which nature is 'left behind' in modern philosophy. Schelling's texts from this period are often quite obscure, and they can rely on outmoded theological models.[11] However, the ideas that lead in the direction of Adorno are relatively simple. Much of the contemporary debate over naturalism seeks, as we saw, to reduce the mental to being part of nature in the formal sense. This kind of identity of mind and nature leaves no role for freedom, and tends to lead to ineffectual appeals to compatibilism. The problem is that if the world is to be fully explained in deterministic terms, it becomes hard to understand why there are moral issues in any meaningful sense at all. The power of such reductionist positions derives from the fact that natural scientific research increasingly reveals the extent of our causal dependence, and social and historical research reveals the ways in which we are influenced by social and historical circumstances. The position suffers, though, from a metaphysical assumption which is not based on such research, or is invalidly extrapolated from it. The direction offered by Schelling and Adorno is important because it does not deny the extent of our dependence on nature (and, in Adorno's case, social causality), but leaves room for ways of making sense of the nature of the living world that are manifest in relations to the world which are not just cognitive. This approach extends the scope of 'nature', taking account, in Wellmer's phrase, of our nature as our 'neediness, its impulses, its potentials and its vulnerability' (Wellmer 2009, p. 220).

The equivalent of contemporary reductive naturalism for Schelling was Spinozism, and its appearance in various versions of the idea of identity of nature and freedom. Schelling suggests that 'if [...] necessary and free are declared to be One, which means: the same thing (in the last instance) which is the essence of the moral world is also the essence of nature, then this is understood as follows: the free is nothing but natural power, a spring which, like all others, is subordinated to the mechanism' (Schelling 1856, p. 342). He sees this as involving 'an incomplete and empty idea of the law of identity' (ibid., p. 345), and thus an incomplete and empty idea of nature. This aspect of his conception is close to Adorno's idea that '[w]hat transcends nature is nature that has become aware of itself', where nature is both that which is subject to necessary laws and what goes beyond it, whilst still depending on it. That freedom depends on nature does not, Schelling argues, mean freedom is not 'real'. Dependence just means that 'what is dependent, whatever it may be, could only be as a consequence of what it is dependent on, it does not say what it is and what it is not' (ibid., p. 346). Otherwise it is impossible to understand why there is an issue about freedom at all.

Schelling's theological argument is intended to get away from the perceived mechanical consequences of Spinozism by seeing 'freedom' as the condition of the emergence from blind nature into the conflicts of living existence. The theological argument here, which has some bizarre and indefensible consequences of a kind also present in a related form in Kant, need not detain us.[12] The useable philosophical substance of the argument is clearly what appealed to Heidegger (see Bowie 1993, Chapter 5). Heidegger's concern is why the world is manifest and intelligible at all in all the diverse ways it is if its essential basis is really deterministic causality that is explained by natural sciences whose explanations themselves rely on a prior 'unconcealment' that cannot itself be explained scientifically. Schelling, distancing himself from Idealism, even though it is in some respects a counter to Spinozism, claims that the problem with the Idealism of Fichte is that by putting freedom at the centre of philosophy it involves 'the most general, but on the other hand the most formal concept of freedom' (Schelling 1856, p. 352). The key to freedom is, however, really 'that it is a capacity for good and evil' (ibid.): only humankind is capable of evil, which therefore is based not, as in Spinozism, on a lack of insight or on sensuous desires, but rather on the same will which can drive one to strive for the good.

What Schelling means by evil connects to Adorno's idea that freedom also relates to awareness of our dependence on nature, rather than being an absolute capacity for self-determination. If God were 'a merely moral world-order' (ibid.), we would lose the reality of freedom, which involves the need to transcend its 'ground' by overcoming an alternative that is a real possibility. If there were no struggle to overcome something which opposes it, why would freedom be so significant? Without the struggle nothing would motivate our will, because it would be in complete harmony with itself. The ground here is our natural being, which is not reducible to the natural laws which we use to describe it in objective terms. Without resistance from this natural basis the value of freedom becomes impossible to understand, and the very debate over determinism and free-will would not even matter: '[O]nly from the darkness of what lacks understanding (from feeling, longing, the glorious mother of knowledge) do illuminated thoughts grow' (ibid., p. 360). Despite the fact that they must ultimately be identical, if there were not some kind of duality between nature and mind, there would be either meaningless, causal change or pure opaque stasis. For this even to be a problem, there must be that which goes beyond that change or that stasis. The duality is therefore based in the inseparability of mind from motivating will. This duality brings about an inherent tension in being, and is the pre-condition of living, manifest being – being in which things *make sense* and so generate tensions and conflicts, rather than being whose functioning is solely to be objectively explained.

The key move with respect to the link to Adorno comes when Schelling talks of evil as occurring when the particular individual will which transcends nature seeks to dominate it. It is not the fact that we have a naturally driven basis that is the source of evil; rather it is that this driven basis can become the core of subjectivity itself: 'Evil does not come from finitude in itself, but from finitude which has been raised to being-self' (ibid., p. 370). Schelling, like Adorno, rejects the Kantian idea 'according to which freedom just consists in the mastery of the intelligent principle over sensuous desires and inclinations' (ibid., p. 371). If one lacks the insight into what can be evil, and simply follows desires and urges, there is no good and evil, just the functioning of the natural ground. The point is to see subjectivity as both based in nature and as what comes to transcend it, but then also to see that this transcendence depends on the same will as motivates our natural impulses. There can therefore never be a wholly transparent distinction between nature and freedom in us, of the kind that is based on nature being the realm of necessary laws and subjectivity the realm of pure self-determination. This is what leads in the direction of Adorno's idea of nature-history, but also to his sense that we must constantly re-negotiate the contradictions that arise from the relationship of nature and freedom in different historical constellations. The Kantian exclusion of our embodied natural impulses from the realm of freedom contrasts here with the idea that freedom must include what motivates us in all the different forms that make up what we are: hence, for Schelling, the need to characterize it as the capacity for good and evil. As Adorno suggests, a freedom which does not include the fulfilment of desires loses its point, but if the fulfilment of desires is essentially linked to domination, rationality and domination are connected, even as what connects them is also what can make embodied life worthwhile.

Schelling still sees these issues in a perspective formed by theological questions of the kind raised by Spinoza and Leibniz. The core thought which frames his reflections is the following apparently rather banal claim: 'For every being can only become manifest in its opposite, love only in hate, unity in strife' (ibid., p. 373). In humankind 'the link of the [opposed] principles is not a necessary one, but a free one' (ibid., p. 374). Freedom is linked to the fact that there is a manifest world in which things are valued, which they could not be if there were not a real opposition between principles that create the differentiations and contradictions of a living reality. Broadly and bluntly: the fact that anything can make sense at all depends on the basic tension between a ground and what seeks to move beyond it, between, for example, an existent state of one's life and the sense that it is not meaningful.[13] There can be no sense without such a dynamic.

The force of this conception lies in how it attempts to respond to the negative sides of human existence, which Schelling sees in thoroughly melancholy terms, while understanding that without them the positive sides could not emerge at all. Schelling helps to make apparent a frequent deficit in many areas of philosophy, namely a proper understanding of why one would adhere to, follow, or establish norms at all. There can be no desire without a lack that gives rise to it and demands fulfilment, and no knowledge and insight without the resistance of the object that generates the motivation to understand it. Unlike a Hegelian account of negation, Schelling's does not necessarily require the idea that negation can ultimately be overcome by philosophical insight. Schelling's 'veil of melancholy' that is manifest in the transience of all natural things cannot be overcome by understanding the necessity of transience. Transience has instead to be able to become what can motivate us to find new ways to live that make sense of it, not least in ways that philosophy cannot predict, even as we may know we cannot finally succeed. Music, the key temporal art, exemplifies what is meant here: it is precisely the way that music generates something beyond the sadness and suffering in which it is often grounded that gives it its power. The alternative for Schelling to the melancholic sense of negation – and here there is an implicit response to Leibniz – is that there would be no world at all, and God would remain in undifferentiated oneness with Himself.

At an existential level, and omitting his attempt to construct a philosophical theology, Schelling suggests how every form of thinking is grounded in some kind of 'desire'. This links it to what happens throughout living being, but it does not involve the rationalist sense of a cognitive identity between the structure of thought and the structure of the object. Hegel sees desire as a stage to be transcended in the process which leads to mutual acknowledgement and the community of free self-legislators. In the Schellingian view desire is not simply *aufgehoben*, because it remains the ground of all development. Without the tensions created by desire, freedom lacks any motivating ground, and that ground is what we share with the rest of nature, even as we may try to move beyond it. If we try to absolutize our attempt to overcome this ground, we fall prey to what Schelling means by evil: 'Evil is in a certain respect completely spiritual [*das reinste Geistige*], for it carries on the most emphatic war against all *being*, indeed it would like to negate [*aufheben*] the ground of creation' (ibid., p. 468). This sense of evil relates closely to aspects of *Dialectic of Enlightenment*'s account of how the subject's aim of self-preservation can lead to the dominance of instrumental reason, which, rather than liberating humankind, does the opposite.[14] As Adorno says in *History and Freedom*: 'To impute that one ever knows, without doubt and unproblematically, what the good is is itself, one might say, already the beginning of evil' (Adorno 2001a, p. 365).

The source of the divergence of both Schelling and Adorno from a Hegelian conception is well suggested in Schelling's *Ages of the World*. He puts the argument in the questionable terms of 'character', as what is decisive in the last instance in moral life. However, if one reads what he says in terms of Adorno's emphasis on '*das Hinzutretende*', the motivation that cannot fully be based on theoretical reflection, the idea that freedom is ultimately to be understood as self-determination by norms can be seen as insufficient. Schelling does not reject a normative perspective: '[A]cting according to reasons and so-called principles [*Grundsätze*] in its place [...] is something splendid' (Schelling 1946, p. 94), but these should not 'make the will the complete servant of the understanding' (ibid.). The element of Schelling's views which can still command attention is the idea that evil is a perversion of reason which is always a potential of reason, rather than either something which can just be overcome by greater understanding, or some kind of mysterious malevolent power. Evil and freedom are therefore necessary complements of each other. As Wellmer puts it in relation to the Holocaust: '[T]he freedom of spirit can also manifest itself in the form of a will which has been radically *perverted* towards evil' (Wellmer 2009, p. 224).

Adorno's use of Freud can elucidate this conception: the super-ego's tendency to 'transfer itself on to things which are no longer compatible with reason' depends on the fact that reason has no force without what is expressed by the idea of the super-ego. Norms make no sense unless they are in some way collectively effective, but they may be instilled in us in ways which involve unconscious compulsion. This is why the super-ego threatens to over-extend the reach of reason. What establishes the norms which supposedly enable us to 'leave nature behind', to move from natural 'sentience' to cultural 'sapience', can therefore become a form of nature-history. It is not that this situation should lead us to abandon the role of normativity in any account of freedom, but it does remind us that an account of freedom without that which goes beyond the normative gives us too few resources to comprehend how modern norms have been used for appalling ends. It is hardly as if the Nazis lacked norms that were collectively assented to, and the likes of Eichmann invoked, however disreputably, a Kantian notion of duty in their self-justifications. Just saying, as we saw Pippin doing, that it is only when 'the recognizers are themselves actually free, where the intersubjective recognitional relation is sustained in a reciprocal way', that freedom is realized does not really address the sheer weight of circumstance that makes this situation so hard not only to realize but also to recognize.

Adorno puts his essential point like this: 'The relation freedom–law is not a well-balanced, not a reasonable equation; rather, dynamic moments are in play on both sides. What is captured by the law is the drive-energy of humankind, which can barely be subdued, but cannot be sublimated without remainder' (Adorno 1996, p. 181). In Schelling's terms we cannot ever finally overcome the ground: without it the point of life would be lost, because what motivates us is the need to transcend the given. The necessary contradiction in human freedom lies in the fact that it depends on an ineliminable ground that makes it possible, but which we are forced to try to overcome, even as a complete overcoming of it would actually destroy freedom. How this contradiction plays out in concrete situations is, as Adorno insists, dependent on adequate historical and sociological understanding: '[S]ocial categories stretch right into the innermost aspects of moral philosophy' (ibid., p. 205). Adorno questions the Kantian imperative because of the consequences of making freedom that which must overcome nature: '[T]his overstretching of the concept of freedom, that it is based on the absolute independence of all being, of all nature, threatens at the same time to turn into unfreedom by the fact that renunciation is enforced on people, and, above all, that they generally do not get back what they have to renounce according to this imperative' (ibid., p. 179). The consequence is that people seek to get back what they renounce in forms which can be manipulated or abetted by the dominant mechanisms of modern societies.

The other problem with the Kantian imperative is that it presupposes that 'the endless ramification of the social totality, thus something infinite, is positively given to me, so that I can produce this connection between my maxim and this universal legislation' (ibid., p. 232). In reality, the link between a maxim and the reality in which one seeks to apply it is rarely, if ever, given in a form which is fully transparent. Just asserting, as Kant does, that the only thing which is unqualifiedly good is a good will is therefore another version of the attempt to leave nature behind. The idea does little to help understand how we might legitimately exercise our freedom in the reality of complex social contexts that are subject to the objective pressures characteristic of modern capitalism, which can distort our desires and needs, even as they produce other desires and needs.

The Kantian and Hegelian attempts to anchor self-determination in social norms can neglect the ways in which norms concretely function: '[V]ery often the motives which we pretend to ourselves are the pure ones, thus those of the categorical imperative, are in truth just motives which come from the empirical world', and 'are really connected with the satisfaction, if I may say so, of our moral narcissism' (ibid., p. 242). Empirically we can never be sure of the transparency of our motives, because the internalization of norms takes places in structures of domination that we cannot definitively step outside.[15] Ownership of norms in the Pippin–Hegel sense – the basic idea of the categorical imperative, shorn of its connection to the idea of an intelligible sphere, is a decisive factor in the self-determining adoption of norms from a Hegelian perspective – can too easily be linked to 'the preparedness to denounce, with the need to punish and persecute others' (ibid.). Adorno is, though, not offering any easy alternative here. The most substantial claim he is prepared to make is that '[w]e might not know what is the absolute good, the absolute norm, or even only what man or the human or humanity is, but we very well know what the inhuman is' (ibid., p. 261). The question is why, if we know it – he is again thinking of the Holocaust – we remain so prone to allow it to dominate, and he argues this has to do with the structures of power in modernity.

The concluding motto of the conclusion of *Problems of Moral Philosophy* is 'modesty', in the sense of a critical awareness of the difficulty of achieving legitimate self-determination. The real alternative, which separates Adorno from the positive philosophical sense in Pippin that one can own one's norms, is between 'positing the group to which one belongs and negating what is different' and 'learning in reflection on one's own relativity [*Bedingtheit*] to also allow legitimacy to what is different and to feel that the true injustice is really always there where one assumes one is right and the other is wrong' (ibid., p. 251). Pippin might counter that this is a merely empirical point that should obviously be built into our awareness of the complexity of moral life. However, this criticism abstracts too much from the historical picture which Adorno uses as the basis of his reflections, where the failure to do what he advocates is the dominant factor in a world which possesses the technical and other means to enable more just and humane life, and yet produces the Holocaust.

Adorno, in a characteristic dialectical twist, favours in one respect the notional purity of the categorical imperative over concrete Hegelian *Sittlichkeit*, because it leaves space for the 'salvaging of the moral norm in relation to the social reality which is precisely not identical and not reconcilable with it' (ibid., p. 246). Pippin argues that Hegelian rationality is non-metaphysical, because the only appeal can be to historically developed norms and their forms of legitimation; any attempt to move beyond this immanent perspective will involve some kind of dogmatism. Adorno argues against Hegel, though, that 'the reason which forms itself in the world and the critical reason which stands opposite it are not only not One, as Hegel would like us to believe, but they are not reconcilable with each other in their consequences' (ibid.). But does Adorno himself not rely on a kind of dogmatism? His critical reason evidently involves its own rigorism, insofar as any action in the context of the interconnected social totality we inhabit can add to the mechanisms of oppression. A trip to the supermarket is fraught with the sense of colluding with the injustices of a global capitalist economic system. Although this stance can be legitimated immanently, to the extent that aspects of the social world offer alternatives to the increase in oppression occasioned by the rigging of markets, Adorno himself at times argues as if the totality is so dominant that no such perspective can emerge.

In contrast to Adorno's sceptical view of the possibilities for self-determined action in modernity, Pippin contends that there are good reasons for adhering to at least an attenuated view of Hegelian *Geist*, because modernity shows that, along with the disasters, there can be real moral development. This is evident in those things which were once acceptable but have come to be inherently unjustifiable, such as slavery, the oppression of women, and racism. All these still exist, but a legitimation of them, of the kind which was possible in the terms of some pre-modern societies, has become impossible, and this testifies to the development of free self-determination that transcends the horrors within which that development takes place. Adorno's view is usually summarized, in contrast, by the notion of a dialectic of Enlightenment, where notional self-determination ends in instrumental reason. The social and economic structures in which self-determination is exercised can often lead to one person's self-determination being the root of another's loss of self-determination. This seems radically opposed to Pippin's view, but things are not that simple.

Adorno would agree that there can be forms of moral progress, but incorporating an account of this into a wider Hegelian *philosophical* claim about self-determination and *Geist* seems to him in danger of hiding the ways in which such progress produces other forms of repression. The concrete development of modernity involves some of the most brutal events of human history, even as moral awareness seems to progress in key respects. If the progress is also connected to what produces the brutality, one needs to show how rationality in the modern world is contradictory, rather than just abstracting a story of its immanent development towards higher stages. The problem is how one should adjudicate on the generalized assessments of modernity involved in the contrast of Adorno and Pippin. What is at issue here is how we interpret the relationship between freedom and history, and how this interpretation informs any conception of a philosophical account of ethics.

Freedom and history

The 'specific vantage point' of Adorno's lectures on *History and Freedom* is 'the relationship between the individual and freedom, which is largely identical with the relationship of the universal, of the great objective tendency, with the particular' (Adorno 2001a, p. 11). The point of orientation is Auschwitz: '[I]f freedom and autonomy had still been substantial, Auschwitz could not have happened' (ibid., p. 14). The basic question is: 'What does it mean: the human species progresses, if millions are degraded to being objects?' (ibid., p. 15).

What is puzzling about the contemporary revival of Hegel's practical philosophy in the USA in particular is that it models freedom on a reconciliation of the individual and the universal which is so patently absent in the USA itself, or, for that matter, most of a world dominated by neo-liberal economic policies which privatize profits and socialize losses. Adorno could here be talking about the contemporary USA, where deprived people regularly adhere to values (and vote for those who advocate them) which lead to their further immiseration: 'The less people are free in history [. . .] the more desperately they insist on asserting their own immediacy as something final and absolute' (ibid., p. 38). Instead of a historical realization of *Geist* which transcends the particularity of the contingent happenings of modern moral life, suggested for Pippin by the examples of what becomes objectively impossible to argue for, Adorno is concerned with a different kind of transcendence, namely of objective economic and social processes over individuals, and the ways in which this produces ideology, as a form of nature-history.

Ideology is a highly controversial term, precisely because it challenges the extent to which people are self-determining with respect to the ideas to which they adhere. This seems to put the critic of ideology in a transcendent position, of the kind which theories like Adorno's should be concerned to question. However, saying, as Rorty does, for example, that ideology therefore should just mean 'bad idea' is likely to obscure the fact that the production and adoption of 'bad ideas' involve accumulated systemic social and economic pressures. These need to be analysed in terms of how individuals are subject to forces beyond their control and yet do not see how they may be led to deceive themselves by such forces. The links between the notion of ideology and the ways in which the super-ego over-extends the need for the renunciation of drives can suggest what is meant here.

The idea that individuals are somehow just passive vehicles for social forces is the main reason for suspecting the notion of ideology of entailing an unjustified objectifying view of social subjects. Adorno, though, thinks social actors are caught in a contradiction, because subjects *must* actively pursue their interests as best they can; the consequence is that 'they become [. . .] the executors of precisely that historical objectivity, which, as it is at every moment ready also to turn against their interests, then also becomes precisely that which enforces itself over their heads' (ibid., p. 41), in forms of nature-history. John Lanchester's description of the crisis in the Eurozone and the wider crisis that began in 2007 makes the problem clear:

> From the worm's-eye perspective which most of us inhabit, the general feeling about this new turn in the economic crisis is one of bewilderment. I've encountered this in Iceland and in Ireland and in the UK: a sense of alienation and incomprehension and done-unto-ness. People feel they have very little economic or political agency, very little control over their own lives; during the boom times, nobody told them this was an unsustainable bubble until it was already too late. The Greek people are furious to be told by their deputy prime minister that 'we ate the money together'; they just don't agree with that analysis. In the world of money, people are privately outraged by the general unwillingness of electorates to accept the blame for the state they are in. But the general public, it turns out, had very little understanding of the economic mechanisms which were, without their knowing it, ruling their lives. They didn't vote for the system, and no one explained the system to them. (Lanchester 2011)

Adorno does not propose a naïve political answer to this kind of situation; objective processes are also what enable human self-preservation, even though they do so at the cost of those who go under or live in misery, so they have, in one sense, a real form of legitimation.

Indeed, and here the connection to Pippin's insistence on the anti-metaphysical construal of Hegel is clear: 'It is the endless weakness of every critical position (and that includes mine, I would like to say) that Hegel simply has the stronger argument in relation to such criticism because there is no other world than the one in which we live' (Adorno 2001a, p. 72). However, Adorno wants to avoid the idea that he is invoking something merely utopian or metaphysical because, in the contemporary world, the at least partial realization of freedom is actually possible: '[T]he state of technology would allow the satisfaction of human needs to such an extent that lack really would not need to exist at all' (ibid., p. 252). The same instrumental rationality which produces unfreedom is also what, in changed economic and social circumstances, could enable its abolition. The problem lies in the ways that changing those circumstances can just produce another version of them. How, then, does freedom ever play a role in such a picture, given what Adorno sees as the dominant modern tendency of people to identify with forms of order which may in fact oppress them?

Separation of the issue of political freedom from the question of the freedom of the will, which is characteristic of a large amount of analytical moral philosophy in particular, can be seen most clearly to stand in the way of an adequate response to these issues. One point is straightforward in this context, and Adorno and Pippin are, via their shared orientation to Hegel, in agreement about it. The attempt to argue, in the face, for example, of the growing neuroscientific knowledge of the natural laws that play a role in the functioning of the brain, whether or not there really is free-will simply misses the point. If the idea of causal closure really meant there was no freedom, would this invalidate all previous attempts to understand human history via concepts like self-determination? The absurdity of such a stance can be suggested by the idea of telling people on Tahrir Square during the Egyptian revolution that what they wanted was not real anyway. The point of Adorno's criticism of Kant for reducing freedom to what 'does not come under natural causality' is apparent here. Any attempt to define freedom in such a way fails to see that freedom 'is a category which is *historical* through and through; that one cannot, for example, formulate and stipulate a concept of freedom once and for all, in the way philosophy has almost always done it' (ibid., p. 248).

The historicity of freedom is apparent in the fact that freedom of the will only becomes a major philosophical problem with the rise of modern individualism. Freedom as just the idea of 'the inner power or freedom of decision', as 'the immanently subjective' (ibid., p. 256), rests on a questionable separation of the internal and the external. Without the 'external' historical change in the status of the individual subject, the issue of whether the internal constitution of that subject is wholly subjected to necessary natural laws would not have arisen in the forms it now does.[16] The 'concept of the will itself [. . .] as concept of the alternative: freedom or unfreedom of the will, only belongs to a relatively late phase of philosophical reflection' (ibid., p. 267), associated particularly with Locke's formulation of the problem of determinism. As the bourgeoisie demanded freedom in opposition to the feudal order, it was 'forced to ground its freedom in the essence of humankind itself' (ibid.). This conception reveals itself, though, as involving the contradictions we have observed in Kant. Reason, as this 'essence', also has a tendency to repression, of the kind suggested in the discussion of the super-ego. This contradiction leads to the following: '[T]he more the theory urges freedom, the more the theory insists that human beings are free in themselves, that their will is absolutely free, that they are absolutely responsible for themselves, the more the theory lends itself to repression' (ibid., p. 272). Adorno cites the example of legal theory, where the more the freedom and responsibility of the subject is insisted on, the more there is a tendency 'to let subjects feel the full weight of the law' (ibid.).

The core of Adorno's conception is dialectical: attempting to understand freedom from either just the subjective or just the objective side fails to see their necessary inter-relationship. He praises Hegel for showing how 'freedom, which appears to us as if it were just a quality of subjectivity, as if its possibility could only be decided and judged in the subjective realm', depends 'on the objective, on the extent to which we are capable at all, via what we do as subjectively formally free beings, of influencing overwhelmingly structured institutional reality' (ibid., p. 282). The recent economic crash exemplifies what he means: those losing their jobs through no fault of their own, while many of those who caused the crash enrich themselves, may be formally 'free' under the law, but when the will has so little space for self-determination, this freedom can be largely empty. The utopian element in Adorno means that 'freedom and unfreedom are not the primary thing, but both are rather derived from the totality, which has supremacy over the individual' (ibid., p. 286). As we saw, this means in one sense that real freedom is only possible when all are free.

It is, though, not clear what this could concretely mean, at least in the extreme version in which the idea appears at times in Adorno. In its less extreme versions, Adorno thinks that freedom can be realized, as we saw, when the means already at humanity's disposal are used to liberate everyone from material want. The contemporary socio-economic and cultural state of large parts of the world is testament to how perennial the failure to realize this situation is. The objective failure to liberate people from the lack of the basic needs for life is why Adorno's focus is on the extent to which the 'primacy of the objective' dictates so much to do with freedom in the modern world. The very emergence of the modern concern with freedom is dependent on the nature of the objective social world, so that 'one could say that in a very real sense freedom gets mixed up in the context of determination' (ibid., p. 338). However, Adorno does not – although he tends to on occasion – wholly reduce his dialectical conception to the primacy of the objective.

The freedom of the subject

As suggested by both the need to develop a strong ego to cope with the demands of modernity, and the ways in which this development relates to the super-ego, the constitution of modern subjectivity may well be a process that depends on the pressure of objective circumstances, but 'all considerations of this kind have a snag: for such an objectification of the subject [. . .] to take place, there must also already be something like the sphere of subjective reflection, like the sphere of subjectivity' (ibid., p. 266). In Pippin's terms this sphere is able to find its echo in and constitute itself via the norms generated by communities' self-legislation. Adorno, while seeking to sustain a dialectic in which the subject plays a necessary role, thinks that such a view takes too little account of the mechanisms of repression involved in the constitution of subjectivity, and their consequences.

Pippin's conception of self-determination is the outcome of the notional, if not always actualized, resolution of contradictions between the individual and the social. These are the product of the development of the split between the individual and the social that results from the disintegration of the idea of a natural social order, which Adorno also sees as constitutive of modernity, and which is a condition of modern conceptions of freedom. Adorno's more restricted conception of self-determination results from the recognition that we must live with contradictions that may not admit of philosophical resolutions, of the kind that take the form of 'giving oneself the law'. The capacity to reflect critically is the best we can hope for, and this is inherently fallible, for the reasons we have seen. In contrast to Pippin's retaining the Hegelian notion of the development of *Geist* made possible by the rise of individualism and the re-negotiation of the relationship between subject and society, Adorno sees this development, aspects of which he acknowledges, as masking the repressions it also entails.

Adorno's suspicion of resolving contradictions is apparent in his discussions of the subject's relationship to freedom. As we saw, he does not think that there is any kind of yes/no answer to the existence of freedom of the will, because that would require the assumption that what is at issue is located wholly within the subject. Once one sees – and here Pippin, Hegel, and Adorno concur – that 'subjective immanence' is always already imbued with objective factors, it is no longer valid to ask the question whether there is an internal capacity, a kind of on/off switch, which is not causally dependent, to say yes or no to a course of action. The reason why is already suggested by the fact that individual freedom of the will only emerges as the main ethical issue via the disintegration of the idea of a natural social order:

> For it is on [the sphere of the objective], on the organization of the world and the state of the world that the extent to which the subject attains autonomy depends [...]. Detached from the state of the world, autonomy is fictitious – or such a thin and abstract principle that nothing at all more can be said with it about the real and actual behaviour of people. (Ibid., p. 308)

Adorno attacks thought experiments, of the kind represented by Buridan's ass, for reducing 'the empirical conditions to such a minimum' (ibid., p. 309) that they have nothing to do with reality. If the real complexity of any such situation is brought into thinking about it, 'what is determining comes precisely from the outside, which, as something external, is precisely supposed to be excluded, because the question of freedom in all these experiments is meant as a merely internal question' (ibid.). Adorno talks in this connection of a 'naïve realism of inwardness, a naïve assumption of a being in itself of the inner world with its freedom or unfreedom' (ibid., p. 315), of the kind Kant himself criticizes in the first Critique's attack on substantializations of the soul in the Paralogisms chapter, but seems to adopt in the *Foundation of the Metaphysics of Morals*.

At the same time, the thought experiment of Buridan's ass, although illegitimate, does point to an aspect of the subject's relation to freedom that Adorno, as we saw above, regards as crucial, and which separates him from Hegelian rationalism. In any serious moral situation there has to be a form of motivating impulse which turns reflection on action into what one actually does, which Adorno referred to as '*das Hinzutretende*'. This is 'a somatic impulse, which goes beyond the intellectualization' (ibid., p. 317) inherent in theories of the will like Kant's. The point of this element lies in its connecting nature and freedom, not as rationally compatible in the Hegelian manner, but in terms of the idea that motivation is not just something initiated by consciousness in the form of a norm-governed reflective choice of a course of action. It is also something which depends on our primal connection to the natural reality we are that is evident in our reflexes and impulses.

The conception is again close to some of Schelling's reflections on the ground of freedom. Adorno suggests he will be accused of taking a moment of what is 'decisive for the constitution of freedom', and, by trying to account for its origin in the nature of human reflexes, ending up with 'something merely determined' (ibid., p. 328), thus denying freedom of the will. But this is precisely the abstraction which Adorno will not accept. Like Schelling, he thinks that this objection fails to see how the ground of something does not determine what it can become. Adorno puts it in Freudian terms: the ego is 'itself split-off libidinal energy which is used for testing reality' (ibid., p. 329). As such, it cannot be wholly different from natural impulse, but is also not just identical with it. When we 'behave spontaneously in this real sense, then we are just as little blind nature as we are on the other hand repressed nature', and we are 'capable, by dint of this impulse, of getting into, leaping into, going into the objective sphere which is otherwise obstructed for us by our own rationality' (ibid., p. 330). This type of connection makes it clear why aesthetics is so crucial to Adorno's thinking. The kind of relation to the objective world present, for example, in musical performance (particularly improvised performance) relies precisely on the way that acquired norms which are necessary to perform at all are, in the moments which really matter, transcended by impulses that occur in concrete situations and which are not governed by those norms. The jazz player's experiences of 'being in the zone', which only sporadically occur, involve a kind of freedom which precisely manifests itself in the disappearance of the conscious need for control and a following of impulse which creates new sense. The – in many respects justified – Hegelian sense that by owning the norms by which one acts one can lead a meaningful life tends to ignore how the kind of motivation which gives content to norms can be more evident in such moments than in a self-determination which harmonizes with a given norm. If freedom were wholly norm-governed, we would again be back with the harmonization of the individual and the social that Adorno refuses to accept under the conditions of modern capitalism – and which may be an unattainable abstraction anyway.

By concentrating on our nature's 'neediness, its impulses, its potentials and its vulnerability', Adorno brings out how the exploration of freedom necessarily leads to contradictions whose significance can only be grasped in particular historical constellations. The same freedom which enables forms of self-transcendence of the kind just described can, in the wrong social, political, and economic conditions, lead to disaster. The structure which helps understand why is the following:

> The more the I controls itself [*sich gebietet*], and the more it controls nature, the more it learns to control itself, the more questionable its own freedom becomes to it, precisely insofar as it is this archaic, non-controlled reaction as something chaotic, so that [. . .] whilst it is only with the development of consciousness at all that something like freedom becomes possible, *at the same time* it is the development of consciousness that pushes freedom back into this archaic-mimetic moment that is essential to it. (Ibid., p. 295)

It is not that Adorno advocates an irrationalist voluntarism of the kind associated with Carl Schmitt, which sees legitimacy as essentially the arbitrary result of the assertion of power. He just does not think that we can ignore what leads to ideas, like voluntarism, that question the absolute status of rational self-determination. The need for self-determining control in terms of collective norms is ineluctable, but so are the resources for responding to impulses which may not be articulable in directly normative terms. Hence the centrality of aesthetic articulation and expression for Adorno's philosophy, and the questions we saw in relation to Brandom's separation of sentience and sapience in Chapter 3.

The idea that informs much of the preceding discussion involves a version of the Hegelian notion that the line between the subjective and the objective with respect to freedom is not something to be fixed by, for example, establishing that there 'really is' a non-determined, spontaneous subjective capacity of free-will that is independent of the way the objective world functions. The difference between Adorno and Pippin's neo-Hegelian view is located not at this level, where they are largely in agreement, but rather in the evaluation of how we understand the contradictory nature of modern rationality. I shall return to this issue in the next chapter, where the question of art's relationship to philosophy further illuminates the contradictions between Pippin's and Adorno's understanding of freedom. I want to conclude this chapter, though, by briefly seeing how aspects of Adorno's conception relate to the arguments of two of his successors, Martin Seel and Albrecht Wellmer, concerning some contemporary aspects of debates about freedom. Seel and Wellmer help to give a more constructive sense of how to think about freedom in the light of Adorno's deconstruction of many of the theories which still preoccupy contemporary philosophers.

Freedom after Adorno

Seel finds a focus for the way freedom has appeared in recent philosophy in the relationship between participation and observation, which has been important in the work of Habermas.[17] This relationship is not the same as the relationship between subjective and objective, for reasons that were apparent in Kant and German Idealism. One key issue in German Idealism, probably seen most clearly by Fichte and Novalis, was how the subject can 'see itself seeing': that is, objectify the (subjective) activity of observation of its own activity in a philosophical explanation. There is always a non-objectifiable aspect of participation in any understanding of what human beings do based on observation: 'Observation is not as such scientific observation, in the same way as participation is not necessarily a solely subjective matter' (Seel 2006, p. 136). This distinction leads to the question which is significant with respect to freedom: 'Is it possible in certain contexts, on the basis of the capacity for both participation *and* observation, to behave in a manner which is exclusively participatory or observational?' (ibid., p. 138). The former, Seel argues, is temporarily possible in playing or listening to music, when one is completely absorbed by what one is doing, but it cannot be sustained indefinitely. The latter is not possible because observing aims at *'observations* which can be passed on and communicated to others. [...] Observers are also participants – potential participants in a practice of justification or presentation of what has been observed' (ibid., p. 139). In consequence: 'It is not only the case for self-observation that a complete distance from oneself is impossible;

this is the case for all observation' (ibid., p. 140). The world cannot be related to in a manner which is exclusively participatory or exclusively observational, because even observation aimed at producing objective theories is communicated in a manner which requires participation. This much is in line with Brandom's inferentialist picture and the use Pippin makes of it.

Seel makes the hermeneutic point that 'no cognitive position can be thought of outside a relation to the real and possible understanding of other people. [. . .] In cognition of whatever kind no path leads out of the intersubjective space of reasons' (ibid., p. 141). Otherwise one would just be making dogmatic metaphysical claims without any consideration at all of whether they can be understood or found legitimate. The further related point with respect to freedom is that '[t]here is no position from which a theoretical distance can be established in relation to the fact of freedom' (ibid.). The reductionist idea of a 'necessary illusion' of freedom in a world that is really wholly deterministic is, as Adorno suggested, inherently untenable. In order even to make the claim that freedom is a necessary illusion, one has to presuppose something which is not wholly determined for the claim to be intelligible at all. Furthermore, making any cognitive claim requires the freedom to judge which reasons one finds compelling, otherwise one has to invoke a wholly mythical picture of the nature of scientific inquiry.

However, this still leaves the understanding of the relationship between 'natural determination' and 'cultural freedom' completely open (ibid., p. 142). Seel argues that three options seem available, none of which really addresses all that is at issue. (1) We will never know what the relationship is, because an explanation of how consciousness could emerge from inert matter is inconceivable. (2) For the time being we don't know what it is, and we must work with the idea that there are two modes of describing what happens in the world, evident in the ideas of participation and observation, whose relationship awaits an empirical explanation. (3) We will be able to know what it is: freedom here comes down, though, to the fact that 'we cannot know what will become of us' (ibid., p. 149). This means that our ignorance makes our sense of freedom compatible with the fact that, from a wholly objective perspective, what we do could be described in deterministic terms. When we participate we feel free; from the absolute observational perspective we are not. The participant's perspective is therefore, as Habermas has suggested, 'swallowed' (ibid., p. 150) by the reductionist observational perspective. This position illustrates precisely what Adorno means by Idealism, because it presupposes an absolute theoretical unity, which actually results from the absolutizing of a subjective perspective, namely that of observation of the world solely as a causal nexus. As Seel puts it, it is 'precisely the idea of an absolute, definitive, ultimate description of "the universe" which is inconsistent' (ibid., p. 152), because all knowledge is of aspects of the real, and would be indeterminate if it were not.

This idea of the ultimate description is itself the fiction which results from the idea that our freedom is fictitious. The fiction relies on the idea that a description of what happens in the intersubjective, participatory, cultural process of the generation of knowledge is finally describable in the language of objective physical processes. The problem is that in order to give such a description of the process of 'reflection and deciding', one has to use a language which cannot belong in a physicalist description, in order to identify what it is that one is describing: 'Thinking is a causal occurrence which cannot be described in the language of physics, and that means that cannot be adequately described as a *causal* occurrence' (ibid., p. 153). Quite simply, a description of what people do as a solely physical, causal event at the level of neuroscientifically observable phenomena does not actually describe what it is for people to *do* something, which involves notions like choose, decide, and so on, and thus what is meant in many contexts by freedom. This follows from the arguments we have seen Adorno and Pippin adapt from Hegel, where the supposedly internal event cannot make any sense at all in isolation from the world of language and action in which it occurs. These objections to the third conception also make it clear why Adorno's refusal to draw a definitive line between nature and history is so philosophically significant.

Seel sums it up neatly: 'If it is not possible to interpret *some* occurrences as doings – as occurrence and doing – it is impossible consistently to interpret the path of nature, the course of the world as *occurrence*, because this interpretation relies for its part on an observation, and so on a doing' (ibid., p. 155). It is not that 'in the last analysis' (ibid., p. 156) we don't know how freedom and determinism relate, because the idea of a 'last analysis' is itself a myth, based on a mistaken construal of what knowledge is and of how it works. Presupposing a scientific version of 'completed knowledge' as a means of arguing that, if we get it, we will know the answer to questions of freedom misses out, as Dewey suggested in his insistence on the historical and temporal character of cognition, the fact that 'we know or can know that knowers only have a limited knowledge at their disposal' (ibid., p. 156). *This* knowledge frees us to make decisions about what we want and what we should do, on the basis of critical appraisal of the shifting limits of how far our knowledge extends. The modesty which Adorno advocates with regard to our capacity for self-determination makes it clear that freedom is not some kind of capacity for absolute beginnings, but, rather, a self-critical awareness of the possibility of interrogating the grounds of what we do. Whether we actually undertake such an interrogation when faced with all the factors that militate against our doing so can depend on the never finally rationalizable moment of impulse on which Adorno insists, and on the structures of power and ideology in a given society.

Wellmer considers these and related issues in terms of the relationship between 'nature' and 'spirit', building on Seel's account of the observation/participation relationship. Significantly, he uses the work of art to explain how we can talk about the nature/spirit relationship, in a manner that echoes Heidegger's essay *Origin of the Work of Art*, which derives in part from Schelling's reflections on the ground of freedom (see Bowie 1997). As an object of scientific investigation, the work 'loses all the qualities that make it a work of art' (Wellmer 2009, p. 214), which belong to what is meant by 'spirit'; but without the material, natural manifestation of what is investigated by the sciences, the work could not exist. The question is therefore how the relationship is to be characterized, which leads to the issues that Seel was concerned with. The neuroscientific account of the causal processes which take place in what, from another perspective, is self-determined action is part of a different 'language game' from the account of 'actions, intentions, reflections, and decisions'. The latter 'cannot by definition occur in the description of purely material processes, in a similar way to how in a physicalist investigation of paintings, the painting becomes, as it were, invisible' (ibid., p. 214).

Wellmer, like Seel, is concerned to resist the reduction of spirit to Kant's formal conception of nature. He argues that language, in which the material manifestation of a sign may remain identical, at the same time as the meanings expressed by the sign continually change, gives an analogy for the relationship between 'mental events and their neurophysiological substrate', because the latter 'cannot determine any meanings' (ibid., p. 219). He then makes the Adornian move of insisting that, with respect to the question of free-will and determinism, nature cannot just be understood in the formal sense, but has rather to be seen in terms of our embodied, sensuous nature. It is here that 'our experiences with freedom and unfreedom of the will' are really located (ibid., p. 220). Our emotions can, for example, prevent us from acting in ways that accord with how we think things should be: '[U]nconscious motives can determine our action behind our backs and finally the norms that have been internalized in socialization [. . .] can and will limit the scope of our will and the reflections that are available to it' (ibid.). It is not, though, that we are therefore wholly subject to these processes, because we can become reflectively aware of them and seek to master them. Wellmer echoes Adorno in changing the Freudian injunction of 'Where id was, ego should become' to 'Where super-ego was, ego should become.' One might suggest that aspects of a Hegelian position can end up seeking to dissolve ego into super-ego, and this is what Adorno objects to, because it takes too little account of how individuals may unnecessarily suffer from dominant social norms, including ones they may see themselves as owning.

Wellmer gives a telling account, based on Adorno, of why the issue of the freedom of the will cannot be understood in reductionist terms, and is inseparable from empirical issues:

> [L]imitations on the scope of self-determined action [...] are always to be related to the perspective of participants in the context of action of the life-world, who, as such, always already acknowledge each other as actors, whose action is determined by reasons and who are responsible for their action. This perspective is therefore the background on which the phenomena of an *unfree* will and also of *weakness* of the will can become the object of experience and the theme of philosophy, of the empirical sciences, and not least also of literature, at all. (Ibid., p. 221)

Some of the best of modern reflective self-understanding is embodied in modernity's great aesthetic works. The idea that this understanding can be obviated by the latest results of neuroscience fails to see that the issue to be understood itself only emerges at all because it takes a form which cannot itself be described in nomological terms, and so gives rise to the depth and complexity of major modern art and the responses to it. It is not the case, Wellmer insists, echoing Adorno's extension of how we think about nature, that 'every causal connection would have to be presented as a context of material events determined by laws' (ibid., p. 223). Social causality inevitably involves interpretative aspects inherent in language-use, where the exercise of coercive power is a constant possibility, and so has to be understood in terms of the complexity of human culture, not as a series of causal laws.

To conclude this chapter, I want to cite a further way in which Wellmer develops a key Adornian point. The emergence of the issue of determinism and the rise, especially in recent years, of reductive naturalism should, in Adorno's terms, be assessed not just with respect to the legitimacy of the arguments proposed, but also as expressions of social and ideological forces. Wellmer contends that reductive naturalism is just false, for the reasons we have seen:

> But even if it is false, it could yet be *effective* – the enthusiasm with which it is often received in the media shows that it is not wholly without effects. But it could thereby come to have fatal consequences as the ideology of a practice of psychic and social-technical manipulation, with deep-seated consequences for the life-context of democratic societies, which *destroy* freedom. (Ibid. p. 225)

What threatens freedom is, then, not, as so many positions in the history of modern philosophy suggest, 'deterministic natural causality' – which evidently is the basis of legitimate natural science – but rather what Adorno addresses through the notion of nature-history, namely 'the causality of social developments which destroy freedom' (ibid.). The importance of such a stance is hard to overestimate. However much we gain, as we undoubtedly will, from the insights of neuroscience and other natural scientific discoveries about the human organism, one of the key tasks of contemporary philosophy is to break the link between such insights and a reductionist metaphysics which easily becomes a form of manipulative ideology.

6
Aesthetics and Philosophy

Modernity, modernism, and aesthetics

The Anglophone reception of Adorno has led to his increasing influence in discussion of modern art, and in aesthetic theory and cultural studies, but it has not made his work a central part of discussion of the leading issues in contemporary philosophy.[1] In this chapter I want to suggest that, in certain respects at least, this situation inverts what ought to be the case. Adorno's stance with regard to modernist art seems to me often implausibly dogmatic, offering flawed, though sometimes still productive, perspectives. At the same time, however, some of his reflections on art can add crucial dimensions to the ideas we have explored so far which do not rely on his own often narrow perception of significant art. More importantly, these reflections can be very fruitful for thinking about the ends of contemporary philosophy.

Part of the reason for the Anglophone neglect of Adorno as philosopher is the peripheral status within much analytical philosophy of questions of aesthetics. The agenda of analytical aesthetics is still mainly set by the agenda of analytical philosophy in epistemology, metaphysics, ethics, philosophy of language, and so on. However, the results of the philosophy of art have no consequences for this agenda, not least because the philosophy of art tends just to tag along behind the dominant currents in analytical philosophy. Until very recently the agenda of the philosophy of art largely consisted of 'conceptual analysis', which is now often seen as really just discussion of how to use words appropriately and effectively, thus as something that cannot be regarded as exclusive to philosophy. I have suggested in more detail elsewhere why this is a problem with respect to art (see Bowie 2007). The issue that matters in the present context can be summarized quite simply. The analytical philosophy of art largely regards art as its object, and seeks to describe the correct ways in which we can characterize that object: hence, for example, the extensive discussions of whether a musical work is the score, a performance, all performances, and so on. This is essentially an exercise in analytical ontology, and has few consequences for those who are actively concerned with art from the productive or receptive end. What the analytical approaches almost invariably lack is any sense that philosophy might learn from art because art articulates things which would otherwise remain hidden to it.

Adorno could be talking about the nature of analytical aesthetics (he is actually talking about the general status of aesthetics in the post-war era) when he says that 'this abstract and largely mechanical derivation of aesthetics from pre-given philosophies seems to me to be the essential reason for the fall of theoretical aesthetics' (Adorno 1961, p. 6525). The consequence he is suggesting is quite straightforward: if philosophy cannot learn from art, and if its job is just to tell us the truth about art in the same way as it does about other issues, then ultimately we won't need art anyway. Analytical aesthetics rarely if at all addresses the question of why art matters, whereas Adorno makes this his central question. This situation points to the kind of dialectic we have repeatedly encountered. The borderline between philosophy and art is essentially contested, and is anyway, as the briefest look at history reveals, not a stable quantity of the kind it is assumed to be by much of the analytical tradition. Rorty's idea that ethics is often most insightfully explored in novels can suggest the point here: isolating a supposed area of philosophical investigation in order to analyse it is not necessarily the path to the greatest insight into an issue. The fact that aesthetics only constitutes itself as a philosophical subject in the second half of the eighteenth century (see Bowie 2003a) is an indication that we are again confronted here with something, like the issue of freedom of the will, which takes a specific form in modernity, rather than something which can be addressed in terms of, say, a conceptual answer to what constitutes a work of art.

So why is aesthetics so central to modern philosophy, and why is the idea of its centrality still anything but widely accepted in contemporary Anglophone philosophy? We have already noted how the rise of the modern natural sciences, where more and more warrantable knowledge replaces mythological and metaphysical accounts of natural phenomena, is accompanied by the rise of sceptical concerns and of the attempts to overcome them in epistemology. The Cartesian sceptical obsession can seem odd because it arises at the moment when the sciences begin to give more and more reasons *not* to be concerned about whether our warranted knowledge is 'in touch with', 'corresponds to', 'truly represents', or whatever – the differing terms each involve their own problems if one attempts to spell out what they mean – 'reality'. It is not as if epistemological objections regularly overturn scientific theories with great explanatory range that enable new practical solutions. As we have seen, Adorno claims that epistemology can also be construed as a symptom of social issues. The reason for the apparently strange conjunction of scientific warrantability and sceptical worries might, then, be said not necessarily to lie in the need to show why realism of some kind is the right epistemological theory. Why would such a need be paramount, when in practical terms few of the myriad theories of realism make much real difference to inquiry in the sciences? Instead, the reason for the conjunction may lie precisely in the sense that a perspective which sees subject/object, language/world, and so on, relationships in purely cognitive terms is not experienced as adequate to our attempts to describe, understand, and make sense of our existence.

Aesthetics is concerned with how changing constellations of the subjective and the objective – such as the modern preponderance of objective causal accounts in more and more domains – lead to the demand to articulate and express our relations to ourselves and the world in ever new ways. As such, it becomes the location of attention to issues that may be underestimated in established forms of philosophy. Wellmer, for example, makes illuminating connections between aesthetic issues and questions of freedom which hardly ever appear in the standard debates over freedom. He suggests a perspective which shows the implausibility of thinking that a view dominated by the paradigm of scientific knowledge, of the kind which informs much of the analytical approach, will ultimately obviate what is at stake in the aesthetic tradition to which Adorno belongs:

> [T]he sphere of the linguistically mediated human mind [is] the location of a continual genesis of ever-renewed novelty: scientific theories, works of art, institutions and new vocabularies with which we describe the world and ourselves, are products of the human mind, via which something new comes into the world, whose *necessary* conditions can admittedly be researched in the form of previous knowledge, of ways of looking at problems, of social constellations, psychic dispositions or biographical preconditions, but which cannot be causally reduced to such conditions. That the new happens shows that the scope of freedom of the human mind is not exhausted by that of the free will; rather, the freedom of the will presupposes this other space of freedom, which is bound to language. The latter manifests itself not least in the sphere of art. For however much we might like to make the genesis of works of art comprehensible via their place in a history of aesthetic problems, social conditions, psychic constellations or biographical influences, the idea of a causal explanation of their emergence appears absurd. (Wellmer 2009, p. 224)

138   *Aesthetics and Philosophy*

The constant changes that languages undergo point to a perennial aesthetic potential for innovation which is not causally explicable: meanings, as we saw Wellmer argue in Chapter 5, change, while the objective manifestations of the signs via which meaning is articulated largely do not. What obstructs that potential is 'the causality of social developments', not our causally determined organism. Assumptions to the contrary are themselves precisely signs of the causality of social developments, in the form of the reductionist neglect of the complexity of human sense-making that we have considered in the preceding chapters. Social causality, of course, plays a decisive role in Adorno's conceptions of art and philosophy, but he does not always deal with it in the most convincing manner.

Adorno's *Aesthetic Theory* has generally, and in some respects rightly, been read as the paradigm of a modernist conception of aesthetics, in which only the technically most advanced artistic production, which is adequate to the 'state of the material' in a particular form of art, can be a valid response to the 'context of delusion' which is the result of the commodified world. The value of advanced modernist art derives from its opposition to forms of expression which conspire with the status quo, by, for instance, providing reassuring emotional experiences that reconcile people to unjust and inhumane situations to which they should not be reconciled. This stance, which does help to understand some key factors in modernism, leads Adorno to reject art works which supposedly do not challenge existing modes of expression: he is, for example, relentlessly critical of the music of Sibelius, Tchaikovsky, and Elgar, among others. The problem is that these judgements often testify to the fact that he has not taken into account how such music may have a different significance in contexts other than the Central European modernism in relation to which he assesses it. Moreover, his hyper-vigilance with regard to the failings which he – sometimes justifiably – finds in the music can derive from hearing it just as a symptom of social contradictions, rather than as something which may also be experienced as a unique expression of something valuable. Those who love the expressive and formal invention, and the unique emotional tone, of Elgar's First Symphony, for example, cannot simply be told, as they effectively are by Adorno, that they are merely hearing the music as a 'consumer good'. Elgar's Symphony's growing international reception clearly shows it is more than the piece of English national music as which, given his general assessment of Elgar, Adorno would regard it. Adorno's overestimation of the intra- and extra-musical significance of the Second Viennese School's rejection of tonality, his valuation of developing variation over most other compositional techniques (such as Elgar's very individual use of melodic development, based on sequencing, rather than on alteration of small melodic cells of the kind present in Beethoven or Brahms),[2] and his failure to understand the often effective, critical potential of the most important forms of jazz also result from what Charles Rosen has termed Adorno's 'ethnocentric' view of modern music.[3]

Aesthetic Theory too often attempts to fit art to a particular philosophical perspective that is based on Adorno's more questionable positions. These are the ones which totalize his negative assessment of modernity, and so obscure resources for seeing ways beyond that assessment. The assumption that the Holocaust is the key to modernity demands that one be very careful about identifying which social trends are really related to what made the Holocaust possible or which may make something similar more likely (cf. Honneth's remarks cited in Chapters 2 and 3). In the case of art works: are they to be interpreted as symptoms of what underlies inhumane developments, or do they have a causal role in such developments? Just rejecting works of art which are insufficiently 'critical', as Adorno often does, means that too many forms of cultural expression that can be legitimately appreciated and critically engaged with in some contexts may be judged from a perspective that is often defined – in contradiction to Adorno's stated aim of doing justice to aesthetic particularity – via a particular philosophical focus.

A further difficulty in *Aesthetic Theory* is that cryptic formulations too often take the place of properly explicated ideas. From one of Adorno's perspectives, this is as it should be, because immediate accessibility is a mark of the culture industry. He thinks, as we saw, that the manner of presentation of philosophical ideas is part of their content. *Aesthetic Theory* might be said, in this sense, to be theory that is aesthetic, and, at its best, it is. Its refusal to accept easy answers to questions concerning modern art and philosophy is on occasion well conveyed by the dialectical shifts of the writing. This is all very well, but the fact is that illuminating versions of ideas only expressed in cryptic form in *Aesthetic Theory* abound in his lecture series on Aesthetics from 1958–9, 1961, and 1963–4. Philosophical form and philosophical content do influence each other, but this can happen in many ways. The form of the lecture seems to me more adequate to the content of Adorno's ideas on art and aesthetics than the mannered style of *Aesthetic Theory*, which has aged in ways that the lectures largely have not. More substantively, the emphasis in the lectures is sometimes on issues that inform the rest of Adorno's philosophy, most strikingly the issue of nature. In contrast to *Aesthetic Theory*, where the topic is a concern, but not such a major one, a very significant proportion of the lectures is devoted to the question of natural beauty, an issue which Hegel and others following him increasingly regarded as irrelevant to philosophical issues concerning art in the modern world. So why would Adorno pursue this theme so extensively?

The reason that aesthetics is so significant in questioning the ends of modern philosophy is that an area of philosophy concerned with *subjective* responses to the natural and cultural worlds necessarily involves a kind of objectivity which differs from that present in warranted scientific knowledge. If culture were supposedly about what gives subjective pleasure to individual human organisms, and what gave pleasure to each organism was radically particular to that organism, there would be no such thing as culture anyway. Culture is constituted by shared, albeit often contested or conflicting, norms, which are evident in forms of expression and institutionally embodied evaluations. The need for norms, which depend on changing forms of language, leads, though, to another characteristic modern contradiction. The culture industry, in which the commodity form has effects on the nature and content of artistic production, undermines individual discrimination by producing ideological norms of judgement and enjoyment that objectively determine whether a cultural product becomes a successful commodity, and thence part of the wider culture. This situation might seem to force one back to the idea of radical subjective individuality in taste as a counter to such objectivity. However, that, for Adorno, would obviate the significance of major art, which he argues must in some sense be 'true'. This demand reintroduces a sense of objectivity into aesthetics.

If what Adorno maintains in this respect can be defended, it means that the currently dominant philosophical model in many areas of Anglophone philosophy, in which questions of truth too often tend to be restricted to semantic issues and questions about realism, fails to deal adequately with crucial ways in which sense is made in the modern world. A lot of Adorno's ideas, such as the notion that truth has a 'temporal core', might, as we saw, lead him to be construed as a 'relativist'. In aesthetics, judgement *is* in some senses necessarily relative to the judging subject; a central aim of Adorno's work on aesthetics is, though, to reject the notion of 'aesthetic relativism', on the grounds that norms for judgement in art are not simply arbitrary and should be discussed in objective ways. This aim suggests how different his approach is from some current philosophical perspectives. The justification for his approach depends on further development of ideas concerning the notion of nature.

Art and the beauty of nature

In the Aesthetics lectures Adorno gives a reason why analytical aesthetics has been so insignificant in contemporary philosophy. He points out that 'the most significant aesthetic theories are to be found in the context of the great philosophical theories, Kantian, Hegelian, in the third book of *The World as Will and Representation*, for example, also in Kierkegaard and Nietzsche' (Adorno 1961, p. 6358). Aesthetics matters not when it is a specialized discipline with its own agenda of questions, but rather when aesthetic issues reveal aspects of other philosophical questions which do not otherwise become manifest. This role depends precisely on the fact that the concrete development of a discipline like philosophy, which, unlike some of the natural sciences, has no definitive, uncontested agenda, is likely to involve the neglect of crucial dimensions of any significant issue on which it focuses. As the history of philosophy tells us, once a train of argumentation about an issue begins, it will exclude perspectives that can later come to be seen as central to the issue. Indeed, it could be argued that this is precisely the case in relation to aesthetics itself, which generally plays almost no role in analytical accounts of the mind/world relationship in epistemology or metaphysics. When, at the end of his essay 'Aesthetic Value, Objectivity, and the Fabric of the World', John McDowell asks: '[H]ow can a mere feeling constitute an experience in which the world reveals itself to us?' (McDowell 1998, p. 130), he is, for the analytical tradition, unlike for the European traditions to which Adorno belongs, saying something quite startling.

The problem with the aesthetic perspective is precisely that it is, as Kant insists, based on a non-cognitive subjective relationship to the world, and so inherently lacks objective determinacy. This lack can, though, in a historical situation where forms of determinacy risk becoming ideological in the ways we have observed, be a source of new kinds of insight. Adorno refers to art works as 'manifestations of society which are not conscious of themselves' (Adorno 1961, p. 6448), and as 'the historiography of their epoch which is not conscious of itself' (Adorno 1997, 7, p. 273). Because the content of art cannot be wholly conveyed in the discursive terms which are the condition of something being 'conscious of itself', it is a reminder to disciplines which are essentially discursive that they may fail to articulate certain dimensions of experience. This is why I suggested that Brandom's strict line between discursive 'sapience' and non-discursive 'sentience' threatened to occlude vital dimensions of meaning which cannot be located either side of that line. It is not that Adorno thinks that art can do without philosophical explication – indeed he sometimes moves too far towards subordinating art to philosophy (see Bowie 2007, Chapter 9). Part of what philosophy has to explicate is, though, precisely the fact that what art conveys is not reducible to what can be said about what it conveys: '[T]he task would not be to grasp art, but first to grasp what is ungraspable about art' (Adorno 1961, p. 6542). Otherwise art would dissolve into philosophical and other explanations.

Natural beauty plays a vital role in Adorno's conception because it relies on a connection between subject and object which, while seeming to be solely based on the internal feelings of the subject, cannot just be based on them. The proof is that, if it were, a major objective historical development would be inexplicable, namely the move during the eighteenth century in which the beauty and grandeur of wild nature and the subject's responses to it become a new focus of European thought. The point that will lead to Adorno's extensive reflections is that this change should not be construed from one side of a subject/object relationship. The pre-modern relationship to natural beauty was, in one sense of the term, essentially an 'objective' one, insofar as natural beauty was generally seen as part of the order of God's creation. As secularization gets underway, this idea of an objective order gives way to the sense that beauty in nature has to do with the feelings of the subject. That change, as Hume and Kant suggest, leads to the problem of how subjective feeling has more than individual significance: 'The general validity of pleasure [in beauty] and yet not via concepts but in intuition is what is difficult' (Kant 1996, p. 137). The attempt to reconcile the subjective and the objective will eventually result in Hegel's argument that appreciation of natural beauty is in fact mediated by the beauty which is a product of spirit. People only appreciate natural landscapes when they become an object of artistic representation in their own right, rather than the scene for human action or the repository of religious symbols.

The discussion of the dialectic of nature and history in the preceding chapters should indicate why Adorno does not think Hegel's position is adequate to the issues, even though he accepts that it registers something important. The change that happens in the eighteenth century cannot only be based on the idea that appreciation of the beauty of wild nature is revealed as merely 'subjective'. This idea would have to involve wild nature arbitrarily moving from being an object of fear and even revulsion to being something else. As we saw with regard to the issue of freedom, concentrating just on the internal moment in the subject misses the point, because it is only when that moment is given content by an objective social and historical context that it means anything. There is, of course, more than an analogy here between freedom and aesthetic issues. It is precisely in the period of the demise of feudalism, when the status of the subject changes, that both freedom and natural beauty become major philosophical topics. This is because the liberation from traditional norms, with respect both to human action and to the natural world, poses the problem of what legitimates new norms. The further point is that concern with natural beauty subsequently tends to diminish both in aesthetics and in modern art, where it is sometimes regarded as likely to lead to kitsch.

Adorno's focus on the beauty of nature results from his awareness that the significance of art in modernity, which he thinks would not emerge at all without what becomes manifest in the issue of natural beauty, must reside in a non-cognitive connection between subject and world. In an Adornian conception the idea that evolutionary theory can account for the relationship of the subject to nature manifest in questions of art and beauty is mistaken because it seeks to found the relationship from the objective side, by giving causal explanations of why nature and art can appear beautiful. The decisive causality involved in these questions, while necessarily involving elements of natural causality, is, however, actually social and historical, as the relationship of the new significance of natural beauty to social and scientific changes in modernity makes clear. The new relationship to nature involves the same kind of causal effects as were present in relation to nature seen in the old way;[4] the difference must therefore depend on changes in the relationship between subject and object that are not explained by natural causality. (Heidegger would see this in terms of a change in the way 'unconcealment' occurs in the modern period.) Such change is evidently not individually subjective, because it is so widespread in European society, and therefore involves aspects of social causality and freedom, in the senses we have been exploring. For Adorno, the reductionist evolutionary perspective would be another result of the modern domination of subjectivity, because it seeks to absolutize a perspective which depends on cognitive ordering of nature. By doing so it loses any sense that what we learn from the issue of beauty takes us beyond reduction to the formal conception of nature towards other relationships to nature which can themselves be conditions of possibility of cognitive explanations. As Heidegger argues, without prior unconcealment which makes things intelligible as problems or concerns, theoretical responses to those problems would have no basis.

Adorno's conception depends, then, precisely on the sense that the modern objectifying relationship to nature, which has its source in the subject's domination of the other, leads to a dialectical counter to the domination. There are problems with his conception, because it seems at times to rely on the untenable idea of a wholesale 'reconciliation' with the nature that has been repressed, but other elements of the conception are not necessarily reliant on this idea. In a discussion of Kant's *Critique of Judgement* Adorno says that 'the idea of art is that of the restitution by spirit which has separated itself from [nature] and subjected it to itself' (Adorno 1961, p. 6357). A lot here again turns on the sense of 'nature', as this passage also suggests: '[A]rt, which in an older phase knew itself as the simply other than, as the simple antithesis of nature, now also knows itself in a certain sense as the advocate of oppressed and distorted nature, as the advocate, incidentally, which it has objectively always been, without knowing it' (ibid., p. 6835). The difficulty in understanding and legitimating Adorno's conception involves, first, making clearer what senses of 'nature' are intended, and, second, seeing how art in modernity can be convincingly given a role as 'advocate' of nature that is oppressed. This is especially difficult when the art in question is very often advanced modernism which sometimes involves no explicit reference to what is (in the wake of Romanticism) thought of as the 'natural world'.

One reason for the renewed attention to Adorno in recent years is that it has become much easier to appreciate the dangers of regarding the natural world as merely a resource for human ends. What exactly is it, though, that is wrong with using nature as a resource, given that we have no choice if humankind is to survive and develop? It is too easy here to slip into a sentimental view of the natural world, not least by subscribing to the myth that it has some kind of inherent integrity that should not be infringed upon. The rhetoric of Adorno's responses to the issue of nature in modernity can suggest that he is not always immune to this myth, but his approach to the issue of nature via the question of natural beauty indicates different possibilities. The nature explored by the modern physical sciences is in many respects essentially the same as it has been throughout history and pre-history. Dewey argued, as we saw, that the mathematical physical sciences are often attached to a metaphysics which denies 'temporal quality' to reality. The very idea of doing damage to nature is unlikely to gain much purchase in these terms, nor is it likely to do so when nature is seen in many theological perspectives.[5] A view restricted to nature in Kant's formal sense leaves no room for what concerns Adorno, and this is a further reason for questioning reductionist philosophical conceptions.

The formal sense of nature is, as Husserl argued in *The Crisis of European Sciences and Transcendental Phenomenology*, a historical product of the 'mathematization of the cosmos', which leads to a neglect of qualitative aspects of nature (see Chapter 3 above). It is precisely when the formal sense starts to dominate and to result in new technical possibilities (and the concomitant problems) that the counter to it also emerges. The counter is present in the feeling, based on the experience of natural beauty, that there is something there to be damaged that is deeply connected to essential aspects of human existence. In this respect the objectifying success of the modern scientific approach is itself the condition of possibility of nature emerging as something as which it previously could not be understood. The relationship is therefore dialectical, in that the objectification is what produces the new subjective dimension. This kind of reversal is crucial for Adorno's consideration of nature. Nature is understood by Adorno, as we have seen, not as a specifiable domain, but as that which is constituted in relation to its changing historical Other.

Nature is in one sense just 'everything', but this is the 'night in which all cows are black'. It therefore either must be defined by its relation to a static counterpart, or has to be understood in terms of the dialectic we have repeatedly encountered. This is why 'nature' can move from being a threat to human existence (which, of course, it always also is, even after the shift in question here) to itself being that which is threatened. The concept of nature can therefore only be given content via exploration of how historical conceptions of and responses to the material world hide nature, even as they reveal other aspects of it. In modernity, in order for what is hidden to become manifest, it has, Adorno thinks, to take on forms which are not primarily conceptual, otherwise it would, as many today think it can, be able to be wholly incorporated into an objective explanation of the world:

> Explanation has the moment of reducing what is unknown to what is familiar, of translating unfamiliar elements into thoughts, experiences, states of affairs which are already present to one. But art gravitates towards what is not known, what does not yet exist. What has not yet been subsumed, what was previously not there emerges precisely in works of art as their content. (Adorno 1973, p. 23)

Nature's historical change of status in Europe is therefore linked to the new status of art in modernity, not as something that celebrates a given order of things, but as something which offers new revelations in response to a rapidly changing world.

Even in *Aesthetic Theory* the unexpected notion of the 'language of nature' (Adorno 1997, 7, pp. 121–2) plays a role in the exploration of the beauty of nature. Notions like the 'book of nature' are familiar from the history of theology, but they are hopelessly inappropriate once theological assumptions lose their force in the face of the descriptions and explanations of nature by the new sciences. Given Adorno's sense that after Auschwitz any notions that suggest a positive metaphysical goal for nature are in danger of adding to the irredeemable harm done to the victims, by pretending that there is metaphysical meaning to existence, why does he persist with the notion of a 'language of nature'? His core idea is suggested by the following: 'There is no other determination of the beauty of nature [*des Naturschönen*] [. . .] than as the appearance of something not made by man as speaking [. . .] as expression' (Adorno 1961, p. 6851). But is this not merely a 'Romantic' metaphor, a version of the pathetic fallacy? If one sees language in essentially analytical terms, it clearly is just metaphorical, because nature does not 'speak', but this misses a vital point.

For anything to come to be understood as language at all, something material must become symbolic, take on 'meaning', by being connected to other things which enable it to make sense. Before this can take place at the level of what become words and larger syntactic units, something must take place at the level of the contact between the subject and the world which is beyond the causal and the instinctual. Brandom's distinction between sentience and sapience is one way of characterizing this, but, as we have seen, it makes the difference too rigid. Adorno talks of one aspect of this contact in terms of 'the non-conceptual affinity of what is subjectively produced to its other, which is not posited by it' (Adorno 1997, 7, pp. 86–7), thus of an affinity which does not depend on knowing nature in objective terms. In German Idealism this relationship of subject and world is seen in terms of the identity of thought and object. Adorno rejects this notion, because it loses sight of the moment which is not dependent on the activity of the subject. At the same time, without a kind of contact with the world which makes the subject invest in the world in ways that cannot be immediately satisfied by the removal of a material lack, it is hard to see how human responses to the world could ever develop in the manner they do. The affinity Adorno refers to has to do with what he means when he talks of nature speaking, of it making sense to us in a manner which is neither in our control, nor a product of instrumental or cognitive thinking. As we shall see in a moment, he understands one aspect of this contact in terms of the 'mimetic'. The mimetic includes gestural responses to the world which do not directly translate into conceptual meanings, but which help establish a structured place for the subject in the world: forms of rhythm and dance are examples of this. Once subjective control reaches the point where modern humankind comes to be able to dominate nature, the repression of nature results in the counter to repression manifest in the new power of natural beauty as something 'not made by man'.

The next question is how this counter relates to the development of modern art. One point that is crucial here is that natural beauty is not a 'property' of nature that was 'there' before people were able to appreciate it, but nor is it something that emerges solely via the subject. As we have seen, the latter idea fails to explain why it becomes widespread 'in' subjects during a series of objective historical changes. The endless attempts in aesthetics (and epistemology) to establish where the line between the subjective and the objective is to be drawn fail to get to grips with the historical dialectic involved in such issues. We have, once again, to grasp 'to what extent even categories which apparently pertain to nature, like that of the beauty of nature, in reality are precisely also historical categories' (Adorno 1961, p. 6844).

Adorno asserts that 'art is imitation of the beauty of nature, but not imitation of nature' (ibid., p. 6851). What is in question here are relationships between subject and world which do not fit the models of a philosophy dominated by epistemological concerns. Adorno suggests that 'I understand a work of art at the moment when [. . .] I understand what it itself is saying, as something that it says to me, and not as something that I just project into it' (Adorno 2009, p. 46). Adorno relates this kind of aesthetic understanding to 'the relationship to nature'. Saying that 'this evening is melancholy' is not 'a mood of the observer', but rather to say, 'admittedly in a constellation with the observer, that the evening itself is melancholic' (ibid.). Clearly, evenings cannot be melancholic without subjects who can feel melancholy, but a subject can be not feeling melancholy and yet appreciate that an evening is melancholic. Indeed, without states of the world which can be connected with emotional states even when one is not in the emotional state in question, affective life would lack dimensions that constitute an essential part of what it is. The world of Heidegger's 'moods'/'attunements' ('*Stimmungen*') is not some kind of contingent addition to the 'real' physical world, but something with its own forms of intelligibility which demands its own forms of reflective understanding.[6] Adorno's idea of grasping what something objective in the world is 'saying', which means it can potentially say it to anyone who understands, already suggests one way of understanding music, and so of seeing how Adorno will connect the beauty of nature to modern art. One can appreciate the emotional content of music without being in an emotional state that corresponds to that content. Adorno contends with respect to the melancholic evening that if one does not have the experience of 'this self-forgetfulness in relation to the object', then one also 'does not know what a work of art is' (ibid.). Only by moving into a relationship with the object that is open to the object and does not seek just to subject it to oneself (e.g. by seeking only objects that reflect or reinforce what one already feels) can one have aesthetic experience in the sense that Adorno seeks to make philosophically significant.

The implications of what Adorno means here take one into contentious philosophical territory: '[N]ature as an object of aesthetic experience seems to say something to us, without our really being able to say what it is' (Adorno 1961, p. 6843). It is precisely this indeterminacy, however, which means that 'the beauty of nature is something like a model, like a standard for what really constitutes art as art' (ibid., p. 6844). From many philosophical perspectives this will seem inherently unsatisfactory: Wittgenstein's 'Whereof one cannot speak, one must be silent' comes to mind. Wittgenstein, though, evidently thought that what one could not speak about mattered, and the question Adorno is addressing is how it matters. The disenchanted nature that results from the sciences replacing mythological and theological accounts of what nature means with causal explanations is increasingly determinate, and much modern philosophy has used this determinacy to try to invalidate other understandings of nature. This exclusion creates the difficulty Adorno confronts when he adverts to what nature says that cannot be made determinate in the form of an explanation. He claims that art 'in a certain respect aims at [*meint*] nature, does justice to repressed nature' (Adorno 2009, p. 47). Art in modernity depends on a relationship of the subject to nature which is produced by the changed status of nature brought about by disenchantment.

In some respects Adorno's view here suffers from the overgeneralization, also encountered in *Dialectic of Enlightenment*, of suspicion of the objectifications that result from the modern sciences and from the commodity form, which we saw Honneth criticize. At the same time, the focus on the beauty of nature and its link to the increased significance of art in modernity gives more plausibility to certain aspects of Adorno's contentions. He suggests that 'the perception of the beauty of nature as something innocent, as it were, something not deformed by man, only became possible because people no longer needed to be afraid of nature, because nature became weaker than humankind' (ibid., p. 50). He links Kant's view of the 'dynamically sublime' apparent in hurricanes, volcanoes, the boundless ocean, and so on, which, when seen from a position of safety, can intensify the sense of humankind's ability to 'measure ourselves with the omnipotence of nature' (Kant), with Beethoven's innovations in music: '[W]hat [Kant] attributes to the sea or to mountains is then what enters art as what is new, for example, in the music of Beethoven' (ibid., p. 51).

The dialectic involved in the Kantian sublime is described as follows:

> On the one hand, there is in nature that moment which is stronger than us and which really as little allows us that contemplation of the beautiful as was possible in older times before progressing mastery of nature; but, on the other hand, after nature is in certain respects tamed and has lost its terror, human consciousness of itself is awoken thereby, and a kind of second affinity, a kind of figurative reconciliation is produced precisely with the nature which humankind has subdued and which it really has done injustice to by subduing it. (Ibid., p. 53)

Rather than aesthetic experience being just 'a harmonious experience of something that is sensuously pleasing', it therefore involves a tension between what is 'stronger' and what is 'weaker' in nature in relation to humankind. Adorno thinks beauty in modern art necessarily involves dissonance for this reason, and he links this dissonance to what he sees as inherent in the notion of beauty since Plato's *Phaedrus*, namely 'a play of forces between desire and the prohibition of desire' (ibid., p. 55). Without the negation of desire, understood as the drive for the appropriation of the object, the 'concept of beauty becomes shallow and empty' (ibid.). This last point further explains why attention to natural beauty is essential both for responding to modern art and for a different focus on issues in modern philosophy.

Natural beauty offers a model of a relationship to things which does not seek to objectify and appropriate them, that allows them to 'speak' to us by making us aware of what we may have repressed. Once nature ceases to be sacred, it is more and more open to the abuses characteristic of the modern period, and this is what generates a different kind of apprehension of nature. Adorno contends that art becomes linked to the idea of the modern secularized form of the salvation of the sacred that he refers to as 'a kind of second affinity, a kind of figurative reconciliation' with nature. The reconciliation is only figurative in art, because for it to be more would involve the realization of a mythical reconciliation of subject and object that would render art redundant – the idea of not needing art any more plays a questionable role in Adorno's more emphatic utopian ideas. But – and here we move into more familiar Adornian territory – how does all this relate to modernist art, which evidently abjures the beautiful in many cases, and what does this tell us about the ends of philosophy?

Being 'absolutely modern'

The severity of Adorno's modernist aesthetic might seem to contradict both his Feuerbachian insistence on sensuous pleasure and the aforegoing reflections on natural beauty. If there is pleasure to be had in beautiful music, why does he seem to wish to deny us it, in the name of music which does not offer what he often (and often unfairly) sees in terms of 'culinary' pleasure? The answer has to do with his insistence on the demand for truth in art, which connects to his suspicion of positive assessments of culture in relation to the Holocaust, but his reflections sometimes make his stance pretty unconvincing. Late in his career Adorno came to realize that he was wrong about radical modernism, because he had not looked sufficiently carefully at the actual reception of differing kinds of cultural production. As he says in 1968, thus putting a lot of his own analyses of modern art in question: 'It is an open question, which can indeed only be answered empirically, whether, to what extent, in what dimensions the social implications revealed in musical content analysis are also grasped by the listeners' (quoted in Dahms 1994, pp. 252–3).

Yet, despite this quite devastating judgement on his own insistence that art has to be understood by immanent analysis of the contradictions that form a work's content, rather than by the concrete historical reception of the work, Adorno's initial questions concerning the effects of the culture industry can still lead to significant insights. The insights relate to his reflections on how 'the relation of works of art to the capacity for desire for its part [. . .] has been manipulated by the market' (Adorno 2009, p. 62). This negative judgement on the working of modern culture contrasts – both moments are essential to his conception – with the situation when 'art, by distancing itself from nature [in the sense, for example, of the nature present in appropriative desire], by making itself no longer immediately an object of desire, but by transferring the happiness of immediacy into the mediation of the imagination, precisely through this act of immanent constitution also tries to assist nature, to preserve something of nature' (ibid., p. 63). In explanation he again refers in this context to the prevalence of dissonance, both literal and metaphorical, in modern art, dissonance being precisely what symbolically expresses the desire for a lacking state of harmony that is present in 'longing'.[7] The essential reason for this view, which is the core of his reflections on modernism, is that dissonance is a way of giving expression to suffering: 'Every dissonance is, as it were, a piece of remembrance of the suffering to which a dominating society exposes nature, and only in the form of this suffering, only in the form of longing – and dissonance is always essentially longing and suffering – only in this does oppressed nature find its voice at all' (ibid., p. 66).

Now this view of art, nature, and society might sound rather far-fetched, especially if one pays too little attention to Adorno's dialectical, dynamic characterization of 'nature'. However, the view does help to address a decisive issue about the reception and production of modernist art. The key phenomenon here is the way that certain forms of aesthetic production cease to 'say anything' important in the face of new developments in art, even though it becomes technically easier and easier to produce something in the older form. A simple manifestation of this is the fact that significant composers don't compose like Mozart any more. A capable composer or musicologist can produce something that sounds convincingly like respectable Mozart. The objection to such a product is not necessarily interesting at the level of authenticity, in the sense of 'it's not really Mozart'. If the piece is strong enough it will actually be musically better than quite a lot of real Mozart anyway. The objection is that the piece no longer expresses anything significant because its context lacks what is involved in real expression. Unlike such a product of just following established musical norms from a particular epoch, the last movement of Mozart's 'Jupiter' Symphony opened up a whole new way of combining fugal techniques of the past with sonata form, and so helped to enable new forms of historically reflexive but expressive musical composition. The Symphony enabled something to be 'said' that transcended the still quite rigid musical forms of its day, even as it employed them. How the Symphony now can still speak to us depends on the nature of performances in new contexts, and the kind of historical and aesthetic awareness that is brought to bear on it, rather than on the musical norms it embodies which can be used to compose in the manner of Mozart.

Adorno often cites Rimbaud's dictum of 'Il faut être absolument moderne', sometimes in a too dogmatic interpretation of the continuous demand in modernism for novelty. However, there is a less dogmatic way of interpreting the idea that the distortions occasioned by modern societies demand forms of expression that do not become complicit with those distortions by repeating established ways of articulating things. Clearly the radical demand for novelty is not always the central issue in many everyday aesthetic practices. However, if art is as significant for modern philosophy as Adorno wishes to claim, one has to take seriously the sense, familiar to modern artists in all areas, that finding appropriate forms of expression is fraught with the difficulties of not just adding to the status quo. Successful new artistic production has critically to challenge what has gone before, thus creating 'dissonance' in both literal and metaphorical senses. Paradigm cases of this in music are Schoenberg and Coltrane, both of whom initially produced relatively conventional music of great power, but who then felt compelled to keep pushing beyond the existing norms towards music many find 'ugly'.

Adorno suggests of dissonance that it is not just an 'expression of negativity, but the happiness of giving nature its voice always at the same time attaches to it' (ibid.). The point is that it 'finds something which has not been registered [. . .] draws something into the work of art that [. . .] is not yet domesticated, that is fresh snow, so to speak, and thereby reminds one of what would be different from the ever-same operation of bourgeois society in which we are all prisoners' (ibid., pp. 66–7). We need a more differentiated view of 'bourgeois society' than this, but the idea that the tensions and dissonances in modern art register something about the repressions which accompany the smooth running of consumer society is anything but absurd. Moreover, it is clear that responses to such repressions play very little role in many forms of philosophy. Adorno insists, in contrast, that 'philosophy should not lag behind the historical experiences of the most modern art in any way' (Adorno 1973, p. 82). As an account of how modernism incorporates more and more of the world into new forms of expression, Adorno's view has much to be said for it, and art can pose an evident challenge for the kind of philosophy which simply returns to the same questions without reflecting on the context of those questions and their effects on those contexts.

The nature that is 'given its voice' in modern art is not, then, nature as a 'romantically' conceived unsullied state of past innocence, but rather what is repressed, both in human beings and in the environment, by forms which no longer allow certain things to speak. Crucial to this conception is Adorno's notion of mimesis:

> [A]rt contains a decisive moment of imitation, but only with a qualification, that it is not as imitation of something, but rather imitation as an impulse to imitation, thus as an impulse to mimicry, the impulse, so to speak, to make oneself into the thing [*Sache*] or to make the thing that stands opposite one into oneself. [. . .] Art is admittedly imitation, but not of an object, but an attempt, through all its gestures and its whole attitude, to restore a state in which the difference of subject and object did not exist. (Adorno 2009, p. 70)

This characterization of mimesis might sound as though it relies on a mythical notion of reconciliation between subject and world, but it can be read more convincingly as a characterization of ways of being in the world which are not essentially objectifying. A pre-linguistic infant apprehends and responds to the novelty of the world and to those who communicate with it in a manner which is prior to objectification, and which involves various forms of imitation. Such ways of apprehending and responding are necessarily lost or transformed in what Lacan describes as the move from the imaginary to the symbolic, but their loss does not mean that the desire for what is lost disappears. It emerges in the suspension or transformation of certain kinds of objectifying relations to things. The experience of pure participation, described by Martin Seel, where one becomes absorbed in playing or listening to music, and so not reflexively aware, but still able to feel that what is happening makes sense, is an example of what happens in the mimetic relationship to things in art.

Importantly, Adorno also acknowledges that 'mimetic' responses can be regressive. When people seek to lose their identity by becoming part of something they feel to be bigger than themselves, they often adopt mimetic forms of behaviour, as the Nazis and others realize. Adorno therefore insists that art must involve a dialectic between mimesis and rationality. He is also clear that art cannot really reconcile subject and object: 'The character of art as appearance means [. . .] in relation to nature that it keeps hold of the image of reconciliation without the reconciliation really being achieved' (Adorno 1961, p. 6885). Part of his advocacy of modernist art depends precisely on the fact that it does not pretend to achieve such reconciliation.

The process that leads from the 'old mimetic ways of behaving' (Adorno 2009, p. 78), of the kind present in traditional rituals, imitative dances to ward off dangerous animals, and the like, to an 'alienation from nature' that allows nature to be controlled means that

> everything conceivable is sacrificed [. . .] from external nature to endlessly many capabilities of humankind itself, for instance all the capabilities which were once mimetic capabilities and which we only perceive in ourselves in a scattered and fragmentary way. Art is now, as it were, the attempt to do justice to what is sacrificed in this progressing concept of the domination of nature. (Ibid., p. 79)

This can only be a symbolic doing-justice, such that art is 'the measure of remembrance of what is suppressed, of what is sacrificed, also the measure of the remembrance of all the powers in human beings that are destroyed by the process of rationalization' (ibid.). Adorno is prone to make all elements of the process of rationalization into forms of repression. He consequently underplays the fact that civilizing processes involving renunciation or sublimation really can liberate us from many kinds of fear and suffering, and, indeed, help to preserve the natural world. It is the shadow of the Holocaust as the epitome of repressive objectification which moves him in this direction, but, once again, there needs to be more differentiation with respect to which forms of objectification lead to inhumanity and indifference to the destruction of nature.

Modern art and philosophy

What justifies some of Adorno's argument about art and nature is the way in which he seeks to answer Marx's question as to why modern societies cannot do without art, even as they gain more and more real, rather than merely symbolic, control over nature. The significance of this understanding for philosophy derives from the fact that it cannot be based solely on cognitive or ethical relations to the world. What art 'says' is precisely not sayable in discursive terms, but, at the same time, it can be affected by such terms, and can itself be necessary to the formation of such terms. This location both outside and inside the dominant ways of relating to the world in modernity constitutes the philosophical importance of art. In the face of the destruction of the sense of meaningful nature by disenchantment, aesthetics becomes the locus of questions about what makes sense that cannot be given metaphysical, scientific, or theological answers.

In his book on Mahler, Adorno talks of the beauty of *Das Lied von der Erde*, a work which is essentially about confronting the transience and insignificance of the earth in the cosmos described by modern science by saying farewell to what have turned out to be illusions. He suggests that the *Lied* shows that '[t]he last metaphysics becomes that metaphysics is no longer possible' (Adorno 1997, 13, p. 297). The question why it is so important to say farewell to something that was in one sense not 'real' anyway is essential to understanding the often melancholy role which art must play in the modern world, where redemption from transience is no longer possible. The paradox of being unable to get rid of the sense of loss even if what is lost is something illusory, in the way that the idea of an immanently meaningful nature becomes illusory, is precisely what Adorno sees as central to modern art. But is the paradox of the last metaphysics merely a contradiction which falls prey to standard philosophical objections, or is Adorno able, by stating the paradox, to express something essential that cannot be made accessible in a non-paradoxical form? The latter option is something which is to be expected in many forms of art, but is inimical to many forms of philosophy.

One way in which Adorno approaches the issues here is with respect to what happens to the sacred when its metaphysical and theological content falls prey to disenchantment. Being sacred confers on an object a specific kind of value, involving a distance between it and the people relating to it, but that value also entails an element of proximity, of identification with the object as the repository of a special meaning. Adorno talks of art as deriving from 'the sacred sphere which has gone through reflection, through the freedom of humankind' (ibid., p. 76), and suggests that '[a]rt wants to honour [*einlösen*] what is promised by the beauty of nature' (Adorno 1961, p. 6959). The question is what sort of a promise this is, if it is not anchored in some kind of metaphysical or theological account. Adorno sees the 'sphere of the sacred' before secularization as involving a 'lie', whereas 'the delimited sphere of art which is separated from the empirical world is liberated [. . .] from the lie of the claim that such a separated-off special realm, which is bracketed from the world in the world, is real' (Adorno 2009, p. 77). The paradoxical status of art derives, on the one hand, from its inheriting something from what was present in the sacred, which leads us to value it for its own sake, and, on the other, from its contribution to the destruction of the sacred by its revelation that the sacred, like art, is actually '*Schein*', 'illusion/appearance'. (The change in the status of religious art from being something whose primary significance was as part of worship to something that may end up in a museum or gallery together with secular art exemplifies this shift.) The promise of the beauty of nature which art is to honour is not a realization of something concrete, but rather the sustaining of a relationship to things that can make sense of them in a way which is otherwise increasingly lacking in the secular world. Whereas cognitive relationships to things specify aspects of them that remain identical, thus enabling them to be better manipulated, aesthetic relationships rely precisely on things being able to become manifest in ways that do not depend on them being conceptually determinable. The idea of our not 'being able to say what it is' that the beauty of nature says is echoed in art's resistance to conceptual determination, and to commodification.[8]

Adorno is addressing a vital, but too rarely adequately addressed, issue in contemporary philosophy, namely how to think about 'meaning' in a non-metaphysical sense, without it becoming reduced to questions of semantics based on word/world relations, of the kind explored in theories of truth conditions, and so on, or to pragmatist inferentialism. Adorno maintains that 'in a certain sense one cannot understand works of art at all' (ibid., p. 33). The reason for this claim is crucial, because it forces us to think about ways of engaging with things that are too often ignored in philosophical reflection about meaning. Adorno suggests that there is a basic alternative with respect to art:

> Either one is inside the work of art, one participates in the work in a living sense, then the question about understanding the work or the meaning of this work of art does not really arise, or one is, via reflection

or development – or perhaps even via something like disgust or excess of artistic experience – now outside the sphere of influence which art represents. (Ibid.)

The consequence is that 'one quite suddenly and abruptly asks oneself: But, what is that really all about, what is that really?' (ibid.). Without a certain kind of engagement with the object which can be a work of art, the object fails to make the specific aesthetic sense which is neither essentially cognitive nor ethical, though it can involve aspects of both.

An acknowledged great work, like a Beethoven symphony, can cease to make sense if, for example, one gets to a point in analysing it where one loses sight of what it was that made it worth analysing in the first place, such as the kind of participation in it generated by hearing a great performance. This situation is what leads Adorno to insist on the 'puzzle-character' of art. In many respects he here echoes, as Karl Markus Michel (1980) has suggested (in a highly critical appraisal of *Aesthetic Theory*), Kafka's last story, 'Josephine, the Singer or the Mouse People'. In the story the narrator (a mouse) seeks to understand why Josephine, the 'singing' mouse, who actually makes the same noise as all the other mice, is regarded as an artist at all. Kafka's text is itself, like the sounds Josephine makes, or the symphony which one finds oneself objectifying, just a version of a form of articulation very like any other, so why should it have any kind of special status? Adorno infers from the perennial possibility of loss of the meaning specific to art that 'works of art themselves, for the sake of their own unfolding, for the sake of their own life, [need] commentary and criticism' (Adorno 2009, p. 35).

This need makes it clear that Adorno's conception is thoroughly temporalized: the participation in art he talks of is inherently 'ephemeral' (ibid., p. 43), in the manner that the beauty of nature is necessarily transient, and needs to be understood in new ways in differing situations. His positive relationship to 'what cannot be fully grasped' (ibid.) puts him at odds with philosophical positions, like Hegel's in the *Aesthetics*, for which the lack of full determinacy and the fleeting nature of things in art are precisely what philosophy is supposed to overcome. For Adorno such overcoming is, though, part of what drives the 'domination of nature', and art's job is to do justice to what is repressed in that domination. That is the source of the meaning expressed by art which cannot be expressed in cognitive or philosophical terms. One of the most difficult things to understand – and one of the most questionable ideas – in Adorno is, though, that he thinks art has to do this by adopting the most advanced technical means within a particular art form. This stance is in part derived from his problematic advocacy of certain kinds of modernism, which is now widely rejected for its ethnocentrism. What counts as most advanced is, simply, not something for which there can be reliable criteria in all social and historical contexts. However, Adorno's reflections on this topic do not all lead to a rigid version of that particular position.

In a world where more and more of nature is explained and controlled, Adorno thinks that art must be able to give a voice to what falls outside of those forms of explanation and control. The result is that art itself, 'by progressive mastering of nature, at the same time [helps] it towards its freedom' (ibid., p. 85), rather than using it instrumentally. Without technical aesthetic mastery of natural 'material', that material will 'fall prey to blindness, obscurity, a kind of mythology' (ibid.). If, for example, an essential aspect of music is the expression of emotion, both aesthetically unmediated direct forms and received forms of expression will fail to express the changing and diverse possibilities of affective life that result from changing historical and social conditions. These possibilities will then not be manifest in a way which makes sense, because they have not been articulated such that they avoid mere repetition, either of unmediated reactions or of pre-existing forms. Adorno thinks the tension involved here is essential to the very meaning of art: on the one hand, art mimics what goes on in the rest of modernity, namely the increasing technical overcoming of the 'Other', because it is constantly forced to develop new techniques; on the other, its way of doing this allows things to speak which other forms of mastery may repress. A psychology of emotions can fail to convey what great music conveys about emotions because its core aim is conceptual identification, rather than differentiated expression which makes new sense of emotions, in the way which the history of music shows is possible in music. Music is, indeed, often about sadness, joy, anger, and so on, thus about the 'garden variety' (Peter Kivy) emotions. However, it is precisely the fact that the music which conveys such emotions constantly changes, and so changes how we can experience those emotions and how they relate to the world, that suggests the paucity of what is achieved by just identifying or explaining them, rather than seeing how, in their aesthetically mediated form, they may make sense of hidden aspects of the world. Why does Wagner continue to exercise the ambiguous power that he does, if this is not the case?

Take also the Kafka story. Much of it can be seen as an ironically disguised version of aesthetic theories from Kafka's era (rather as Kafka's 'Report for an Academy' ironically rehearses Darwinism). What Josephine does is described, for example, in terms which echo the Russian formalist notion of *ostranenie*: it is the same as what others do, but she draws attention to it and so makes it 'strange'. There are also reflections on secularization and mass politics in relation to the mouse people's reception of her singing in times of trouble. In this respect the story incorporates conceptions and problems of its time. Rather than subscribing to any one of the explanations of what constitutes

Josephine's art, the story synthesizes observations of supposed aesthetic phenomena, elements of aesthetic theory, and a narrative which, of course, itself has an absurd aspect, projecting human issues onto 'the mouse people'. The story therefore does not constitute any kind of judgement on what it is about, but it would be invidious to suggest that it gives no insight into aesthetic issues, not least because it is itself a masterly work of literature which embodies so many of the ambivalences inherent in modern art. Adorno thinks of art as 'judgementless synthesis', and this description is an apt characterization of what happens in the story. Basing a philosophical interpretation on such a notion evidently poses a challenge to the kind of philosophy which is essentially based on judgement.

Before we can elucidate this topic, the question of how to understand art's form of mastery of 'nature' in such examples needs to be addressed. This would seem from many perspectives really to be about 'culture', because the material of art is always already socially mediated. The simple answer is that what Adorno means by nature is precisely that which cannot be subsumed into existing forms of identification, which he associates with 'Idealism'. This view of 'nature' might seem likely to contradict all the ways in which mind and nature are seen as interconnected in the post-Hegelian position he developed, because it threatens to establish a static opposition between mind and its non-conceptual, 'natural' Other. However, the success of Adorno's approach depends on its exploration of the ways in which forms of thinking and articulation can obscure what he thinks of in terms of 'non-identity'. The two sides of nature and its Other are not fixed, and they are in the kind of dialectical relationship we have repeatedly encountered. The formal conception of nature defines nature in terms of the opposition between what is bound by necessary laws and what isn't, but this is only one, historically specific, way of characterizing nature.

Adorno thinks of nature in modernity as what is not adequately expressed by the main forms of objectification that societies use to manipulate the material world. These forms keep changing, and art cannot be a stable quantity because it is a response to these changes. What art means, like nature in the move from the theological view to the modern view, is transformed by historical shifts which lead to received forms ceasing to 'speak'. The failure to give definitive answers to aesthetic questions points, then, to kinds of experience and to aspects of the world without which art would not 'speak'. These can be illuminated by conceptual analysis but not replaced by it. Just as natural beauty speaks without us being able to translate it into discursivity, works of art speak by making sense of things, without us finally being able to specify their meaning in semantic terms. That is why art can also, for Adorno, be a repository of hope. Hope resides not in what we know and control, but in the sense that the world may yet offer something beyond what we know and control. Such hope can be generated by an experience in nature, or by a profound aesthetic experience. This idea further elucidates what Adorno means by things 'speaking' to us: a connection between ourselves and aspects of the world which were previously neglected is established by the experience of art.

Adorno insists that art should not be 'reduced undialectically to a formula like "the voice of nature"' (ibid., p. 90), because it must also involve the aspect of control of natural material that it shares, albeit in a very different form, with science and technology. The key notion here is 'expression', and the point is that what is repressed needs the technical means that develop in art to be expressed. Forms of expression can, though, themselves become repressive when they become standardized, and they therefore demand innovation. This depends on technical advances of the kind that lead, for example, from simple songs to complex symphonic movements. Adorno often talks of a dialectic of expression and convention in this context, because convention, although it plays a role in all forms of art, is also what can lead to those forms ceasing to speak (see Bowie 1997). Without conventions, such as sonata form, new expressive means would make no sense, because they would lack what allows them, by challenging the understandings which have been expressed by the existing forms, to reveal what has been excluded or repressed. At the same time sonata form, as a mere norm to be adhered to, can lead to the kind of schematic sonatas characteristic of some second-rate Romantic music in the nineteenth century.

Adorno makes too much of the idea that 'art in a certain sense helps to give what has been oppressed and what suffers its voice' (Adorno 2009, pp. 96–7), because the idea has to gather so many diverse phenomena in a single framework. With respect to some of the most significant art of modernity, though, the framework does help to understand how modern art has increasingly included more and more material that was initially regarded as outside the aesthetic sphere, from dissonances and noise in music, to what become 'ready-mades' in the plastic arts. The drive of very many modern artists in all forms of art not to allow what is socially excluded to be excluded from art is at least in part congruent with the idea of giving a voice to what suffers.[9]

Although Adorno himself seemed largely incapable of seeing it, the history of jazz exemplifies what he means. Jazz instrumental playing gains its life from developing and incorporating expressive elements which were excluded by a dominant musical culture (one which Adorno himself in certain respects sought to make too dominant). This musical culture was (and in some ways still is) linked to the political and social culture from which many of those who developed jazz were excluded on racial and other grounds. Such an incorporation of excluded modes of expression is, in Adorno's terms, also a form of 'domination of nature', because it requires its own techniques and it gains control over something which is initially merely unmediated expression, thus something 'mimetic' that lacks rationality. The vocal aspect of jazz instrumental playing at its most intense incorporates screaming and other immediate expressions into new techniques. Once this has happened the techniques can then tend to rigidify into convention, and so renew the demand for inclusion of something else that has been excluded. What is most characteristic here from an Adornian perspective is the claim that it is only when art is emancipated from tradition and develops highly differentiated technical means of expression that it really is able to express 'nature': '[N]ature in art is the precise opposite of the idea of a so-called art which is "close to nature"' (ibid., pp. 107–8) that is appealed to in anti-modernist views of art. The latter views repress the fact that all forms of art are historically mediated products, and so the appeal to their naturalness is mere ideology.

Adorno's development of this position in relation to his favoured forms of modernism is, as I have suggested, not always convincing. Moreover, it has tended to get in the way of the more significant issue, namely of how his reflections can question philosophy's often exclusive equation of truth with what is articulated in judgements. The two related notions involved here are that art is 'judgementless synthesis', and that truth is inherently connected with expression, which can be repressed by judgement: '[T]he art work, so to speak, restores the aspect of truth which is generally lost to truth precisely by the simple form of the judgement' (ibid., p. 327). The initial assumption is that assertion that 'x is such and such' articulates truth by the exclusion of all the other things which x can be. Clearly this is questionable, because the form of the predicative judgement is an ineliminable condition of intelligible thought. Why can one not just accept that this form is recursively applicable and so not inherently problematic, because we know we can always predicate something else of something, and so repair the damage done by a particular predication? Adorno's position depends, though, on not accepting this consequence (which he is evidently aware of) as the last word on the issue, and it is here that the idea of 'judgementless synthesis' is important.

In a criticism of the idea that Kafka's work is really a manifestation of 'vulgar existentialism's' view of the awfulness of the modern world, Adorno suggests of the elements of Kafka's world, such as sadism, guilt, and myth, that

> [t]he synthesis into which these moments are brought by Kafka is precisely not one of 'That is how it is'; no consequence is drawn [...] no judgement inferred, but precisely the judgement-less and, if you like, the ambiguous combination of these moments allows the artwork to take up into itself that fullness of being [*des Seienden*] which is otherwise cut off by the logic of the judgement. (Ibid., p. 328)

How, though, is truth, which is normally linked to the judgement-form, to be understood in such a perspective? Adorno suggests that art and philosophy are closely connected in a key respect. As I suggested in the Introduction, one of the puzzling aspects of much analytical philosophy is that it generates little but conflicting claims to truth, in a way that successful natural science often does not, because scientific claims can rest on successful prediction and control, as well as on the evidence (which may, of course, generate possibly irresolvable conflicts of interpretation). Analytical philosophy generates contradictions whilst precisely relying on assertion, on proposing arguments for theories that aim to be true. It is not that such arguments cannot illuminate aspects of the issue being dealt with, because the conflicts between theories may open up what is at issue in new ways. They can, though, hardly be said to result in a definitive sense of 'That's how it is', even though the manner in which the arguments are generally presented precisely implies such a sense by the reliance on assertion. Most analytically oriented philosophers are happy to agree that philosophy does not definitively settle issues, but often fail to reflect in any depth on the fact that philosophy's content militates against assertoric form. This is a situation that led the early German Romantics to think that irony is essential to philosophy: one cannot but assert things, but one needs at the same time to suggest that what is asserted is in all likelihood inadequate (see Bowie 1997, 2003a). The analytical approach depends on isolating aspects of a problem or phenomenon, and, as we saw in the case of language, this can lead to a failure to appreciate that the approach may itself generate a false image of what it seeks to analyse. If one thinks in terms of the *conflicts* between analytical theories themselves revealing something of the issues they address, one already starts to move in a direction which connects to the role of art as judgementless synthesis.

The notion of incorporating the 'fullness of being' cut off by an analytical approach might seem much too vague to serve as an alternative. However, if one's approach to philosophy depends more on understanding 'how things hang together' or make sense in concrete historical circumstances than on proposing specific theories to answer supposedly perennial philosophical questions, then resources offered by the development of art can suggest ways of illuminating philosophical issues. The point of a synthesis which is 'judgementless' is that, instead of isolating aspects of the issue in question and identifying them in terms of a theory, it brings together differing, even contradictory, aspects of what is in question. These can convey the complex experience of responding to real-world issues, without seeking to escape the fact that such issues may be inherently contradictory. As Adorno says of the work of art: 'Judgements might occur in it, but the work does not judge, perhaps because it has, since Attic tragedy, been a negotiation' (Adorno 1997, 7, p. 152). The social form in which conflicting validity claims concerning contentious issues, from disputed science to disputed public policy, are dealt with is 'negotiation', and negotiation is always threatened by the illegitimate use of power. As such, a form which withholds from judgement at the same time as seeking to articulate the complexity of the conflict in question must be significant for a self-reflexive approach to philosophy.

Rather than seeking to resolve, say, questions of the philosophy of mind by advocating an eliminativist theory, or a theory which insists on the irreducibility of self-consciousness to such a theory, a judgementless synthesis might consider how such theories express the contradictory ways in which humankind's place in nature is manifest in modernity. Adorno suggests, in a Hegelian vein, that 'you should from the outset free yourself from that concept of philosophy [...] which is supposed to consist of epistemology and aesthetics [...] as a kind of special science, and really arrive at the position of seeing philosophy really as the self-consciousness of the epoch or as precisely the self-reflection of consciousness' (Adorno 1961, p. 6467). That self-reflection is apparent in the conflicting ways in which nature is thought about that are reflected in the conflict between eliminativism and its opponents. This approach is not, however, intended as some kind of definitive way out of traditional philosophical argument. Adorno is aware that one has to work immanently on the consistency and plausibility of arguments in an essentially analytical manner in some situations. However, his approach, as we saw in the notion of the constellation in earlier chapters, may constitute the best concrete response to an issue in certain situations, because just committing to one of a number of incompatible alternatives may blind one to vital aspects of the issue. A basic fallibilism underlies his stance on positive claims. What counts, and here Adorno comes close to the pragmatist heritage of Hegel, is what happens in practice as a consequence of one's philosophical commitments.

By moving away from seeing nature just in terms of saying 'that's how it is', one can begin to understand why the effects of the restriction to seeing nature just in the formal sense may be part of what gives rise to some of the pathologies of modernity. Adorno does not think his approach can be based on a positive alternative theory: '[P]ure, untouched nature cannot be known or formed by art in its immediacy – then the only possibility of helping what is repressed to have a voice is negativity, i.e. alienation itself' (Adorno 2009, p. 126). What Adorno means is explained by his (somewhat unorthodox) version of Hegel's idea of 'determinate negation': the truth arises when 'we measure every phenomenon, confront every phenomenon, with what it claims to be on its part'; in this way 'we can get in touch with its untruth and, if we wish, in this way also get in touch negatively with its truth' (ibid., p. 127). This idea is predicated on the simple historical fact that articulated positive awareness of mistaken and distorted understandings of the world often does not develop until well after the mistaken understandings should have been apparent. The ecological crisis was not a theme for natural science until the crisis was already massively advanced. The realization of the threat posed to civilized life on earth is not necessarily most effectively communicated by scientific or philosophical theories, even though such theories must play a role in the change of awareness required. The decline of a certain kind of celebration of nature in Romantic music that is present in some of the later Mahler and in the rise of dissonant modernism, exemplified in Berg's *Wozzeck*, already pointed to something problematic in the relationship of modern societies to nature, in ways that were largely absent from the science and much of the philosophy of the earlier twentieth century.

Adorno cites Brecht's use of '*Verfremdung*' ('alienation', in the sense of 'making strange', which Brecht adopted from Russian formalism) as a way in which the familiar which obscures the real state of affairs can be countered in art, suggesting that there is a close affinity between this and what takes place in philosophical determinate negation. It is by taking account of 'the really existing alienation between subject and object' in the form of an artistic response that 'restores something like the ability to see nature' (ibid., p. 128). Art should involve the 'dismantling of the conventional, the dismantling of everything which, so to speak, is interposed between the thing itself and consciousness' (ibid., p. 128). This idea is not intended in an epistemological sense, as a version of philosophical realism. Rather the contact with the thing is precisely at the aesthetic level that Adorno's reflections are seeking to illuminate. Beckett's plays' and novels' relentless stripping away of illusions about our ability to transcend our natural status, by directing our attention towards the inevitable decline of the body, tells us about modernity's destruction of nature by bringing to light the repression of finitude on which it is often based. The aesthetic form expresses the suffering that too many social processes and ways of thinking can commit to oblivion, and so help to perpetuate. Adorno sums up his stance as follows: '[T]he consistent technique of aesthetic alienation [*Verfremdung*] restores something like the ability to see nature ['*den Blick auf Natur*'] at the dialectical stage of alienation [*Entfremdung*, in the sense of the split between subject and object] in which we find ourselves' (ibid., p. 128).

The direction Adorno seeks to open up against dominant philosophical trends, which suggests why he thinks art has to be thought of in terms of truth, is evident in his assertion that '[t]he need to give suffering a voice is the condition of all truth' (Adorno GS 6, p. 29). If art indeed expresses suffering in the ways that we have explored, there are good grounds for taking this position seriously, though one might question whether 'all truth' involves this. One does not have to give up on semantic considerations and other philosophical questions about truth to see that the ways of making sense of the most troubling aspects of human existence present in modern art are anything but arbitrary or insignificant. What Adorno seeks is echoed in Rorty's contention that the primary aim for philosophy should be to diminish cruelty. One looks first to how the way we think can be damaging to others and to what is being thought about, before being concerned with notional objectivity. Such an approach does not question the results of well-warranted science, but instead insists that we first think about how we locate what science tells us in relation to the other ways in which the world is disclosed to us. That is why Adorno wants to incorporate the 'fullness of being' evident in great art into our responses to the world. As Hilary Putnam, Nelson Goodman, and others have often pointed out, one can grind out endless objective theories that can be experimentally confirmed in relation to any object in the world. The prior question should therefore be about how what one does affects the world, which is not something determinable by objective theories. The aesthetic aspect of this approach is philosophically significant because we 'behave aesthetically at the moment when we [. . .] are not realistic, when do not look cleverly to our advantage, our getting-on, or any aims we seek to achieve, but rather give ourselves over to something in itself [*einem Ansichseienden*] [. . .] without concern for the realm of purposes' (ibid., p. 146), in the manner we have seen in the discussion of natural and artistic beauty.[10]

Adorno's claim here can be read as just repeating the critique of instrumental reason that forms the basis of *Dialectic of Enlightenment*, and so as questionably totalizing the idea that means/ends action is the essential problem in relation to nature in modernity. As he himself also admits, his position involves an aspect of 'art for art's sake', which is hardly novel or philosophically interesting in itself, though the emergence of that idea in the nineteenth century is a sign of a change in how modern societies relate to the world that accompanies growing commodification. However, Adorno's claim can be read in other ways, which make the critique of commodification and objectification more plausible, by suggesting how they are linked to certain approaches to philosophy.

In his influential essay 'Aesthetic Problems in Modern Philosophy' (Cavell 1976), Stanley Cavell argued for the importance of the aesthetic in understanding why philosophy should not always focus on cognitive matters, a focus based largely on the idea that aesthetic judgements lack the logical certainty of cognitive judgements. Referring to Cavell's main source, Kant, Adorno similarly suggests that the main task for contemporary aesthetics should be to 'resolve this quite drastic, quite crude contradiction' in judgements of taste between the 'logical function', which relies on a limited number of specific forms of judgement, and what is 'merely perceptual ['*bloss anschaulich*', in the sense of Kant's 'intuition' (*Anschauung*) as the mode in which the world is given to us]' (Adorno 1961, p. 6541), which is indeterminately diverse.

The split between the logical and the perceptual is crucial, because, as we saw in Chapter 3, the latter is often associated with the 'myth of the given', the untenable idea that perception provides basic elements which can ground cognitive judgements. If the 'perceptual' is always necessarily mediated by language, there can be no such foundational justificatory elements, and validity and truth therefore, as Brandom contends, depend on inferential articulation of what is judged. However, as we saw, if one thinks of the 'immediacy' of what is here termed the 'perceptual', not in terms of the mythical empiricist sense, but in the sense in Schelling, Heidegger, Merleau-Ponty, and others of fundamental kinds of contact with the world that make sense, the split Adorno sees as essential to aesthetics takes on a different significance. The approach both Cavell and Adorno develop acknowledges the necessity of inference in understanding, but seeks to take account of other ways in which things are given to us, thus of how we can respond to things in a manner which does not belong exclusively either to sapience or to sentience. The point here is that, as we saw Wellmer suggest, language is also bound up with freedom, because it may enable expression which makes suffering tolerable, or give a new way of relating to things that opens up new aspects of the world. Neither of these possibilities is primarily dependent on fulfilling inferential commitments, though what results from them may often involve that.

Meaning is, for Adorno, seen as inherently bound up with all the ways in which the world engages us, rather than as essentially consisting in subsumption of the particular under the universal. As such, meaning has to involve ways beyond disenchantment that are neither illusory nor arbitrarily subjective, even though they are based on the 'pre-logical' (ibid.). This is also the point behind Cavell's reflections, which we will look at in more detail after establishing why Adorno can be understood in the light of what Cavell says. If aesthetics is to be concerned with truth, the core problem is that in art 'one experiences something singular, something particular in its necessity, without the universal which would guarantee this universality being positively given in advance, so that one could just apply it to the particular [in the way that a concept is applied in a cognitive judgement]' (ibid., p. 6552). This combination of necessity and singularity is decisive, because it demands forms of attention and analysis which do not match the forms of judgement that concern most philosophy.

Adorno says of 'bourgeois art' that 'one can regard it, since there has been the form of the novel or also since there has been great music, as a single effort to draw the contingent [*das Zufällige*] into this context of meaning [*Sinnzusammenhang*]' (ibid., p. 6562). If the meaning of 'the contingent' were to be rendered conceptually determinate, though, it would potentially fall prey to objectification and commodification, rather than opening up new ways of seeing things. Instead 'the acknowledgement of this contingency itself becomes a moment of the artistic content of meaning [*Sinngehalt*]' (ibid., p. 6563). The history of modern art shows that it is likely that the contingency will subsequently become incorporated into artistic convention, when its significance will become something more akin to that present in conceptual meaning. Adorno often cites the example of the diminished seventh chord moving from being a revelatory shock in Beethoven to being a cliché of salon music used for standardized expressive purposes. The meaning of what is contingent is not what can be made determinate by analysis: '[T]his indeterminate aspect in the work of art is at the same time determinate, only in a completely different direction from determination in a concept. And what we call artistic form is really [. . .] to be grasped as the aesthetic determination of the indeterminate' (ibid., p. 6864). Aesthetic form is, then, what allows contingent material to make its own unique sense.

Artistic form can be a kind of expression of truth, but it is a truth which takes the form of something singular. By configuring material, such as the notes of the diatonic scale, into something with its own unique kind of internal necessity, something emerges which can then make possible a new kind of necessity beyond the particular work. Once Beethoven shows the new expressive possibilities contained in such means as developing variation and the use of rhythm as a major structuring device, new music which takes no account of how received musical techniques have thereby been transformed risks ceasing to 'speak' in the sense we have seen. Similarly, once Ornette Coleman and others show how melody can be made to work in certain respects independently of harmony, jazz improvisation is faced with the demand to incorporate notes which were previously just 'wrong' in ways that make sense, without relying on existing harmonic norms. The truth of Beethoven or Coleman is manifest 'negatively', via the way in which music after them may cease to speak if it does not find its own way of engaging with what has become possible. This is not, as Adorno's reference to determinate negation suggests, wholly different from what happens in the cognitive domain: once a 'paradigm shifting' discovery is made, it redefines the scope and nature of what can be considered valid. Adorno's approach is, though, in danger of neglecting what it is in art, like that of Beethoven, which enables it to speak beyond the context of determinate negation in which its truth became apparent. To suggest that the aesthetic pleasure to be gained from Beethoven in the present is more culinary than anything else brings Adorno too close to something like the Kantian moralism we saw him criticize in the last chapter.

Adorno adopts Novalis' idea (which is shared by Hegel) that there is no such thing as bad art, because bad art is not art at all, art being what says something true in the 'negative' manner just described. Without this idea the scope of the notion of 'art' becomes largely indeterminate, and leads precisely to the kind of relativism we shall consider in a moment. The problem with Adorno's version of the idea is that, in the name of making art significant for philosophy, some of what matters in art can be neglected. From a strictly construed Adornian perspective these other dimensions – often those having to do with the affective resources offered by art to the individual – have no great philosophical significance.[11] The crucial factor for Adorno is to find ways of doing philosophy which reveal the truth-content of art by understanding the 'aesthetic determination of the indeterminate' involved in the constant process of formal change in modern art. This perspective can be highly illuminating, but it is not adequate to all that is at issue. For the history of 'classical' music from Monteverdi and Bach to Stockhausen, or the history of jazz from King Oliver to the present, one can see that the idea of determinate negation is essential. Be-bop, for example, reacts against commercial swing, which is often indifferent to the social and political tensions of the world in which it is located. The founders of be-bop create a music which channels energy and technique in new expressive forms that are not immediately marketable to a mass audience, and which establish a musical autonomy for jazz that lays the foundation for its development as in many respects the most consistently creative music of the second half of the twentieth century and beyond. Jazz had previously been seen by many as predominantly a form of entertainment, whereas it now helped contribute to what became the Civil Rights movement, not necessarily by making direct political statements, but by the creation of art with its own integrity that established a critical cultural identity. This pattern of rejection of a form of art which has become established and popular, in the name of something which develops new kinds of expression, can be observed in many areas of Western music, and other forms of art.

The idea of the manifestation of truth-content in art as a historical process of determinate negation seems plausible, then, in such contexts. Art incorporates new material and makes sense of the material by the way in which it constitutes new forms, without that sense being able to be conveyed independently of concrete engagement with and participation in the art in question. If semantically conceived truth depends on the capacity to adopt the stance of assenting to or rejecting the content of assertions, art can intelligibly be said to be true if it reveals how existing forms of articulation and expression fail to disclose anything of the world which is not already known or familiar. An elaborate theoretical argument is not necessary to defend this view; the history of art in modernity shows a version of it at every turn, and this fact itself helps to obviate many questions concerning how the subjective realm of aesthetic judgement can have objective content.

For Adorno, a world dominated by commodification increases the extent to which fixed forms become the norm and so encourage passive acceptance of the status quo. The philosophical significance of art in his emphatic sense lies, therefore, in its offering a way of relating to the world which can be lost if the world is dominated by economic and technical imperatives. These imperatives can (cautiously) be linked to the effects of the dominance of the cognitive relations to the world which form the major focus of discussion of truth in many kinds of philosophy. Despite Adorno's insistence that all notions of what nature is are mediated, and so belong in some sense in the inferential 'space of reasons', there must, for art to be intelligible at all, be an immediate connection between subject and world in the experience of natural beauty:

> Thus if this experience of beauty, as something immediate, which is before aesthetic sublimation, before the separation from what is there, before the separation from the beauty of nature or from the appearance of beautiful people or whatever it might be, if the concept of the beautiful is not gained and sustained from this [immediate experience], then it, as it were, loses its substance. (Ibid., p. 6944)

The goal in much cognitively oriented philosophy is the explanation of how to match concept and object, in order to overcome the separation of mind and world that arises with the modern sceptical problematic. By contrast, the goal here is, in the face of growing disenchantment, to sustain and create meaningful relations to things, of the kind that are present in everyday life, but which increasingly are neglected when control and exploitation of nature and the associated commodification of the objective world become the dominant aim. Art that matters creates a context of meaning which draws on the most basic experiences of being in a world that makes, albeit transient, sense. Such experiences can be of the kind which children have that determine their subsequent responses to the world, which we have when gripped by a natural scene of great beauty, or when we experience the world in a way which makes new sense by falling in love. The difficulty of modern art is in this respect a reflection of the extent to which such experiences have become lost, neglected, repressed, or commodified in many areas of modern society, and so need new ways of being articulated and expressed.

Adorno's idea that the relationship originally manifest in these direct experiences of beauty is, in the kind of society which is capable of producing the Holocaust, only really sustained by the most radical expressive art need not, however, follow from the rest of his position.

His more extreme position is understandable in the face of the fact that rejection of aesthetic modernism was a feature of the nightmare politics of the Nazis and others, but it tends to exclude too much art from a possible contribution to human flourishing even in extreme circumstances. Although he is right to be vigilant about the perennial possibility of art becoming part of a 'context of delusion', measuring all art against the extreme negative image of the world that informs *Dialectic of Enlightenment* fails to do justice to the ways in which even art that may not achieve the highest standards can have a transformative effect on society and on individual lives.

If what is aimed for in both art and philosophy is a wholesale critical response to the totalizing nature of the commodified world, the danger is that they will mirror what they oppose. This can lead to a demand for radical responses which leave too little space for the fact that critical reactions to commodification can take many forms in differing contexts. That is one of the reasons Adorno failed to understand jazz. Adorno's aesthetic purism is often at odds with the pragmatic possibilities opened up by many of his approaches. His idea that art should be seen in terms of truth does seem to me justified in the terms we have explored. However, the way in which he sometimes seeks to justify the idea – such as by the assumption that there is an 'objective state of the material' to which true art must correspond – had real negative effects, for example, as Hans-Werner Henze and others have argued, on musical composition after the war. In such cases Adorno's insistence on the need for philosophy to bring out the truth-content of art actually introduces the flaws of a Hegelianism which his criticisms elsewhere are so good at revealing, by elevating what is in fact a local perspective into the supposed truth of the totality.

It is here that Cavell has something important to offer. Cavell develops a version of what we saw above in Adorno's insistence on the moment of immediacy in beauty that sustains a demand for objectivity. He argues that in a discussion about the aesthetic value of art, unlike about the truth of a cognitive judgement, where the evidence can be established by inferentially based identification, 'if you do not see *something*, without explanation, then there is nothing further to discuss' (Cavell 1976, p. 93). The question is what we do with this moment of immediacy. The suspicion with respect to Adorno is that, in trying to counter the sense that aesthetic assessments are merely subjective, he adopts a too emphatically objectivizing philosophical perspective. One has, though, to be careful here. Major art does involve a kind of rightness which reveals what is wrong with art which does not possess this rightness. Aesthetic flaws in this sort of situation are akin to logical flaws, because it can be shown why they are not right in the context in which they occur. The dynamic aspects of Adorno's approach also allow for the fact that what may be a flaw in one context may be the opposite in another, there being no norms which can be applied independently of the concrete manifestations of art itself. However, this is a complex issue.

Consider the following, which is the kind of example also cited by Cavell: 'A quartet by Mozart is not just better made than a symphony of the Mannheim School, but also ranks higher, as better-made, more right, in the emphatic sense' (Adorno 1997, 10.2, p. 634). In such a case it makes sense to argue to someone who says they prefer the Mannheim symphony that they might be missing something by their just attending to, say, a tune they like, rather than thinking about the piece as a whole. Without such argument serious musical education would be inconceivable. Adorno does not equate superiority in the command of the material of a kind of art with the 'progress of art itself' (ibid.). He does suggest that once the move to perspective in visual art in Europe has been made, it would be 'objectively false' (ibid.) to retain the old representation of space. At the same time, however, works made in the older manner may prove themselves over time, not because they belong to a timeless artistic canon, but because they can come in certain circumstances to reveal something missing in the art that succeeds them.

It is with respect to certain kinds of European modern art, like music, that Adorno adopts a questionable version of the idea that once a certain technique is established it will reveal how approaches that employ other means are false. The moves from Bach to Schoenberg follow a pattern that can be construed – for example with respect to the tempering of the scale into equal intervals and the growing integration of musical material into compositional forms by developing variation – in terms of increasing technical and rational control of musical means, and thence linked to a dialectic of Enlightenment (see Bowie 2007). This approach leads Adorno to over-elaborate dialectical reflections on how technique in art should always be advanced, so as to constitute an adequate response to the inexorable development of technology in the practical realm. He assumes that there is a very substantial connection between the two, and he tries to underpin the connection with too many merely metaphorical links between technology and techniques in art, when the structures involved in each are often very different.

The grand historical story of modern art and philosophy on which Adorno sometimes relies does provide a framework which illuminates a variety of important phenomena. However, Cavell shows how, with a more cautious version of the story of modern art, one can challenge the agenda which both dominates too much contemporary philosophy, and is an expression of wider social and cultural problems. What Cavell argues is congruent with much that we have considered in previous chapters: at the same time as rejecting the myths of exclusive objectivity produced by reductionist approaches, he, like Adorno, keeps the goal of an objectivity that goes beyond the solely cognitive.

The reason this goal is so important is that a culture which increasingly functions in terms of the notional validity only of what can be 'scientifically proven' distorts the human world. What is regarded as open to rational appraisal can become reduced to various forms of quantification, from the economic to the natural scientific. It is not that this reduction is itself actually scientific, because the justified esteem which accrues to well-warranted science can be invalidly transferred to issues where it has no place. The catastrophic effects of this transfer in economics, as we saw, are now leading to a long-overdue reappraisal of the subject in some areas. In certain respects this misuse of notional objectivity is so obvious as to seem almost too banal to describe, but the extent of the problem seems to grow in many spheres of contemporary life. The 'fact/value' distinction is regularly invoked in order to consign anything which cannot be quantified to the realm of the merely subjective, so cutting off debate about essential social, cultural, and political matters, even though that distinction is more and more called into question by philosophical reflection (see Putnam 2004). The bureaucratic standardization of practices in institutions can destroy patterns of trust and good-will developed in a particular context over time. These patterns are what enable people to make complex judgements involving factors which often can only be analytically separated at the expense of what constitutes their real substance. The resulting 'audit culture' has, for example, invaded British higher education, with consequences which in the long run will be disastrous to critical intellectual life. By treating intricately connected processes of learning as though they are equivalent to manufacturing processes that can be analysed into separate components, the resulting institutionalized forms of learning start to break down the capacity for making complex links between issues that can lead to creative insight. These are phenomena which evidently relate to issues concerning instrumental reason and the modern world, and the philosophical issues raised by aesthetic questions need to be seen in relation to these concrete phenomena.

Cavell considers the issue that debates about aesthetic judgements may go on indefinitely because there is no agreement, may come to seem pointless, and so on. Aesthetic judgement does not have the same logical status as well-warranted cognitive judgement; indeed, in this respect, it seems not to involve anything logical at all. The fact that much of what Cavell then says about aesthetic debate applies equally well to what tends to happen in philosophy suggests the perspective I want to develop here. The familiar consequence associated with disagreement on aesthetic judgements is that there are therefore no real grounds for argument about aesthetic issues – the issue that goes back to Hume and Kant. Like Adorno, though, Cavell sees a necessity in aesthetic judgements, which is 'partly, a matter of the *ways* a judgement is supported, the ways in which conviction in it is produced: it is only by virtue of these recurrent patterns of support that a remark will count as – will be – aesthetic, or a mere matter of taste, or moral, propagandistic, religious, magical, scientific, philosophical' (Cavell 1976, p. 93). The idea of specific kinds of support for kinds of judgement leads to his remark that there can be no aesthetic discussion unless there is some shared immediate, unexplained sense that there is something worthy of discussion. The point is that this kind of sense is built into the fabric of communication of a society and can be appealed to by those advancing an aesthetic judgement.

Adorno suggests the possible consequences of this fact in *Aesthetic Theory*: 'That people incessantly get involved in aesthetic disputes, no matter what position they take up with regard to aesthetics, proves more against relativism than its philosophical refutations: the idea of aesthetic truth gets its justification despite its problematic nature and in its problematic nature' (Adorno 1997, 7, p. 419; see Bowie 2004). As soon as one is concretely involved with an aesthetic issue, the relativist claim is revealed as depending on not actually attending to the issue, because by really engaging with a work of art as a work of art one cannot remain external to the demands it makes. The idea that taste is 'just subjective', and so outside the sphere of social legitimation, is contradicted almost everywhere by the fact that people get so agitated about issues of taste: just read the comments by readers in newspapers about new architectural plans, for example. Either we see each such critical readers as just a locus of 'will to power', seeking to assert themselves against the other by having their subjective preference approved, or we realize that they are part of a culture of judgement which, for all its problems, can result in something socially valuable. If this were not the case, why would people be so concerned to argue for their assessment, rather than simply bathing in solipsistic self-righteousness, or assuming that such matters are 'merely subjective'?

Adorno's point here links him to views, like those of Habermas and Brandom, which argue that the attempt to claim that communication is essentially grounded in the will to power relies on a dogmatic assumption that cannot be validated in the space of reasons without thereby demonstrating the priority of normative assessment. Adorno's difference from these views lies in his making the aesthetic in one sense more decisive than the cognitive, because it depends on a different kind of link to the world to that in objective knowledge. Inferential justification in the cognitive realm relies on observational data that can be agreed on in discussion: 'If we mean by red what is located in the following part of the spectrum, then this object counts as red.' Aesthetic justification also involves inferentially articulated assertions: 'If you play the first subject of this sonata a lot more quickly than the second, the movement begins to make no sense,' but without the moment of 'seeing' or – probably more importantly – feeling '*something*, without explanation' the reason for making the inferential case is lost. Why does it matter at all that a sonata should make sense? What is at issue are fundamental kinds of engagement with the world which can be affected by giving reasons, but which need to be in play in a substantial way before giving reasons can have any grip. This is not a 'myth of the given', because it entails no claims about foundational cognitive justificatory status with respect to what is involved in this engagement, just the awareness that without it the phenomenon of art and its complex relationship to modern philosophy themselves make no sense.

Cavell makes a crucial point:

> If we say the *hope* of agreement motivates our engaging in these various patterns of support, then we must also say, what I take Kant to have seen, that even were agreement in fact to emerge, our judgements, so far as aesthetic, would remain as essentially subjective, in his sense, as they ever were. Otherwise, art and the criticism of art would not have their special importance nor elicit their own forms of distrust and of gratitude. (Cavell 1976, p. 94)

It is not, then, that aesthetic judgement would only be fully validated if it could be assimilated to cognitive judgement, thus eliminating its subjective aspect. Rather it opens up different kinds of understanding of and response to the world which have their own kind of importance, precisely because they involve the 'essentially subjective', and this is where Adorno's ideas about nature are so important. It is the *subject* that can suffer and for which beauty can offer ways of coming to terms with suffering, and too often this aspect of the world is relegated to 'unreality' by the assumptions of reductive naturalism. However problematic Kant's idea of the 'universal voice', which distinguishes a judgement of beauty from one of agreeableness, may be, it addresses a crucial element of the questions here. It does so by showing how the subjective may demand its own form of validity that cannot in the last analysis rely on any kind of explanatory foundation and must rely on a culture of 'patterns of support' which draws on experiences that require aesthetic forms of expression.

Adorno's critical assumption in this context concerns the extent to which subjects are so formed by the objective pressure of commodity society that any aesthetic judgements they make actually become ideological, rather than being rooted in the moment of immediacy that pertains to the individual's experience of beauty. However, if his remark about aesthetic disputes proving more against relativism than the standard easy logical rejoinder in philosophy is given the weight it seems to me to deserve, this takes Adorno beyond the idea that we live in an impenetrable context of delusion. Cavell suggests that the 'air of dogmatism' involved in the kind of aesthetic claim couched in the form of 'We want to say' or 'We are dissatisfied', which assumes some kind of community which does not actually exist, 'is indeed present in such claims; but if that is intolerant, that is because tolerance could only mean, as in liberals it often does, that the kind of claim in question is not taken seriously' (ibid., p. 96). By taking it seriously one restores a sense that validity is not something that can just be left to the physical sciences, where the hope for substantial agreement is in many respects and many contexts quite justified, and is institutionalized into self-critical expert cultures.[12] Instead, agreement or negotiated disagreement also has to be reached in areas where a sense of dissonance between subjects and between subjects and the world seems constitutive.

In a post-traditional society, where normative authority is no longer just presupposed, ideas about what kind of world would make people feel 'at home' – the concern with which, as the emergence of the metaphor of homelessness in Romanticism suggests, is part of what gave rise to the modern development of aesthetics – necessarily become massively contentious. Conflicting wishes and hopes concerning how one's world can be meaningful, which very often coexist *within* the individual subject, are reflected in the way that significant art incorporates more and more dissonance as it seeks to open up ways of living with the kind of inescapable contradictions that form the focus of Adorno's thinking. What can be shared, in terms of a conception which makes the aesthetic relationship to the world central to philosophy, is precisely the sense that negotiating differences that are rooted in our most fundamental responses to the world is an imperative that cannot be eliminated by the kind of lazy tolerance rejected by Cavell, a tolerance which often relies on the sense that only scientifically warranted claims possess a logical status which means they must be taken seriously. The point about such tolerance, as Adorno and Marcuse would argue, is that it is 'repressive', an ideological means of sustaining a status quo which involves structural injustice.

In a more emphatic interpretation, the agenda of certain areas of Anglophone philosophy in particular can be seen as reinforcing the structures in question by their neglect of questions about 'meaning' in the senses we have outlined, in the name of the obsession with epistemology and semantics. However unnecessarily exaggerated some of Adorno's global judgements on 'positivism' may be, the kernel of truth they contain is apparent here. Recent moves in philosophy against a reductive naturalism that is an echo of disturbing social and political trends are in line with what underlies Adorno's most apt criticisms.[13] The lack of any real dialogue between many working at the reductive naturalist end of Anglophone philosophy and people working in the humanities is a manifestation of the deeper connection between certain reductive directions in philosophy and dangerous social trends of the kind exemplified by the attempts to reduce issues of culture and social justice to issues of economic management and technological control. The contemporary widespread irrational rejection of good science that is particularly striking in the USA is a manifestation of the way Adorno sees the philosophical tensions as expressions of wider social and cultural developments. By failing to see that resources for meaning take the kind of forms we have been discussing, metaphysical faith in natural science as the only source of warrantable truth helps to create the space for the arbitrary rejection of precisely the science which those who have such faith argue for so emphatically. While abstraction and objectification are essential to scientific progress, making them the basis of the understanding of all other forms of relationship to the world adds to the social alienation which results from the dissonances between scientific and social and political developments in modernity. Adorno's insistence on attention to the truth of expressive forms of sense-making offers resources for cultural politics that are still missing in too much contemporary philosophy.

These reflections on the role of expressive forms help one gain a clearer sense of why 'non-identity' plays the central role it does in Adorno's thinking, and why it militates against a view of philosophy as consisting essentially of arguments about the supposed 'problems of philosophy'. In the face of the increasing specialization in many areas of Anglo-American philosophy the contemporary choice tends to be either to engage in a very specific area with its own core agenda, or to seek to illuminate issues that substantially affect contemporary life by reflecting on connections between differing philosophical approaches. Those now looking for existential orientation or insight into how to respond to questions which have an unavoidable metaphysical dimension are very unlikely to seek it in the specialized end of contemporary analytical philosophy, and are far more likely to seek it in the arts.[14] However, that is not to say that elements from specialized philosophical debates will not be significant with respect to matters of cultural politics. The question is what resources philosophy now offers for making the connections between detailed technical arguments and critical reflection on social issues. The reason the aesthetic perspective is so important is that it suggests how conflicting forms of articulation and conflicting perspectives can be brought into contact with each other, without assuming that there can be a definitive resolution of those conflicts. Adorno's concern with his specific notion of experience results from his sense that in engaging with any significant issue the contradictions involved can be more revealing than the attempt to resolve them. The idea with respect to art that the attempt to be definitive is both necessary and doomed to failure informs Adorno's whole approach to philosophy.

Conclusion

The themes of the present book, such as nature-history and the philosophical implications of art in relation to the 'fall' of metaphysics, lead in a different direction to much of contemporary philosophy, from attempts to restore metaphysics and reductionist naturalisms in the analytical tradition, to aspects of the new Hegelianism and recent directions in French philosophy, including new approaches to metaphysics, in the European tradition. The underlying issue which connects these disparate directions is the understanding of 'meaning' in the face of a world whose workings are explained more and more effectively by the modern sciences.

Heidegger already mapped out some of the tensions in contemporary philosophy in his 1964 essay on 'The End of Philosophy and the Task of Thinking'. He focuses his interpretation of the 'end of philosophy' on the idea that 'metaphysics', as conceived of in the Western philosophical tradition since the Greeks, has actually become modern natural science. The explanation of the ground of what there is that was sought by philosophy is now achieved with unparalleled success by experimental science. The emergence of 'cybernetics', information theory, which Heidegger sees as the core of a technological approach based on modern scientific method, replaces philosophical investigation of 'the ontologies [in the sense of the grounding background assumptions that constitute the meaning of these regions] of the respective regions of entities (nature, history, law, art)' (Heidegger 1988, p. 65). The fact that philosophical investigation based on the results of scientific methods is essentially linked to technological control, based on theory and prediction, means that what Heidegger himself seeks is to be thought of no longer as philosophy, but rather as what he terms 'thinking'. Heidegger is concerned here with kinds of understanding which are reducible neither to scientific explanation, nor, looking at what underlies his approach in a contemporary perspective, to description in revised metaphysical terms which seek to find 'what fundamental kinds of things there are and what properties and relations they have' (Williamson 2007, p. 19). The question here is what the status is of these kinds of understanding – which Charles Taylor, in the wake of Heidegger, terms 'disclosive' – given the privilege accorded to well-warranted science and the orientation of so much analytical philosophy towards representationalist accounts of cognition.

Adorno can show how some of the contemporary concern with naturalism and metaphysics should also be understood as part of 'nature-history', rather than solely in terms of its own aims. This can be suggested via the history of the reception of the Vienna Circle. The move within analytical philosophy from the Vienna Circle's desire to overcome metaphysics in the name of empirical science to versions of the contemporary analytical aim of a new metaphysics is an example of nature-history which can be understood via a perspective not involved in either of the differing approaches. Why, quite simply, do the logical empiricist vision and its developments dominate philosophy for a significant period, but then diminish so radically in importance? The answer in the terms we have considered via Adorno does not lie at the level of the refutation of the philosophical arguments.[1] Albeit in very different ways, both Heidegger's move towards 'thinking' and the recent versions of the idea that armchair metaphysical reflection can tell us something about the sort of 'fundamental kinds of things there are' are predicated on a sense that restricting ourselves to scientific accounts of the world does not obviate some important questions about the world. In *The Evolution of Modern Metaphysics* A.W. Moore suggests that the latter, unlike the former, however, see it 'as their business to reflect on how reality must be, as opposed to finding out empirically how it happens to be' (Moore 2012, p. 324), and assume that the metaphysical account will be 'a pursuit of truth *of fundamentally the same kind as the natural sciences*' (ibid., p. 584).

As I have suggested, natural science seems better than recent analytical metaphysics at telling us what fundamental kinds of things there are, because what it tells us has enormous effects on what we do, of a kind such metaphysics demonstrably does not. Whether knowing what fundamental kinds of things there are is really the decisive task for philosophical thinking is, of course, itself open to question, not least the question of what the idea means. Fundamental can, for example, just mean that the things are understandable in ways which make us generally able to make predictions about them and control them. But this understanding is, of course, also a potential source of blindness, as Adorno and Heidegger suggest, and this is where I think the philosophical issues lie. Moore suggests that the difference between contemporary naturalist metaphysics and early modern metaphysicians, such as Hegel, is that the latter 'brought a due regard, not only for the things, and not only for the things together with the sense made of them, but for the making of that sense. Metaphysics in the early modern period had a distinctive kind of self-consciousness that naturalistic metaphysics lacks' (ibid., p. 342). The real issue here is, then, once again, how one thinks about meaning. What is in question is the nature of philosophical responses to Max Weber's idea of the disenchantment of the world in modernity, hence the divergences over questions of meaning between, on the one hand, narrow semantic and realist approaches which try to develop theories which mimic those in the sciences while doing no empirical research and, on the other, approaches, like Adorno's, that have a much wider sense of what it is for something to mean something.

Both Adorno and Heidegger make disenchantment central to their thinking. The Adornian question is how one responds to what is lost, and gained, from disenchantment, a question which is central, for example, to Charles Taylor's recent work on secularization (see Taylor 2007). From the point of view of philosophy which defines its role in relation to the ways that the natural sciences increasingly occupy formerly philosophical territory, what is at issue here may seem either to lack the perceived rigour of the arguments in metaphysics or epistemology that constitute their own agenda, or to be harking back to something that is irredeemably lost once what gives rise to disenchantment shows itself to be so successful. Questions about meaning of the kind that concern Heidegger and Adorno do not lend themselves to being dealt with as another 'location problem', of the kind we saw in relation to freedom. The problem as seen in the analytical debate is how to explain meaning and other notions not obviously construable in the representational terms that are seen as apt for natural objects – terms which involve looking, for example, for what it is in the world as described by physics, chemistry, and biology that makes our sentences true – as part of a 'naturalist' picture of the world.

However, we saw via Bilgrami's comments in the Introduction, and elsewhere above, that the debate over these issues has tended to lead to the neglect of the more urgent sense that the dominant ways in which humankind relates to nature in modernity can now be said to be in crisis. As Charles Taylor puts it: '[T]he whole ecological movement draws on the sense that there is something wrong, blind, hubristic, even impious in taking this [instrumental] stance to the world, in which the environment is seen exclusively in terms of the human purposes to which it can be put' (Taylor 2011, p. 357). If, following the Adornian approaches we have been exploring, we read the tensions within debates over naturalism, and between these debates and what they fail to attend to, as expressions of contradictions in a contemporary world, where some forms of objectification turn out to have serious unforeseen problematic consequences, we can suggest ways in which the wider import of philosophical issues might be better understood. The indefensible exaggerations of *Dialectic of Enlightenment* should not blind one to the realization that it is prescient with respect to how modern science leads to dilemmas which scientific methods help to analyse, but which, as Heidegger (1961) suggests in his dictum that 'science does not think', causally based scientific explanation cannot itself bring to light. In this perspective the ability of philosophy, suggested in Adorno's reflections on non-identity, to bring to light what is hidden by the dominant modes of responding to the world, which are institutionalized in disciplinary and other structures and practices, matters more than the anyway constitutively contested aim of establishing positive epistemological and metaphysical theories.[2]

The fact that both Heidegger and Adorno give such a central role to art in relation to modern philosophy is an indication of something that should be more regularly questioned in the focus of much contemporary philosophy.[3] The initial issue here has to do with thinking about truth in ways which are not adequately covered by a semantic perspective. In *Heidegger and Unconcealment* (2011), Mark Wrathall suggests a model of how this should be done, and much that he says is congruent with the approaches we have explored in Adorno.[4] Contemporary reductive naturalism assumes that, in the long run, every phenomenon can be located as part of an articulable causal order that will systematically connect physics, chemistry, and biology, hence the frequent assumption that there is no location for 'freedom' in such thinking. Such a conception is, though, as Seel argues (see Chapter 5), based on the dogmatic myth of the 'last analysis', which ignores the fact that critical reflection on knowledge, where some sense of freedom is indispensable, necessarily involves an awareness of knowledge's inherent limits. Wrathall shows how Heidegger's idea of unconcealment can be used to back up such a view: any way in which things are made manifest is never definitive, because being is inherently always also concealing. Scientistic conceptions reduce the world of human meanings that make sense of life to a subordinate or effectively illusory status, in the name of specific truths which have experimental and observational warrant. Dewey's view, as we saw in Chapter 4, is an effective counter to this kind of reduction, which does not involve questioning the legitimacy of good science, a legitimacy which in many respects is more plausibly explained by Brandom in his account of the game of giving reasons, than by philosophical attempts to prove the truth of realism.

However, as the Romantics already suggested, if analysis becomes the dominant modern relationship to the world, it can lead to disintegration of the life-world, and thence to the adoption of mythological forms of meaning as a way of coping with the effects of disenchantment. The crucial issue is how analysis relates to the wider understanding of the world in which the analysis is located, and here the implications of aesthetics for the rest of philosophy become crucial. The dialectical shifts we have examined in the relationship between 'nature' and 'culture' can be understood in terms of the ways in which knowledge of natural laws relates to meanings in the social world. The latter cannot be explained away in terms of the former, both because, as Heidegger shows, knowledge of natural laws could not come about at all without prior understandings of being, and because such meanings often have to be manifested in expressive forms which are not reducible to the ways in which they can be discursively analysed.[5] The tensions that result here form precisely the domain in which there is still a role to play for philosophy that moves in the direction we have been exploring via Adorno.

Responses to the dissonance between the success of the sciences and the enduring divergences in epistemological accounts of how knowledge is constituted (or of what knowledge is) are a significant indicator of the differing ways in which the ends of philosophy are understood, both within analytical and European approaches, and between them. Since German Idealism in particular, the sense that such divergences are the result of a misconception of the nature of the mind/world relationship has recurred in philosophy, and contemporary Hegelianism is a further manifestation of the need to seek ways beyond the divergences. Brandom offers some plausible reasons why a reinterpretation of the German Idealism-influenced pragmatist tradition, which gives primacy to practical intentionality over representationalist intentionality, offers one way beyond the dissonance between the successes of science and the failures of epistemology: 'For the first time, the rational practices embodying the paradigmatic sort of reason exercised by scientists understanding natural processes become visible as continuous with, and intelligible in just the same terms as, the physical processes paradigmatic of what is understood' (Brandom 2011, p. 40). Aspects of the kind of 'naturalism' present here are not wholly at odds with Adorno's version of a 'naturalistic' perspective.[6] At the same time, what Brandom outlines *is* a kind of identity philosophy, which Adorno criticizes for its tendency to neglect how the subject's practices may not be fully transparent to the subject. The crucial question is how one conceives of nature, and I have tried to show that the neo-Hegelian attempt to 'leave nature behind' in the name of norm-governed self-determination raises issues about why rational practices can result in such irrational consequences. I do not have a decisive argument to defend this claim, and Adorno would not have claimed to have one either. It is the sheer force of the historical experience of how modern rationalized societies can go so wrong that lies behind the pressure for a philosophical approach which does not lose sight of the historically concrete ways in which rationality can turn against itself.

The neo-Hegelian approach, and particularly Brandom's emphatically rationalist version of it, does not always sufficiently reflect how divergences between philosophical theories of knowledge and the progress of the sciences relate to the differing meanings that forms of knowledge acquire in new social and historical contexts. The divergences point to the idea that conflicting understandings of what is rational are not just philosophical disagreements, but expressions of real contradictions between what we do and what we take ourselves to be doing. Disputing the criticism that in his *Debt: The First 5,000 Years* (2011) he is unnecessarily antagonistic to impersonal mechanisms of exchange of the kind that Adorno makes central to his reflections on commodification and its effects on consciousness, David Graeber suggests with respect to the assumptions of economics as presently constituted:

> [E]conomics is a field that largely creates the reality it describes and then naturalizes it, and by doing so, [economists are] doing us all a world of harm. [. . .] [T]he reason is because they do not actually eliminate human passions or moralities. They just select one or two – the passion of acquisitiveness, the morality of debt – and treat them as if they are the only ones relevant to the transfer of goods and services, or even, for the most ambitious economistic thinkers, the only ones relevant to anything at all. I don't think that there are impersonal mechanisms and the problem is they sometimes go crazy. I think the main problem is there is a craziness already lying behind what we take to be impersonal mechanisms. (Graeber 2012)

From Adorno's vantage point, contradictions in forms of explanation of the world and forms of exchange, from the material to the symbolic, resist being resolved into an overall philosophical picture of the development of rationality, and thus point to a different image of the ends of philosophy. The revelation of the irrationality of social mechanisms may only be possible in terms of moving imaginatively and expressively beyond the given in art, or, as in Graeber's book, in terms of alternatives, discovered by historical and anthropological research, that have been forgotten or repressed to such an extent that the present state of things has come to seem natural.[7] The urgency of rethinking what has come to be seen as rational in the contemporary world is well captured by Slavoj Žižek's observation that it seems easier for contemporary culture to imagine the end of the world than to imagine the end of the present unjust and destructive world economic order (Žižek 2011; see also Hammer 2006).

Twentieth-century history involves a repeated failure to appreciate how dominant rationalizing trends, while enabling many essential advances, also produce effects that conflict with the putative rational aims of those involved. Critical Theory originated precisely, as we saw, from the intellectual failure to appreciate the real sources of the catastrophic nature of the First World War. Adorno insists on a vigilance based on the assumption that philosophy may neglect other kinds of non-cognitive relationship to the world – of the kind Honneth suggested in Chapter 2 – that are crucial in understanding the pathologies of modernity. This stance can be seen in certain respects as complementary to Brandom's and others' questioning of representationalist epistemologies in the name of versions of pragmatism – the shared Hegelian heritage, in which holistic considerations are central, suggests why – but it also poses other questions about the ends of contemporary philosophy.

Should philosophy, for example, still focus predominantly on explanatory theory construction, or should it instead try to interpret the very obvious radical conflicts between perspectives which are characteristic of the actual practice of contemporary philosophy? In the first case, philosophy still mainly seeks to ground the cognitive ways in which we determine what there is; in the second, philosophy, while in one sense also seeking to do this, is concerned with how we can critically relate to a world in which some forms of attempted determination of what there is can themselves have damaging consequences. As Wellmer maintained with respect to reductive naturalism: 'But even if it is false, it could yet be *effective* – the enthusiasm with which it is often received in the media shows that it is not wholly without effects' (Wellmer 2009, p. 225). We don't know when philosophical theories are true in the way we sometimes know scientific ones are, insofar as they enable real advances in technological and other capacities. The second approach consequently builds in what Adorno sees in terms of non-identity, namely the sense that positive determination of what there is always remains liable to blindness, and so needs to think against its own forms of determination. It is not that philosophy should, as trivially it always must, just be self-critical, but that it should build the sense of its own potentially repressive nature into the way in which it is presented. This is not something that Adorno himself always succeeds in doing.

The latter critical option might seem to demand precisely the kind of meta-perspective which it itself rejects. However, this is not necessarily the case. In my *Music, Philosophy, and Modernity* (2007), I suggested, following Herbert Schnädelbach (1987), a distinction between 'metaphysics[1']' and 'metaphysics[2']'. It should be clear, then, that what is suggested here is opposed not to 'metaphysics' *per se*, but to the idea of metaphysics suggested by Heidegger and Adorno, which seeks a definitive picture of reality in opposition to a world which they see as denying the very possibility of such a picture. A.W. Moore suggests: '[I]t simply may not be possible to make (some kinds of sense) of things. We must take very seriously Adorno's question of what the prospects are for metaphysics after Auschwitz' (Moore 2012, p. 6). Consequently, the real issue lies not in the name 'metaphysics', but in the kinds of sense that philosophy seeks to establish.

Metaphysics[1] is what Heidegger sees as culminating in the replacement of metaphysics by natural science. Schnädelbach, echoing Adorno's sense of 'experience', refers to metaphysics[2] as 'negative metaphysics': 'the warranted reminder that discourse does not have complete control of the true and the good: that there is something here which cannot be anticipated by a method, but which must show itself and be experienced' (Schnädelbach 1987, pp. 171–2). In a sign of his awareness of how issues linked to aesthetics pose a challenge to the Hegelian story in the way I have tried to suggest, Robert Pippin suggests an example of what is meant here when he reflects:

> At some point the Hegelian categories just run out, and then you get the Frankfurt School's account, and the accounts of structuralism, post-structuralism, Freudian or Lacanian psychoanalysis, all of them trying to get at what's going wrong in the basic, fundamental structure of human desire formation. Let's say that the problem is deeper than one Hegel could deal with. Nietzsche was one of the first to see that the problem in sustaining a massive common culture is that the resultant form of life sustains no great desire. It is flat, boring, and uninspirational. Hegel did not fully understand the nature of this issue. It would have astonished him that, just as Enlightenment rationalism was beginning to pay off on all its great claims, with decreased infant mortality, public health, the rule of law, and so on, all the great artists and intellectuals of 19th century Europe rose up in disgust and said, 'No, it's not what we wanted.' It was the beginning of the great bourgeois self-hatred that you see so much of in art. (Pippin 2011)

Pippin is rightly critical of the Adorno who overestimates the significance of high modernism, but his subsequent remarks on why art is central to the understanding of modernity are very much in line with the neglected elements of Adorno I sought to highlight in Chapter 6:

> So much of the modern layout of the problem, the hard-to-pin-down but pervasive sense of the 'wrongness' of society, seems to bypass politics by pointing to a level of engagement that is so deep behind consciousness that we cannot reach it. Art, precisely because it is a mode of non-discursive intelligibility, which does not consist in propositions, arguments, and syllogisms, nonetheless makes sense of ourselves in a way that actually resonates with what is now coming onto the scene as more important than the conscious deliberative capacities of individual subjects. (Ibid.)

What Pippin is addressing here is precisely what leads Adorno to rethink the idea of 'nature', as that which can suffer, be damaged and repressed, against the reduction of nature to the 'formal' sense, of the kind that is epitomized by contemporary reductive naturalism.[8]

The key here is how philosophy attends to what can be hidden by dominant forms of articulation, from the sciences, to philosophy itself. Precisely because art's ways of making sense involve non-discursive forms of engagement with the world, they can make more accessible what is otherwise likely to be concealed. Many very diverse philosophical approaches these days accept that some kind of 'naturalism' is inevitable, if implausible metaphysical commitments are to be avoided and due weight is to be given to the results of modern natural science. What Adorno offers in this respect are ways of incorporating the 'level of engagement' inherent in our status as needy, impulsive, vulnerable natural beings into how we should think about naturalism. Reductive naturalism presupposes an objective nature which is fully 'present', awaiting its incorporation into the ever-expanding domain of explanatory science. The result is the 'Idealism' that is Adorno's constant target, because it inflates one perspective for interpreting the world into the basis for all others.

The core of Adorno's approach to meaning is that meaning also results from the need to transcend given states of the world. That is why he is suspicious of the philosophical concentration on epistemology, and attributes such importance to what art may reveal. An exclusively analytical focus renders effectively impossible the kind of location of knowledge within a wider totality demanded by Adorno. What is at issue here is how 'worlds' are constituted – Markus Gabriel refers to 'domains of sense' (Gabriel 2011)[9] – which Adorno, as we saw, addressed in terms of the notion of historical constellations in which things become intelligible. Part of any constellation may well be the best scientific accounts we have, but these have to be examined in terms of the meanings of the world in which they are located, which can change the meaning of what we know. This can be illustrated by the history of psychology, where the understanding of a notional pathology differs radically in relation to the constellation in which it is located, hence the startling conflicts in the interpretation of psychological phenomena in changing social and political contexts.

How, then, should conflicts of interpretation themselves be responded to in philosophy? Arguing against Badiou, and in line with Adorno's attention to the centrality of art for philosophy, Gabriel suggests that

> [t]here might be a universe of purely quantifiable objects, but this universe is smaller than the world, because the world encompasses a plurality of domains, the universe of physics or mathematics being just some domains of objects among others. The formation of a set of senseless, uninterpreted (mathematical) objects cannot furnish us with the

> ontology of all domains, because there is no such thing as an underlying pure multiplicity in a work of art (to name but one example). Works of art do not have a unified structure of sense; they do not form a single world in Badiou's sense, but open up different worlds. (Gabriel 2012, Introduction, Location 502)

The Heideggerian idea that art opens up worlds is congruent with much that we have seen in Adorno, but there is a specific dimension not specifically addressed in Gabriel's transcendental ontology which is the source of Adorno's particular – controversial – status in relation to contemporary philosophical discussion.

Underlying Adorno's work is the awareness that the modern world is capable of the radical destruction of sense, in ways which were not possible prior to modernity. This awareness of the fragility and the dangers inherent in how sense is made in a disenchanted world often singles Adorno out from related perspectives in the European tradition, and is almost totally lacking in analytical reflection on questions of meaning. Adorno offers a reminder that it can be more urgent for philosophy to ponder sources of blindness and the destruction of meaning than to concern itself, for example, with epistemological problems in areas where scientific focus on specific areas of nature leads to more and more warrantable insight. When Adorno makes his reflections into a general verdict, of the kind present in his inversion of the Hegelian dictum that the 'whole is the true' into 'the whole is the untrue', he opens himself to the sort of criticisms which have prevented his best ideas becoming part of mainstream philosophy. Not all Adorno's approaches can be mobilized for a change in the agenda of contemporary philosophy. Some of his ideas can, however, focus the implications of the kind of unease addressed by Pippin in his remarks on how the 'wrongness' of modern society needs the kind of forms of articulation present in modernism, which philosophy can obscure.

The bizarrely narrow focus of the philosophy of art in the analytical tradition is, in this context, a symptom of something which is significant in a way such philosophy of art itself is not. Its lack of reflection on how art might ask serious questions of philosophy offers an example of how philosophy itself can obscure our access to vital aspects of modern life. We may well question Adorno's specific interpretations of the classics of high modernism, from Kafka and Beckett, to Mahler and Webern, and beyond, but his attempts to see how they deal with the disintegration of so many established ways of making sense do address important questions which too much philosophy never even goes near. I have quoted this passage on Mahler's *Das Lied von der Erde* before, in the Adorno chapter of *Music, Philosophy, and Modernity*, because it epitomizes why metaphysics[2] seems an ineliminable element of what philosophy should concern itself with:

> The first song says that it [the earth] stands firm for a long time – not eternally – and the one who says farewell even calls it the dear earth, as it is disappearing. For the work [i.e. *Das Lied*] it [the earth] is not the universe, but what fifty years later someone flying at a great height may have caught up with, a star. For the gaze of the music which is leaving the earth it curves into a surveyable sphere, in the way it has in the meanwhile already been photographed from space: not the centre of creation, but something tiny and ephemeral. [. . .] But the earth which has moved far away from itself lacks the hope which the stars once promised. It is submerged in empty galaxies. On it beauty lies as a reflection of past hope which fills the dying eye until it freezes under the flakes of now unlimited space. The moment of rapture at such beauty dares to stand up to the spell of disenchanted nature. That metaphysics is no longer possible becomes the last metaphysics. (Adorno 1997, 13, p. 297)

The point about such a paradoxical passage is that it gestures towards forms of meaning which can only be properly understood through simultaneous engagement with the non-discursive form of the specific music which the passage is addressing. It is this demand to take in all forms of possible sense-making that is decisive.

For Adorno metaphysics, *qua* making ultimate sense of the world, can no longer be articulated in a positive form, but what, like Mahler's *Lied*, expresses that impossibility now plays the role of making sense of the lack of ultimate sense. This situation constitutes in one respect the 'end' of philosophy that seeks to make universal sense of the kind that would give life *per se* meaning. In 'Meditations on Metaphysics' from *Negative Dialectics*, Adorno maintains that thought that 'does not measure itself against the most extreme things which escape concepts' is like the music the SS used to 'drown the cries of their victims' (Adorno 1997, 6, p. 358). The extremity of the demand seems to me in this case justified with respect to what should be expected of contemporary metaphysics, even if the demand cannot be fulfilled. But how can philosophy even try to measure itself in this way? The 'triumph and failure of culture' (ibid., p. 359) lies in its repression of the underlying lack of ultimate sense and the horrors that are part of finite, embodied existence, which leads Adorno to the 'materialism' discussed in Chapter 4. The repression which enables us to cope with the awareness of inevitable decay can easily conspire with what leads to reification and cruelty, in the form of attempts to dominate nature of the kind that are the constant concern of Adorno's critical approaches. So how are we to achieve more than what the Nietzsche of *The Birth of Tragedy* saw as the creation of beautiful illusion?

Adorno sees culture and repression as inextricably linked. All that is possible is critical and imaginative reflection on the consequences of the link. That is the task of philosophy, which needs art to help it with the task, and art in turn needs the capacity for critical reflection to avoid merely adding to the delusions that lead to the 'extreme things'. The challenge to philosophy which seeks to salvage what can be salvaged from the end of redemptive metaphysics is that '[t]hose who plead for the preservation of radically guilty and shabby culture make themselves into accomplices, while those who refuse culture directly promote the barbarism as which culture revealed itself' (ibid., p. 360). This claim might seem to block any possibility of change for the better, but Adorno's rejection of timeless concepts applies here as well: the challenge is to work towards forms of culture which diminish barbarism precisely by attending to 'the most extreme things' and responding to them more adequately. Even death, he insists, is different in differing historical circumstances: '[S]ince Auschwitz being afraid of death means fearing what is worse than death' (ibid.). The negative point about death also allows for the possibility of a reversal. The reason is that nothing can be definitively established by a philosophical answer to what things really are, because there can always be a moment which forces one beyond the given: '[N]othing could be experienced as truly something living that did not also promise something which transcends life' (ibid., p. 368). Later Adorno says: 'What is said by finite beings about transcendence is its appearance/illusion [*Schein*], but, as Kant realized, a necessary appearance/illusion. That is why the salvaging [*Rettung*] of appearance/illusion, the object of aesthetics, is incomparably relevant to metaphysics' (ibid., p. 386).

Instead of the Kantian epistemological question of whether metaphysics is possible, Adorno thinks the question should be 'whether metaphysical experience is still possible' (ibid., p. 365). He exemplifies metaphysical experience by childhood happiness, which relates to the unique particularity of things, such that 'happiness, the only thing in metaphysical experience that is more than impotent craving [*Verlangen*], grants the interior of things as being at the same time something which is removed from them' (ibid., p. 367). The child's fantasy of the special place – he cites Proust's reflections on childhood fantasies about place names – is not realized by reaching the place, but such fantasies make sense by the way in which they offer a renewable promise of something beyond the mundane. Metaphysical experience is the promise that children see in things, which may not be fulfilled, but which need not disappear when the fulfilment does not occur. The broader point of what might seem to be the endowment of something very local with too grand a significance is that instead of meaning in the emphatic sense at issue here being something which is achieved by a definitive grasping of sense and by conceptual resolution of a dilemma, it is what is manifest when the world promises something beyond the given. This is not as paradoxical as it might sound: it is, for instance, obviously congruent with Adorno's reflections on aesthetics.

Moreover, Adorno thinks that general philosophical answers to questions about the meaning of life create the problem they are supposed to solve, by seeking to arrive at a unified, definitive sense, when this is itself precisely what may empty individual lives of meaning. The mistake lies in the form of the question: '[T]he thesis that life has no meaning is, as a positive thesis, just as absurd as its opposite is false' (ibid., p. 370). Adorno suggests that it is pointless to tell someone contemplating suicide the supposed meaning of life, but 'abstract nihilism' which asserts that life has no meaning must face the question as to why the person advancing this view is still alive. The passages in which these reflections occur become almost impenetrably complex, acknowledging forms of meaning, including theological ones, only to reveal their complicity with delusion. However, in this case the complexity is, in a way that in other cases it often is not, the result of Adorno's justified refusal to think that clear philosophical answers resolve metaphysical questions. We can approach such questions only in the concrete process of revealing both what generates meaning and what it is in this generation that can also contribute to delusion and the destruction of meaning. This combination, which can only be realized by immersing oneself in all the specific ways in which sense is made in human culture, is still too rare in contemporary philosophy.

The elements of Adorno's work which suggest that we live in a 'total context of delusion' and which claim that modern life is irredeemably damaged need to be seen in relation to the reflections on meaning just cited, which make it clear how totalizing claims lead to contradictions. Adorno's extreme views are the understandable product of the defining events of his time, events which play no real role in Anglophone philosophy's reflections on the nature of meaning. At the same time, some of what he claimed in an exaggerated fashion in his era has now come to seem less exaggerated: the culture industry's relentless promotion of the saleable over the aesthetically significant, ecological devastation, rapacious capitalism, can all hardly be said to have become less of a threat in the meanwhile.[10] The extremes here cannot simply be resolved into a complacently rational philosophical judgement on the making of sense. The point with respect to contemporary philosophy is that Adorno both questions metaphysical claims to establish how things make sense as a whole, on the grounds that in the modern world such totalizing claims can be too closely allied to the negative effects of reification and rationalization, and yet at the same time demands resources for sustaining more than local sense in a world where so many factors conspire to destroy it.

The history of modern philosophy can be crudely seen as involving an oscillation between the extremes of the idea that all sense is ultimately generated by the subject, and the idea that what enables the subject to do this is actually objective nature. John McDowell's desire to escape from the oscillation, characteristic of key areas of contemporary philosophy, between Davidsonian 'coherentism' and the 'bald naturalist' 'myth of the given' is just one recent example of the responses to the ramifications of this history that much of Adorno's work is an attempt to get beyond. There is, though, another, related oscillation that is arguably culturally more significant, and less focused on epistemological considerations. This is between the appeal to kinds of transcendence that are a source of the meanings that motivate human lives, on the one hand, and the idea that the very idea of transcendence is mere illusion that is invalidated by the fact of disenchanted nature, on the other. Many contemporary cultural and political conflicts can be understood in terms of the effects of such oscillation. The future philosophical significance of Adorno will, I suspect, depend on the extent to which his work can inform the growing awareness that too much contemporary philosophy is blind to how focus on meaning based too exclusively on semantic and cognitive considerations may obscure our understanding of meanings that can both motivate and sustain lives and inhibit, distort, and destroy them.

Such a generalized formulation of different approaches to meaning may seem impossible to concretize in a philosophically adequate fashion. The difficulty of the demands that emerge from Adorno's manner of doing philosophy is evident in his own failures with respect to the assessment of some concrete issues. These failures do not, though, invalidate the motivation that leads to them, which is the attempt to make sense in a world whose complexity and contradictory nature constantly threaten our ability to comprehend it. The attention to technical analysis of very specific philosophical issues that dominates academic philosophy in most of the Anglophone world can be a resource for our attempts to comprehend the modern world, but without highly developed means of connecting specific issues to their role in their wider cultural context, such resources are likely to remain ineffective. For all his faults, Adorno offers reminders of why we must make such connections, and some still useable models of how this can be achieved.

Notes

Introduction: Contemporary Alternatives

1 Bilgrami does not mention Adorno, but his sources include Nietzsche, who was a major influence on Adorno.
2 Lee Braver (2007) shows how the debate can be seen as central to modern philosophy, but much of the analytical debate lacks Braver's historical perspective.
3 It would, though, be worth making a list of the specialized areas which have effectively disappeared from philosophical view even in the last fifty years. See Bieri (2007), who argues that many concerns even of contemporary analytical philosophy have ceased really to matter.
4 Following Bernard Williams, A.W. Moore makes a further distinction between history of philosophy and history of ideas, seeing the former as 'in the first instance philosophy, not history' (Moore 2012, location 380).
5 The tendency in analytical philosophy is to see such matters in terms of beliefs about persons. We don't, though, just relate to people in terms of – often contradictory – beliefs about them, but rather do so in terms of complexes of feelings which may well resist verbal articulation.
6 It is, though, open to dispute as to just how far the positions of Popper and Adorno are fundamentally incompatible (see Bowie 2000).
7 Some of these lectures appeared in pirated editions, many of which are now very hard to find, some of which are reliable, others not.
8 This is a photocopy of the unpublished lectures in the Adorno Archiv, Akademie der Künste, Berlin. The complexity and diversity of views in the Vienna Circle is often forgotten, in the name of pursuing just those issues which made it onto the agenda of mainstream analytical philosophy (see Bowie 2000; Friedman 1999).
9 Zygmunt Bauman (1991) makes a similar point about the Holocaust with respect to the focus of attention of sociology.
10 I am not proposing an abandonment of careful attention to the use of key concepts, but rather an emphasis on what this sort of attention can exclude, if it fails to take account of historical considerations.
11 See Bowie (2007) for an exploration of this tension in which music is seen

as playing a central role in modern assumptions about language, an idea which is almost wholly absent from analytical philosophy. It is not as if arguments pointing to the deficits of the 'mathematically inspired tradition' did not exist until they were formulated in an analytical idiom: Hamann already suggested in 1784 that Kant fell prey to the reduction of language in this manner (see Bowie 1997, 2003a; Forster 2010).
12 The latter is too often omitted from consideration of conceptions of freedom and is not simply a form of self-determination.
13 I will capitalize the word when it is used in Adorno's sense.
14 'Determinate negation' means that the refutation of a theory leads not to nothingness, but to another theory that could not exist without the one that it refutes. No Galileo without Ptolemy. There are, for Hegel, no positive foundational theories, only the process of negation itself.
15 Rorty suggests that whereas we have norms for talking about snow, we don't for talking about 'Reality', and this would be in line with Adorno's view here.
16 On this see Bauman (1991) – however contentious this account may be, it poses questions which cannot be ignored.
17 That is the main reason why I have not engaged in any detail with the now extensive secondary literature on Adorno. My focus is on how Adorno can be used to criticize the agenda of contemporary philosophy.
18 Although my approach is quite different, its concentration on underplayed aspects of Adorno echoes Seel (2004).

Chapter 1 Negative Philosophy?

1 Adorno generally opposed Heidegger, often in a not necessarily very adequate way, but at key points he makes explicit his agreement with certain core ideas, especially in the earlier Heidegger.
2 In some respects Adorno's exaggerated evaluations of the modernism of the Second Viennese School (Toulmin discusses the School in this context) might be considered to be related to this development. His position is, though, broadly in agreement with Toulmin's diagnosis in other respects.
3 But see reflection 46 of *Minima Moralia* (Adorno 1997, 4, pp. 82–3), which suggests that even this stance can be problematic.
4 On reification, see the discussion in Chapter 2.
5 This phrase is also central to Adorno's pupil Habermas in his *Knowledge and Human Interests* (Habermas 1973).
6 As a cyclist in Cambridge I never cease to be amazed at the vitriolic attitude of motorists to cyclists, when it is the former who can kill the latter, and not vice versa. Adorno would interpret this in terms of how reification can determine consciousness. He often argues that such apparently trivial examples are the key to non-trivial instances of inhuman behaviour in changed historical circumstances.
7 This sounds somewhat dismissive, but it is a notable factor of these approaches that arguments which dominate for a period soon come to be seen as irrelevant or completely outmoded. The lack of reflection on this fact

within most analytical philosophy is a source of bemusement for those who are suspicious of an exclusively analytical approach.
8 The word 'truth-content' appears 293 times in Adorno's *Collected Writings*, and is notoriously hard to explicate.
9 This example is discussed in more detail in Adorno's unfinished book on Beethoven (Adorno 1993).
10 The notion of 'idea' in Benjamin's version of the notion of truth-content has clear metaphysical and theological implications, based on Benjamin's perennial desire to redeem the transience inherent in modernity. Adorno does not rely on these implications for what he intends.
11 There is some similarity between this idea and Badiou's 'truth-event'

Chapter 2 Contradiction as Truth-Content: Adorno and Kant

1 For a critical reading of Adorno on Kant, see Pippin (2005). Pippin concentrates on *Negative Dialectics*, which often states Adorno's case in a misleadingly extreme way. The version of Kant in the lectures is not susceptible to all the critical points made by Pippin (see Chapter 5 below). Pippin argues that Adorno's own position is Kantian in many respects, and Adorno says the same in the lectures 'Introduction to Philosophy', and this suggests the problem with Adorno's overly emphatic stances in *Negative Dialectics*. See also O'Connor (2004), Chapter 4.
2 It is Fichte who makes the ability to reflect in this way the absolute moment in subjectivity. Kant scholars differ on the extent to which this is an adequate interpretation of Kant. However, the idea of the absolute status of the capacity for reflection is crucial for German Idealism, and Robert Pippin, for example, argues for the absolute status of reflection. Adorno can legitimate this account from aspects of Kant's text, but he is most interested in how the idea becomes historically effective.
3 The role of Jacobi in the genesis of German Idealism is vital here, as a thinker who was very aware of the sceptical tradition (see Bowie 1997; Frank 1997).
4 See Johnson (2008) for the best response to reductionist, representationalist neuroscience – which itself uses neuroscience that is philosophically plausible
5 This is unfair to McDowell: in other respects he has quite a broad focus, but my comment is not inappropriate for this specific issue.
6 Pippin (2005) makes the unsuccessful approaches very clear.
7 The book's political reliance on the idea of the Communist Party as that which would channel the critical insights of the proletariat is now so discredited that we can safely ignore it. The book's most important contentions do not depend on its mistaken political diagnosis.
8 Such hatred can be encouraged by modern structures of thought and action, as the fact that it is intensified or diminishes in relation to economic changes suggests, but it should not be reduced to these structures.
9 This view echoes McDowell's questioning of Davidson's 'coherentist' claim that 'nothing can count as the reason for holding a belief except another belief' (cited in McDowell 1994, p. 24).
10 Adorno does not discuss the *Critique of Judgement* in this context, which

would provide further back-up for his contentions about the ambivalences in Kant. Kant's hints of a different kind of connection to the natural world in the third Critique will relate to what Adorno says about 'mimesis'.

Chapter 3 Immediacy and Mediation: Hegelian and Adornian Dialectics

1. O'Connor (2004) deals with Adorno and Hegel from the metaphysical perspective on Hegel, but not from the non-metaphysical perspective.
2. This conflict is apparent in the differing aims with regard to Hegel of Frederick Beiser, who takes a historicist view, and Robert Pippin (see below), for example, and the conflict is a manifestation of a tension in contemporary society about how to relate to the past, which connects to many political and social tensions.
3. On the centrality of suffering in Adorno, see Foster (2007).
4. Pippin is least open to this criticism, as I suggest at various points later, especially in the Conclusion. My divergences from Pippin are based on a lot of agreement in key areas.
5. Pippin's remarks on modernism as an expression of a sense of 'wrongness' in modern society, discussed in the Conclusion, suggest he is aware of the deficit here.
6. On this see Bernstein (2001).
7. The objection here is that nobody can ever be sure of the consequences of his or her actions in any kind of society. There is, though, a difference of degree between action in a traditional society which does not have extensive links to the rest of the world or substantial technological resources and action in the interconnected world of global commodity exchange and modern technology. In the latter the subject's ability to see through circumstances to the right course of action is systemically obstructed. See Chapter 5 below.
8. Adorno's use of the 'primacy of the objective' can be a problem: he sometimes should say the 'primacy of being', but the sense here is clear (see Bowie 1995).
9. The idea derives from Walter Benjamin, but Adorno often uses it in a more pragmatic way than Benjamin, who tends to see it in metaphysical terms, as a way of restoring a substantial link between signifier and signified (see Bowie 1997, Chapter 8).
10. As Honneth and others point out, Adorno links the idea of the constellation to a reinterpretation of Weber's use of 'ideal types' in understanding social phenomena (see Adorno 1997, 6, p. 167).
11. Brandom argues something similar, but then gives priority to expressing claims as the key to understanding language, whereas Adorno does not prioritize a particular dimension of language, because he sees it as always involving a tension between the logical and the mimetic.
12. On Adorno and Husserl, see O'Connor (2004), Chapter 5.
13. Brandom is clear that culture is endlessly diverse, but he thinks what founds it is the game of giving and asking for reasons.

Chapter 4 Nature

1. But see Bowie (2010) for a different view of 'unconscious productivity', which seeks to counter the accusation of dogmatism.
2. On Adorno and nature see Cook (2011), who makes links to ecological thinkers, like Arne Naess.
3. See the summary of the analytical debates in Aydede (2013), which, characteristically, only touches on the moral issue at the very end.
4. Alvin Plantinga and others try to show that even such events do not legitimate the argument that God should not have made a creation in which such things are possible (see Gutting 2007). Adorno thinks that trying to use philosophical arguments in theology to come to metaphysical terms with the horror does an injustice to those who suffered it by trying to give their suffering meaning.
5. For Adorno's positive response to Dewey, see Adorno (2003), p. 128.
6. I have given the page numbers of the English translation, but have myself translated most of the quoted passages from a manuscript kindly provided by the author.
7. See Pippin (2000), who argues that what Fichte aims at is showing the mythical status of 'the given'.
8. See Bowie (2007) for a critical appraisal.
9. Atonality has now become just one musical tool, rather than having any kind of necessarily progressive status. This situation does not fit Adorno's more dogmatic contentions about music, where he seems at times to espouse a progressivism that his other thought abjures.
10. Whether the criticism is adequate to Heidegger's approach depends on how Heidegger is to be understood. Cristina Lafont offers a case that would back up Adorno's view, claiming that Heidegger thinks there is a fixed horizon of possibilities of understanding being: 'The "world-disclosure" – the unfoldedness – which language "contains in itself" regulates and distributes the possibilities within which the other sources of disclosure (such as moods) can move' (Lafont 1994, p. 74). Pragmatist readings, like those of Hubert Dreyfus, Mark Okrent, and Charles Taylor, see world-disclosure and historicity in less rigid terms. Mark Wrathall (2011) does a lot to counter Lafont's reading. On Heidegger and Adorno, see Mörchen (1981).
11. The former is the published title, the latter the literal translation of the title.

Chapter 5 Freedom

1. On Adorno and ethics, see Bernstein (2001); on Adorno and freedom, see Hearfield (2004).
2. The history of the succeeding editions of the *Diagnostic and Statistical Manual of Mental Disorders* reflects what is at issue here. What counts as a mental illness, and the consensus on the means of treating mental illness, shift in relation to a whole series of social and ideological pressures. As brain science develops in explanatory power and sophistication, the move towards chemical intervention in the *Manual* might seem to be backed

by 'good science', but this move is also influenced by the pharmaceutical industry.

3 Whether Pippin offers an adequate account of Hegel is not the issue here. He rightly argues that 'pious paraphrase' and 'radical text-free reconstruction' (Pippin 2008, p. 33) are not the best alternatives, and sees his work as a 'philosophical engagement' with Hegel. Adorno talks in similar terms. That aspects of Hegel's *Philosophy of Right* are highly questionable seems indubitable, so the issue is how far what Hegel says can illuminate contemporary moral philosophy. The interpretative charity Pippin uses with respect to Hegel is, though, often rather lacking when he talks about Adorno.

4 In many analytical debates both sides often have something plausible to offer moral reflection and understanding, which suggests, as Pippin implies, that the manner of arguing in such debates is inadequate to the reality of moral life.

5 See Raymond Geuss' essay 'Outside Ethics' (2003), which frames the issue of an alternative approach to the 'What should I do?' question very effectively.

6 The title means literally 'On the Doctrine of History and Freedom'.

7 On Adorno and Freud, see Sherratt (2002), but see the critical remarks in Cook (2003).

8 Kant's aesthetic ideas in the *Critique of Judgement*, where moral attributes are symbolized in empirical form, can be read as a response to this problem.

9 The last point seems less apposite these days, given the changing roles in the family, but the point about the internalization of norms does not depend on what may be something historically relative.

10 For reasons of space, I have deliberately skirted the now very substantial debate about Habermas' critique of Adorno. Habermas' critique seems apt in relation to works like *Dialectic of Enlightenment*, but the two often appear, especially in the light of some of the lectures, to be closer together than the debate sometimes suggests. The weakness in Habermas' approach, I would argue, lies in his attempt to circumscribe cognitive, moral, and aesthetic spheres of communicative action in modernity, when each of these can have effects on the others. Habermas' recent interest in the semantic resources of religious forms derives from his lack of a convincing account of what binds people to norms of communicative action. Adorno is less prone to this problem because he is more alert to aesthetic possibilities of making sense (see Chapter 6).

11 Whether Schelling's use of theological concepts means that he is actually arguing theologically is still disputed; something similar applies, of course, to Hegel.

12 Notably the idea that nobody 'has chosen his character; and yet this does not stop anybody attributing the action which follows from this character to himself as a free action' (Schelling 1946, p. 93). This means that there is some kind of essential decision in the timeless intelligible domain in each person which explains why children can have a 'tendency to evil' even before they are morally aware (Schelling 1856, p. 386).

13 Wolfram Hogrebe has connected this idea to a theory of predication, where the ground is what is designated by the singular term, and what it comes

to be is designated by what can be predicated of that term, which takes it beyond its self-enclosed nature (see Bowie 1993, Chapter 5).
14 Peter Dews first made this point to me.
15 In one respect Kant agrees: the very structure of his conception means that the relationship between what we know about what we do and its moral value cannot be transparent. Even the most selfless act may have a lurking element of empirical pleasure for the one who performs it, which disqualifies it from being pure.
16 Something similar is apparent in Marx's account of alienation: misery and the desire to escape it are ubiquitous and perennial in human life, but it is only when immobile social structures begin to dissolve that the specific modern sense emerges – which connects to the modern issue of freedom – of not being able to realize what one could be.
17 Pippin (2010) has written on this in a related manner.

Chapter 6 Aesthetics and Philosophy

1 On Adorno's aesthetics Huhn and Zuydervaart (1997), Paddison (1997), Roberts (2006), and Zuydervaart (1991).
2 Thanks to David Owen Norris for the clarification of what is specific to Elgar.
3 See Bowie (2007) for a detailed critical appraisal of Adorno's assessments of modern music. In the notes for *Towards a Theory of Musical Reproduction* (Adorno 2001b), Adorno starts to change his mind about jazz in key respects.
4 I do not mean to suggest by this that perception is essentially causally explicable, which is plainly not the case, just that there is an objective level which can be apprehended in terms of photons hitting retinas, and so on.
5 The idea of a lack of respect for God's creation is clearly a significant part of some theological traditions, but it is only when the means for having massive effects on nature emerge that the idea of damaging nature *per se* becomes significant: in Goethe's *Faust* Part II the mediaeval sense of transgression in the Faust legend takes on the thoroughly modern form of transgression of nature by reclaiming land from the sea and using force on those who are in the way.
6 An analytical approach which is compatible with this is suggested by Huw Price, especially in the essay 'Moving the Mirror Aside' (Price 2011).
7 The notion of 'longing' is central to the work of Friedrich Schlegel, and the argument here brings Adorno close to the early German Romantics (see Bowie 2003a).
8 Art works evidently are commodities too, but their value as art works is not their exchange-value. Adorno sees them as 'absolute commodities' because they reject any appearance of use-value, but this claim relies too much on his totalizing assessment of commodification.
9 Auerbach's *Mimesis* (1959) can be read in this perspective, because it shows a tendency for important literature from the beginning in Europe to become more inclusive by taking seriously the experience of more and more levels of society.

10 In such remarks Adorno, as is more often the case than he would admit, comes close to Heidegger's sense of 'letting things be'.
11 These resources can be found in trivial and meretricious art – Adorno himself acknowledges the power of some trivial music – but the Kantian distinction between the beautiful, which involves more than arbitrary preference, and the agreeable, which doesn't, is relevant here. Part of the power of Mahler's music lies in the way in which it salvages the trivial, giving it a kind of truth.
12 One can give too rosy a view of such cultures, which also involve the power struggles present in almost any human enterprise, but the accumulation of well-warranted science is an undeniable fact of the contemporary world. Critical questioning should be directed at the scientist over-extension of the results of areas like biological research into the social realm.
13 See Bowie (2000) for a more differentiated appraisal of the significance of the Vienna Circle of the kind that Adorno seemed incapable of making, despite his initial enthusiasm for some of the ideas of the Circle.
14 Lest this sound merely vague, it is worth remembering that Sellars thought that philosophy should be about 'how things in the broadest possible sense of the term hang together in the broadest sense of the term' (Sellars 1962, p. 35). It should be clear, then, that I am not referring to metaphysics of the kind that stays at the level of narrow reflections on realism (see Moore 2012 for an analytical approach that is congruent with this view).

Conclusion

1 Garry Gutting (2007) gives other examples of such moves where the supposed arguments are not in fact decisive for the move, though he interprets them in a manner more sympathetic to analytical modes of philosophizing.
2 In this respect the later Foucault, for example in the essay on 'What is Enlightenment?' (1980), comes close to Adorno.
3 I will be further investigating the issues here in a forthcoming book on the questions posed by aesthetics for the rest of modern philosophy.
4 I have no interest in highlighting the tensions and contradictions between Adorno and Heidegger, tensions that Adorno himself, for complex (and sometimes justified) reasons, sought to emphasize. The present reflections will underplay areas where there may be problems in Heidegger's conception of the kind Adorno suggests.
5 Compare also Wellmer's observations in Chapter 5 on how materially identical signs give rise to differing meanings in different social contexts.
6 I am using 'naturalism' in a very wide sense here, not in the reductive sense I am concerned to criticize.
7 Whatever one thinks of its more controversial contentions, Graeber's book offers scholarly resources for making up the deficit in anthropological research on issues of symbolic and material exchange which so mars *Dialectic of Enlightenment*.
8 The formal conception is obviously of crucial importance; the issue is what it can conceal if it is understood in a scientistic manner.

9 Gabriel offers an interesting alternative, based particularly on Schelling, to the kind of set-theoretical ontology proposed by Badiou.
10 The case of the culture industry is hugely complex. We live, especially with respect to music, in a time of unparalleled riches. The availability of great music of every conceivable kind is one of the huge benefits resulting from technological advances. At the same time, being unconcerned about the manipulation of musical taste by the culture industry is not an option.

References

All quotations from German sources are in my translations.

Adorno, T.W. (1959–60) 'Einleitung in die Philosophie', unpublished lectures, Adorno Archiv, Akademie der Künste, Berlin
Adorno, T.W. (1961) 'Ästhetik', unpublished lectures, Adorno Archiv, Akademie der Künste, Berlin
Adorno, T.W. (1963–4) 'Fragen der Dialektik', unpublished lectures, Adorno Archiv, Akademie der Künste, Berlin
Adorno, T.W. (1973) *Vorlesungen zur Ästhetik 1967–8*, Zürich: H. Mayer Nachfolger
Adorno, T.W. (1993) *Beethoven: Philosophie der Musik*, Frankfurt: Suhrkamp (English: *Beethoven: The Philosophy of Music*, Cambridge: Polity, 1998)
Adorno, T.W. (1995) *Kants 'Kritik der reinen Vernunft'*, Frankfurt: Suhrkamp (English: *Kant's Critique of Pure Reason*, Cambridge: Polity, 2001)
Adorno, T.W. (1996) *Probleme der Moralphilosophie*, Frankfurt: Suhrkamp (English: *Problems of Moral Philosophy*, Cambridge: Polity, 2001)
Adorno, T.W. (1997) *Gesammelte Schriften* (20 vols), Frankfurt: Suhrkamp
Adorno, T.W. (1998) *Metaphysik. Begriff und Probleme (1965)*, Frankfurt: Suhrkamp (English: *Metaphysics: Concepts and Problems*, Cambridge: Polity, 2001)
Adorno, T.W. (2001a) *Zur Lehre von der Geschichte und der Freiheit*, Frankfurt: Suhrkamp (English: *History and Freedom: Lectures 1964–1965*, Cambridge: Polity, 2006)
Adorno, T.W. (2001b) *Zur Theorie der musikalischen Reproduktion*, Frankfurt: Suhrkamp (English: *Towards a Theory of Musical Reproduction: Notes, a Draft and Two Schemata*, Cambridge: Polity, 2006)

Adorno, T.W. (2003) *Vorlesung über negative Dialektik*, Frankfurt: Suhrkamp (English: *Lectures on Negative Dialectics: Fragments of a Lecture Course 1965/1966*, Cambridge: Polity, 2008)
Adorno, T.W. (2008) *Philosophische Elemente einer Theorie der Gesellschaft*, Frankfurt: Suhrkamp
Adorno, T.W. (2009) *Ästhetik 1958–9*, Frankfurt: Suhrkamp
Adorno, T.W. (2010) *Einführung in die Dialektik*, Frankfurt: Suhrkamp
Andrews, F.E. (1997) 'On Reading Philosophy after Analytic Philosophy', *Animus*, Vol. 2 (*http://www.mun.ca/animus/1997vol2/andrews2.htm*, accessed 4 March 2013)
Auerbach, E. (1959) *Mimesis. Dargestellte Wirklichkeit in der abendländischen Literatur*, Bern: Francke (English: *Mimesis: The Representation of Reality in Western Literature*, Princeton: Princeton University Press, 2003)
Aydede, M. (2013) 'Pain', in E.N. Zalta, ed., *The Stanford Encyclopedia of Philosophy* (Spring 2013 edn) (*http://plato.stanford.edu/archives/spr2013/entries/pain/*, accessed 6 March 2013)
Bauman, Z. (1991) *Modernity and the Holocaust*, Cambridge: Polity
Bennett, J. (1966) *Kant's Analytic*, Cambridge: Cambridge University Press
Bernstein, J.M. (2001) *Adorno: Disenchantment and Ethics*, Cambridge: Cambridge University Press
Bernstein, R. (2010) *The Pragmatic Turn*, Cambridge: Polity
Bieri, P. (2007) 'Was bleibt von der analytischen Philosophie?', *Deutsche Zeitschrift für Philosophie*, Heft III, pp. 333–44
Bilgrami, A. (2010) 'The Wider Significance of Naturalism', in M. de Caro and D. Macarthur, eds, *Naturalism and Normativity*, New York: Columbia University Press
Bowie, A. (1993) *Schelling and Modern European Philosophy*, London: Routledge
Bowie, A. (1995) 'Non-Identity: The German Romantics, Schelling and Adorno', in T. Rajan and D. Clark, eds, *Intersections: Nineteenth-Century Philosophy and Contemporary Theory*, Albany: SUNY Press
Bowie, A. (1997) *From Romanticism to Critical Theory: The Philosophy of German Literary Theory*, London: Routledge
Bowie, A. (2000) 'The Romantic Connection: Neurath, the Frankfurt School, and Heidegger', Parts 1 and 2, *Journal for the History of Philosophy*, Part 1, Vol. 8, No. 2, pp. 275–98; Part 2, Vol. 8, No. 3, pp. 459–83
Bowie, A. (2003a) *Aesthetics and Subjectivity: From Kant to Nietzsche* (2nd edn), Manchester: Manchester University Press
Bowie, A. (2003b) *Introduction to German Philosophy from Kant to Habermas*, Cambridge: Polity
Bowie, A. (2004) 'Adorno, Pragmatism, and Aesthetic Relativism', *Revue internationale de philosophie* special edn on 'Adorno', Vol. 227, No. 1, pp. 25–45

Bowie, A. (2007) *Music, Philosophy, and Modernity*, Cambridge: Cambridge University Press

Bowie, A. (2010) 'The Philosophical Significance of Schelling's Conception of the Unconscious', in A. Nicholls and M. Liebscher, eds, *Thinking the Unconscious: Nineteenth-Century German Thought*, Cambridge: Cambridge University Press

Brandom, R. (2008) *Between Saying and Doing: Towards an Analytic Pragmatism*, Oxford: Oxford University Press

Brandom, R. (2009) *Reason in Philosophy*, Cambridge Mass., and London: Harvard University Press

Brandom, R. (2011) *Perspectives on Pragmatism: Classical, Recent, and Contemporary*, Cambridge Mass., and London: Harvard University Press

Braver, L. (2007) *A Thing of This World: A History of Continental Anti-realism*, Evanston, Ill.: Northwestern University Press

Bronk, R. (2009) *The Romantic Economist*, Cambridge: Cambridge University Press

Brunkhorst, H. (1999) *Adorno and Critical Theory*, Cardiff: University of Wales Press

Buck-Morss, S. (1977) *The Origin of Negative Dialectics: Theodor W. Adorno, Walter Benjamin, and the Frankfurt Institute*, Hassocks, UK: Harvester Press

Cavell, S. (1976) *Must We Mean What We Say?*, Cambridge: Cambridge University Press

Claussen, D. (2003) *Theodor W. Adorno. Ein letztes Genie*, Frankfurt: S. Fischer

Cook, D. (2003) Review of Yvonne Sherratt, *Adorno's Positive Dialectic*, Notre Dame Philosophical Reviews, 6 April (http://ndpr.nd.edu/news/23357-adorno-s-positive-dialectic/, accessed 12 March 2013)

Cook, D. (2011) *Adorno on Nature*, Durham, UK: Acumen

Cooper, D. (2003) *Meaning*, London: Acumen

Dahms, H.-J. (1994) *Positivismusstreit: die Auseinandersetzung der Frankfurter Schule mit dem logischen Positivismus, dem amerikanischen Pragmatismus, und dem kritischen Rationalismus*, Frankfurt: Suhrkamp

de Nora, T. (2003) *After Adorno: Rethinking Music Sociology*, Cambridge: Cambridge University Press

Dewey, J. (1958) *Experience and Nature*, New York: Dover

Eldridge, R. (1997) *Living a Human Life: Wittgenstein, Intentionality, and Romanticism*, Chicago: University of Chicago Press

Forster, M. (2010) *After Herder: Philosophy of Language in the German Tradition*, Oxford: Oxford University Press

Foster, R. (2007) *Adorno: The Recovery of Experience*, Albany: SUNY Press

Foucault, M. (1980) 'What Is Enlightenment?', in P. Rabinow, ed., *The Foucault Reader*, New York: Pantheon

Frank, M. (1997) *'Unendliche Annäherung'. Die Anfänge der philosophischen Frühromantik*, Frankfurt: Suhrkamp
Friedman, M. (1999) *Reconsidering Logical Positivism*, Cambridge: Cambridge University Press
Gabriel, M. (2011) *Transcendental Ontology: Studies in German Idealism* (Kindle edn), London: Continuum.
Gadamer, H.-G. (1993) *Ästhetik und Poetik I. Kunst als Aussage*, Tübingen: J.C.B. Mohr
Gascoigne, N. (2002) *Scepticism*, London: Acumen
Geuss, R. (2003) 'Outside Ethics', *European Journal of Philosophy*, Vol. 11, No. 1, pp. 29–53
Gibson, N. and Rubin, A. (eds) (2002) *Adorno: A Critical Reader*, Oxford: Blackwell
Graeber, D. (2011) *Debt: The First 5,000 Years*, London: Melville House
Graeber, D. (2012) 'Seminar on *Debt: The First 5,000 Years* – Reply', Crooked Timber, 2 April (*http://crookedtimber.org/2012/04/02/seminar-on-debt-the-first-5000-years-reply/#more-23912*, accessed 11 March 2013)
Gutting, G. (2007) *What Philosophers Know: Case Studies in Recent Analytical Philosophy*, Cambridge: Cambridge University Press
Habermas, J. (1973) *Erkenntnis und Interesse*, Frankfurt: Suhrkamp (English: *Knowledge and Human Interests*, Cambridge: Polity, 1987)
Habermas, J. (1981) *Theorie des kommunikativen Handelns* (2 vols), Frankfurt: Suhrkamp (English: *The Theory of Communicative Action* [2 vols], Cambridge: Polity, 1986, 1989)
Habermas, J. (1985) *Der philosophische Diskurs der Moderne*, Frankfurt: Suhrkamp (English: *The Philosophical Discourse of Modernity*, Cambridge: Polity, 1990)
Hammer, E. (2006) *Adorno and the Political*, London: Routledge
Hearfield, C. (2004) *Adorno and the Modern Ethos of Freedom*, Aldershot, UK: Ashgate
Hegel, G.W.F. (1959) *Enzyklopädie der philosophischen Wissenschaften im Grundrisse (1830)*, Hamburg: Meiner (English: *The Encyclopedia of the Philosophical Sciences (1830)*, Parts 1–3, Oxford: Oxford University Press, 1970, 1975, 2004)
Heidegger, M. (1961) *Was heisst denken?* Tübingen: Niemeyer (English: *What Is Called Thinking?*, New York: Harper, 1976)
Heidegger, M. (1988) *Zur Sache des Denkens*, Tübingen: Niemeyer (English: *On Time and Being*, Chicago: University of Chicago Press, 2002)
Honneth, A. (2005) *Verdinglichung: Eine anerkennungstheoretische Studie*, Frankfurt: Suhrkamp (English: *Reification: A New Look at an Old Idea*, Oxford: Oxford University Press, 2012)
Honneth, A. (2008) *Pathologie der Vernunft: Geschichte und Gegenwart der Kritischen Theorie*, Frankfurt: Suhrkamp (English: *Pathologies*

of Reason: On the Legacy of Critical Reason*, New York: Columbia University Press, 2009)
Huhn, T. (2004) *The Cambridge Companion to Adorno*, Cambridge: Cambridge University Press
Huhn, T. and Zuydervaart, L. (1997) *The Semblance of Subjectivity: Essays in Adorno's 'Aesthetic Theory'*, Cambridge, Mass.: MIT Press
Husserl, E. (1976) *Die Krisis der europäischen Wissenschaften und die transzendentale Phänomenologie: Eine Einleitung in die phänomenologische Philosophie*, The Hague: Nijhoff (English: *The Crisis of European Sciences and Transcendental Phenomenology*, Evanston, Ill.: Northwestern University Press, 1970)
Jäger, L. (2005) *Adorno: A Political Biography*, New Haven: Yale University Press
Jarvis, S. (1998) *Adorno: A Critical Introduction*, Cambridge: Polity
Jay, M. (1984) *Adorno*, London: Fontana
Johnson, M. (2008) *The Meaning of the Body*, Chicago: University of Chicago Press
Jungk, R., ed. (1961) *Off limits für das Gewissen. Der Briefwechsel zwischen dem Hiroshima-Piloten Claude Eatherly und Günther Anders*, Reinbek: Rowohlt
Kant, I. (1968) *Kritik der reinen Vernunft*, Werkausgabe III and IV, Frankfurt: Suhrkamp
Kant, I. (1996) *Schriften zur Ästhetik und Naturphilosophie*, ed. M. Frank and V. Zanetti, Frankfurt: Deutscher Klassiker Verlag
Lafont, C. (1994) *Sprache und Welterschliessung*, Frankfurt: Suhrkamp (English: *Heidegger, Language, and World-Disclosure*, Cambridge: Cambridge University Press, 2000)
Lanchester, J. (2010) *Whoops! Why Everyone Owes Everyone and No One Can Pay*, Harmondsworth: Penguin
Lanchester, J. (2011) 'Once Greece Goes ...', *London Review of Books*, Vol. 33, No. 14 (*http://www.lrb.co.uk/2011/06/30/john-lanchester/once-greece-goes*, accessed 8 March 2013)
Langton, R. (1998) *Kantian Humility: Our Ignorance of Things in Themselves*, Oxford: Clarendon Press
McDowell, J. (1994) *Mind and World*, Oxford: Oxford University Press
McDowell, J. (1998) *Mind, Value, and Reality*, Cambridge, Mass., and London: Harvard University Press
McDowell, J. (2008) *Having the World in View: Essays on Kant, Hegel, and Sellars*, Cambridge, Mass., and London: Harvard University Press
Michel, K.M. (1980) 'Versuch, die "Ästhetische Theorie" zu verstehen', in B. Lindner and W.M. Lüdke, eds, *Materialien zur ästhetischen Theorie Th. W. Adornos. Konstruktion der Moderne*, Frankfurt: Suhrkamp
Mill, J.S. (2011) *On Liberty* (Kindle edn), n.p.: Mobile Lyceum
Mitscherlich, A. and Mitscherlich M. (1967) *Die Unfähigkeit zu Trauern.*

Munich: C. Beck (English: *The Inability to Mourn*, New York: Grove Press, 1975)

Moore, A.W. (2012) *The Evolution of Modern Metaphysics: Making Sense of Things* (Kindle edn), Cambridge: Cambridge University Press

Mörchen, H. (1981) *Adorno und Heidegger, Untersuchung einer philosophischen Kommunikationsverweigerung*, Stuttgart: Klett-Cotta

Müller-Doohm, S. (2005) *Adorno: Eine Biographie*, Frankfurt: Suhrkamp (English: *Adorno: A Biography*, Cambridge: Polity, 2008)

O'Connor, B. (2004) *Adorno's Negative Dialectic. Philosophy and the Possibility of Critical Rationality*, Cambridge, Mass.: MIT Press

Paddison, M. (1997) *Adorno's Aesthetics of Music*, Cambridge: Cambridge University Press

Pippin, R. (1997) *Idealism as Modernism: Hegelian Variations*, Cambridge: Cambridge University Press

Pippin, R. (1999) *Modernism as a Philosophical Problem: On the Dissatisfactions of European High Culture*, Oxford: Wiley-Blackwell

Pippin, R. (2000) 'Fichte's Alleged Subjective, One-Sided Idealism', in S. Sedgwick, ed., *The Reception of Kant's Critical Philosophy*, Cambridge: Cambridge University Press

Pippin, R. (2005) *The Persistence of Subjectivity*, Cambridge: Cambridge University Press

Pippin, R. (2008) *Hegel's Practical Philosophy*, Cambridge: Cambridge University Press

Pippin, R. (2010) 'Participants and Spectators', On the Human: A Project of the National Humanities Center, 19 April (http://onthehuman. org/2010/04/participants_and_spectators/, accessed 8 March 2013)

Pippin, R. (2011) 'After Hegel: An Interview with Robert Pippin' [by O. Hussain], *Platypus Review*, 1 June (http://platypus1917.org/2011/06/01/after-hegel-an-interview-with-robert-pippin/, accessed 11 March 2013)

Price, H. (2011) *Naturalism without Mirrors*, Oxford: Oxford University Press

Putnam, H. (1990) *Realism with a Human Face*, Cambridge, Mass., and London: Harvard University Press

Putnam, H. (2004) *The Collapse of the Fact/Value Dichotomy and Other Essays*, Cambridge, Mass.: Harvard University Press

Redding, P. (2007) *Analytic Philosophy and the Return of Hegelian Thought*, Cambridge: Cambridge University Press

Redding, P. (2012) 'Georg Wilhelm Friedrich Hegel', in E.N. Zalta, ed., *The Stanford Encyclopedia of Philosophy* (Summer 2012 edn) (http://plato.stanford.edu/archives/sum2012/entries/hegel/, accessed 6 March 2013)

Roberts, D. (2006) *Art and Enlightenment: Aesthetic Theory after Adorno*, Lincoln: University of Nebraska Press

Schelling, F.W.J. (1856) *Sämmtliche Werke*, ed. K.F.A. Schelling, I Abtheilung Vol. 7, Stuttgart: Cotta

Schelling, F.W.J. (1946) *Die Weltalter*, ed. M. Schröter, Munich:

Biederstein (English: *The Ages of the World*, New York: State University of New York Press, 2000)

Schnädelbach, H. (1987) *Vernunft und Geschichte*, Frankfurt: Suhrkamp

Seel, M. (2004) *Adornos Philosophie der Kontemplation*, Frankfurt: Suhrkamp

Seel, M. (2006) *Paradoxien der Erfüllung: Philosophische Essays*, Frankfurt: Fischer

Sellars, W. (1962) 'Philosophy and the Scientific Image of Man', in R. Colodny, ed., *Frontiers of Science and Philosophy*, Pittsburgh, Pa: University of Pittsburgh Press

Sherratt, Y. (2002) *Adorno's Positive Dialectic*, Cambridge: Cambridge University Press

Stone, A. (2006) 'Adorno and the Disenchantment of Nature', *Philosophy and Social Criticism*, Vol. 32, No. 2, pp. 231–53

Taylor, C. (2002) 'Foundationalism and the Inner–Outer Distinction', in N.H. Smith, ed., *Reading McDowell. On 'Mind and World'*, London and New York: Routledge

Taylor, C. (2007) *A Secular Age*, Cambridge, Mass., and London: Harvard University Press

Taylor, C. (2011) *Dilemmas and Connections*, Cambridge, Mass., and London: Harvard University Press

Toulmin, S. (2003a) *The Uses of Argument*, Cambridge: Cambridge University Press

Toulmin, S. (2003b) *Return to Reason*, Cambridge, Mass., and London: Harvard University Press

Wellmer, A (2004) *Sprachphilosophie*, Frankfurt: Suhrkamp

Wellmer, A. (2007) *Wie Worte Sinn machen: Aufsätze zur Sprachphilosophie*, Frankfurt: Suhrkamp

Wellmer, A. (2009) 'Bald frei, bald unfrei' – Reflexionen über die Natur im Geist (MS). (English: 'On Spirit as a Part of Nature', *Constellations*, Vol. 16, No. 2, pp. 213–26.)

Williamson, T. (2007) *The Philosophy of Philosophy*, Oxford: Oxford University Press

Wilson, R. (2007) *Adorno*, London: Routledge

Wrathall, M. (2011) *Heidegger and Unconcealment*, Cambridge: Cambridge University Press

Žižek, S. (2011) 'Slavoj Žižek Speaks at Occupy Wall Street: Transcript', *Impose*, 10 October (*http://www.imposemagazine.com/bytes/slavoj-zizek-at-occupy-wall-street-transcript*, accessed 14 March 2013)

Zuydervaart, L. (1991) *Adorno's Aesthetic Theory: The Redemption of Illusion*, Cambridge, Mass.: MIT Press

Index

aesthetics 20, 52, 59, 67, 82, 83, 127–8, 135–74, 179, 186
analytical philosophy 2–3, 4, 5, 15–16, 28, 41, 55, 70, 73, 135–7, 140–1, 160–1, 173, 183, 184, 188, 190–1 n. 7
art 35–6, 42, 87, 91, 95, 132, 133, 135–74, 182–4, 185

Badiou, A. 183–4
be-bop 166
Beckett, S. 162
Beethoven, L.van 35–6, 138, 148, 165
Benjamin W. 34–5, 82, 90
Berg, A. 162
Bernstein, R. 65
Bilgrami, A. 1–2
Brandom, R. 16, 56, 61, 62–3, 65, 72, 73, 145–6, 171, 179–80, 192 nn. 11 and 13
Brecht, B. 162
Bronk, R. 28

Cavell, S. 101, 163–4, 168–74
Coleman, O. 165
Coltrane, J. 151
compatibilism 96–7, 114
constellation 35, 39, 70–4, 89, 128, 183, 192 n. 10
contradiction 3, 5–7, 12, 17, 24, 26, 38, 39, 40, 41, 43, 45, 53, 56, 70, 93, 94, 103, 104, 107, 108, 111, 123, 126, 160, 174, 180, 187
Cooper, D. 63
culture industry 140, 149, 187, 197 n. 10

Dewey, J. 26, 51, 61, 66, 78, 83–6, 88
Diagnostic and Statistical Manual of Mental Disorders 193–4 n. 2
dialectic 17, 23, 27, 31, 33, 39–40, 55, 58, 66–9, 72, 81, 113, 125, 144, 158, 179

disenchantment 1–2, 46, 59, 74, 147, 153, 164, 177

Elgar, E. 138
epistemology 23, 30, 32, 41, 45, 49–51, 91–2, 136–7, 146, 173, 179, 183, 188
evil 115–16, 118

Fichte, J.G. 80–1, 129, 191 n. 2
freedom 15, 40, 45, 60, 67–8, 69, 73, 74, 86, 95, 96–134, 137–8
 of the will 97–8, 100, 105, 116, 124, 126, 132–4, 137, 142
Freud, S. 30, 60, 118, 132

Gabriel, M. 183–4
Graeber, D. 180

Habermas, J. 111, 130, 171, 194 n. 10
Hamann, J.G. 25
Hamlet 105
Hegel, G.W.F. 13, 17, 24, 26, 33, 45, 50, 53, 54–74, 89, 93, 98–9, 100–1, 103, 108–9, 110, 117, 121, 123, 132, 142, 155, 177
Heidegger, M. 20, 25, 51, 64–5, 88, 115, 132, 143, 147, 175–6, 178, 179, 184, 190 n. 1, 193 n. 10
Holocaust 14, 18–19, 46, 48–9, 59, 73, 77, 94, 99, 102, 120, 122, 139, 181–2
Honneth, A. 49, 51–3, 59–60
Husserl, E. 71–2, 144

Ibsen, H. 103
Idealism 13, 17, 36, 40, 43, 45, 46, 55, 57, 63, 64, 65, 66, 68, 74, 78, 79, 80, 84, 85, 92, 93, 94, 106, 108, 113, 115, 129, 130, 146, 157, 179, 183, 191 nn. 2 and 3
ideology 87, 122–3, 134, 140, 172, 173

immediacy 45, 59, 61, 62, 63, 64, 65, 67, 72, 76, 77, 87, 91, 122, 149, 161, 164, 168, 172

Jacobi, F.H. 46
jazz 128, 139, 158–9, 166, 168
Johnson, M. 16

Kafka, F. 155, 156, 159
Kant, I. 15, 33–4, 36, 38–53, 55–6, 68, 78, 81, 95, 98, 103, 105–13, 119–20, 127, 142, 143, 148, 163–4, 172, 195 n. 15

Lafont, C. 193 n. 10
Lanchester, J. 27, 123
Langton, R. 40
language 15–17, 26, 27, 66, 70–1, 132, 137–8, 145, 164
literature 133, 157
Locke, J. 124
Lukács, G. 47, 51, 90

McDowell, J. 34, 40, 43, 44–5, 78, 82, 141, 187–8
Mahler, G. 153, 184–5, 196 n. 11
Marx, K. 22, 51, 82, 195 n. 16
meaning 15–17, 27, 56, 62–4, 90, 117, 137–8, 154–5, 164–5, 167, 173–4, 175, 177, 183, 184–8
mediation 40, 53, 57, 59, 61, 63, 64, 65, 72, 76, 91, 149
metaphysics 17–20, 29–30, 39, 40, 42, 55, 59, 60, 74, 77, 83–4, 90–1, 134, 153–4, 174, 175–7, 181, 184–7, 196 n. 14
Mill, J.S. 97–8
mimesis 63, 70, 94, 146, 151–2
modernism 7, 10, 26, 138, 143, 149, 150, 151, 155, 159, 162, 168, 182, 184
Moore, A.W. vii, 176, 181–2
moral philosophy 14, 28, 76, 98, 101, 102, 103, 112, 122
Mozart, W.A. 150
music 10, 16, 60, 63, 86–7, 117, 127–8, 147, 149, 156, 166, 169, 189–90 n.11, 197 n. 11

naturalism 71, 94, 114, 177, 179, 183
reductive 34, 44, 78–9, 130, 133, 172, 173, 177, 183
nature 1–2, 15, 40, 72–4, 75–95, 102, 106, 107, 112, 113–16, 127, 139–40, 143–7, 150–3, 156, 157, 159, 161–2, 172, 179, 182–3
beauty of 140–9
see also second nature 82, 86, 87
nature-history 80–95, 112, 113, 118, 131, 134, 176

Nietzsche, F. 62, 111
non-identity 25, 43, 64, 69, 95, 111, 157, 174, 178, 181
Novalis 42, 129, 166

pain 76–9
Peirce, C. 65–6
Pinkard, T. 54
Pippin, R. 43, 46, 58, 59–60, 62, 74, 75, 98–102, 103, 110, 112, 119, 120–1, 123–4, 126, 129, 182
pragmatism 58, 65, 161, 179, 181
Proust, M. 186
psychoanalysis 49, 69, 95, 109–10, 127
Putnam, H. 84, 170

realism 3, 24, 83
Redding, P. 56
reification 31, 32, 47–52, 59, 65, 84
relativism 6, 12, 20, 35, 42, 84, 140, 171
Rorty, R. 23, 92, 122
Russell, B. 54

sapience 62-3, 65, 67, 72, 74, 75, 76, 92, 118, 128, 141, 145, 164
scepticism 12–13, 17, 32, 44, 45, 51, 55–6, 83, 136, 167
Schelling, F.W.J. 61, 76, 81, 108, 114–18, 127
Schlegel, F. 42
Schmitt, C. 128
Schnädelbach, H. 181–2
Schoenberg, A. 151
Schopenhauer, A. 61
second nature 82, 86, 87
Seel, M. 129–32
Sellers, W. 57
sentience 62, 63, 65, 72, 118, 128, 145, 164
Student Movement 9–10

Taylor, C. 65, 177
Toulmin, S. 25, 26
truth 12, 20, 39, 41, 42, 43, 59, 83, 92–3, 140, 149, 159–60, 162–3, 164–8, 174
truth-content 21, 34–6, 39, 40, 43, 166

Vienna Circle 13, 18, 23, 17

Wagner, R. 62
Weber, M. 71
Wellmer, A. 79, 86, 88, 132–4, 137–8
Wittgenstein, L. 5, 16, 71, 147
Wrathall, M. 178

Žižek, S. 180